CAMBRIDGE TEXTS IN THE
HISTORY OF POLITICAL THOUGHT

Political Writings

CAMBRIDGE TEXTS IN THE HISTORY OF POLITICAL THOUGHT

Series editors

RAYMOND GEUSS

Lecturer in Social and Political Sciences, University of Cambridge

QUENTIN SKINNER

Professor of Political Science in the University of Cambridge

Cambridge Texts in the History of Political Thought is now firmly established as the major student textbook series in political theory. It aims to make available to students all the most important texts in the history of western political thought, from ancient Greece to the early twentieth century. All the familiar classic texts will be included but the series does at the same time seek to enlarge the conventional canon by incorporating an extensive range of less well-known works, many of them never before available in a modern English edition. Wherever possible, texts are published in complete and unabridged form, and translations are specially commissioned for the series. Each volume contains a critical introduction together with chronologies, biographical sketches, a guide to further reading and any necessary glossaries and textual apparatus. When completed, the series will aim to offer an outline of the entire evolution of western political thought.

For a list of titles published in the series, please see end of book.

VOLTAIRE

Political Writings

EDITED AND TRANSLATED BY
DAVID WILLIAMS

*Professor of French,
University of Sheffield*

CAMBRIDGE
UNIVERSITY PRESS

Published by the Press Syndicate of the University of Cambridge
The Pitt Building, Trumpington Street, Cambridge CB2 1RP
40 West 20th Street, New York, NY 10011-4211, USA
10 Stamford Road, Oakleigh, Melbourne, 3166, Australia

First published 1994

Printed in Great Britain at the University Press, Cambridge

A catalogue record for this book is available from the British Library

Library of Congress cataloguing in publication data
Voltaire, 1694–1778.
Political writings / Voltaire; edited by David Williams.
p.   cm. – (Cambridge texts in the history of political thought)
Includes index.
ISBN 0 521 43116 6. – ISBN 0 521 43727 X (pbk.)
1. Political science – Early works to 1800. I. Williams, David,
1938– . II. Title. III. Series.
JC179.V65 1994
320'.01–dc20   93-28512, CIP

ISBN 0 521 43116 6 hardback
ISBN 0 521 4372 7 X paperback

WV

WV

Contents

Contents

Abbreviations

Best. D   *Voltaire: correspondence and related documents*, ed. Theodore Besterman, in *The complete works of Voltaire* (Geneva: Institut et Musée Voltaire and Banbury/Oxford: The Voltaire Foundation, 1968–77)

Kehl   *Œuvres complètes de Voltaire*, ed. Condorcet *et al.*, (Kehl, 1784–9)

Moland   *Œuvres complètes*, ed. Louis Moland (Paris: Garnier, 1877–85)

Works by Voltaire (with date of first publication)

CLDP   *Commentaire sur le livre des délits et des peines par un avocat de province. Commentary on the book On crimes and punishments, by a provincial lawyer* 1766

ABC   *L'A B C, ou Dialogues entre A B C; traduits de l'anglais de m. Huet. The A B C, or Dialogues between A B C, translated from the English by Mr Huet* 1768

DH   *Les droits des hommes et les usurpations des autres. Traduit de l'italien. The rights of men and the usurpations of others. Translated from the Italian* 1768

DP   *Dictionnaire philosophique portatif. Pocket philosophical dictionary* 1764

E(DP)   *Etats, gouvernements. States, governments*

G(DP)   *Guerre. War*

L(DP)   *Lois (Des). Laws*

P(DP)   *Patrie. Homeland*

vii

DPC	*Dialogue entre un philosophe et un contrôleur général des finances. Dialogue between a philosopher and a comptroller-general of finance* 1750
IR	*Idées républicaines par un membre d'un corps. Republican ideas by a member of a public body* 1765
LHQE	*L'Homme aux quarante écus. The man in the street* 1768
PA	*Pensées sur l'administration publique. Thoughts on public administration* 1752
QE	*Questions sur l'Encyclopédie. Questions on the Encyclopaedia* 1770–2
D(QE)	*Démocratie. Democracy* 1771
E(QE)	*Economie. Economy* 1771
G(QE)	*Gouvernement. Government* 1771–4
H(QE)	*Homme. Man* 1771
I(QE)	*Impôt. Tax* 1771–4
P(QE)	*Politique. Politics* 1774

Chronology

1694	François-Marie Arouet baptised at the church of Saint André-des-arts in Paris on 22 November. Exact date of birth unknown.
1704–11	Educated at the Jesuit college of Louis-le-grand.
1713	Secretary to the French ambassador at The Hague.
1717	May. Imprisoned in the Bastille for a scurrilous satire.
1718	Reputation as a dramatist established with the successful performance of his tragedy, *Oedipus*. Now signing himself 'Arouet de Voltaire' (Best. D72).
1726	Quarrels with the chevalier de Rohan-Chabot, who has Voltaire thrashed by his lackeys. Unable to seek redress against this nobleman, he is exiled from Paris. In May goes to England, where he stays until 1728.
1734	Publication of the *Philosophical letters*, the 'first bomb to be launched against the *ancien régime*', according to Gustave Lanson. It was condemned by the Paris *parlement*. Flees to Cirey where he stays with Madame Du Châtelet for the most of the next decade, working on his translation of Newton.
1736	Starts corresponding with the Royal Prince of Prussia, Frederick.
1740	Publishes Frederick II's *Anti-Machiavelli*.
1743	Goes to Berlin on a secret mission in connection with negotiations to end the War of the Austrian Succession.
1745	Appointed Royal Historiographer to Louis XV.
1746	Elected to the French Academy.

1747	The first of his satirical tales, *Zadig*, is published. In November loses his favoured position at the French court, and flees to the court of Stanislas at Nancy. Leaves Alsace after the death of Madame Du Châtelet in 1750, and accepts invitation to Frederick the Great's court at Potsdam.
1750	Publication of *The Voice of the wise man and of the people.* Condemned by the Church and placed on the Catholic Index of Forbidden Books.
1751	Publication of first edition of *The Age of Louis XIV*, and *DPC*.
1752	Publication of first edition of *PA*.
1753	Breaks with Frederick. An unhappy period of rootlessness follows.
1754–55	Settles at Les Délices in Geneva.
1756	Publication of the *Essay on the customs and the spirit of nations*.
1757	Acts as diplomatic intermediary in secret negotiations between France and Prussia after the outbreak of the Seven Years War in 1756.
1759	Publication of *Candide* and the *History of Russia under Peter the Great*. Moves to Ferney on the Franco-Swiss border where he remains until his return to Paris in the last weeks of his life.
1762	The Calas affair starts. This is the first of the great public causes in which Voltaire challenges the power of the State in the defence of the individual's rights to justice, and which were to inform most of his polemical writings from now on. Jean Calas was broken on the wheel by order of the Toulouse *parlement* in 1762. Also involved in the campaign to rehabilitate Sirven, falsely accused of the murder of his daughter by the Bishop of Castres.
1763	Publication of the *Treatise on tolerance*.
1764	Publication of the first edition of *DP*.
1766	La Barre convicted at Abbeville. Tortured and executed in July. Two weeks later dedicates his *Account of the death of the chevalier de La Barre* to Beccaria. Publication of *CLDP*.
1768	Publication of *LHQE*, *ABC*, *DH* and *IR*. By now heavily involved in Genevan political quarrels.

1771	Publication of *QE* starts.
1777	Publication of the *Commentary on the Spirit of the laws*.
1778	Returns to Paris. Dies in Paris on 30 May.
1791	11 July: state burial in the Panthéon.

Introduction

In politics as in philosophy, Voltaire was no system-builder. He had a deep suspicion of 'systems', and his political writings do not combine readily to reflect a systematically argued world-view. 'I write to act', he once informed Jean-Jacques Rousseau (Best. D13221), and as a political thinker he tended to respond to events rather than metaphysical abstractions. He was remarkably well-informed, however, and his reading was wide. He knew the work of Grotius, Pufendorf, Hume, Bolingbroke, Montesquieu, Machiavelli, d'Argenson, Mably, Saint-Pierre, Quesnay, Le Mercier, Melon, Hobbes, Mandeville, Buffon, Beccaria, Rousseau and Locke although, astonishingly, evidence suggests he knew little of the latter's *Two treatises on government* (see Perkins 1965, Appendix 2, Crocker 1983, Thielemann 1959, Kotta 1966).

He drew constantly on this rich hinterland, but his allusions are deceptively casual, and often expressed in an ironic, tangential way. As he puts it in *ABC*, 'we take what we like from Aristotle to Locke, and don't give a damn for the rest'. Only with Montesquieu, and to a lesser extent Rousseau, does he offer anything like a prolonged commentary on another theorist, even when we are led to expect one, as in the case of Beccaria. Voltaire's technique is to entertain, to provoke and to inform by means of satirical anecdote, outrageous vulgarisation and lively dialogue. Among his many gifts as a persuasive polemicist is his unrivalled ability to breathe life and a sense of human reality into the driest issue. Voltaire was a politically engaged propagandist. He wrote to exert pressure for change, and he possessed the rare gift of distilling from small events those vast implications for political life whose urgent complexities continue to over-whelm us.

Power and the state

Almost certainly the most powerfully formative experience behind the evolution of Voltaire's views on the legitimacy and exercise of power was his brief stay in England between May 1726 and November 1728 (see Pomeau 1985, ch. 13; Fletcher 1986 ch. 2; Perry 1977). The post-1688 settlement that gave England constitutional monarchy offered Voltaire a working model of government. England was to become a repeated point of reference in his political writings, and it is no accident that one of the interlocutors in *ABC* is an Englishman. Voltaire never envisaged the possibility of simply engineering a transfer of the English model to France. There was no House of Commons in France, no possibility of a 1688-style revolution, no freedom of speech or of the press, no equality before the law. In any case, Voltaire was never an advocate of revolution. The upheavals of 1789 would have appalled him, the power of the mob terrifying him as much, if not more, than that of autocrats. He remained very much opposed to any idea of devolving power to the masses, as can be seen in his repeated opposition to Montesquieu's famous antithesis between republics and monarchies. He wrote in sympathetic but very general terms about republics, but only one example of a personal commitment to 'republican philosophy' has been found, and this is in a letter written to his friend Thieriot in 1726 while he was in England (Best. D303). It stands alone (Besterman 1969, ch. 24; but see Gay 1988 for the counterview).

More typical are the views expressed by C in *ABC*: 'The people are not fit to govern. I could not bear my wig-maker to be a legislator. I would prefer never to wear a wig.' In France Voltaire saw clearly that the practical alternative lay between power exercised by a monarch, or power exercised by the *parlements*. The Paris *parlement*, which was really a court of law, was nothing like the English parliament, and Voltaire's opposition to any further transfer of power to it, or to the provincial *parlements*, was unremitting and unreserved (see Tate 1972). He thought all the *parlements* were dangerous to progress and liberty, and that their record as repositories of justice, and as courts of appeal, was abysmal. It might seem paradoxical at first glance, but Voltaire was sure that the only viable system of government for

France was that of an absolute monarchy (see Gay 1988 ch. 7). This much debated *thèse royale* is explored in *PA*, as well as in *ABC*. Voltaire was never at ease personally with monarchs or with their courts, but he maintained firmly and consistently that absolutism did not necessarily mean tyranny. He saw concrete advantages accruing to a state ruled by a supreme monarch, provided that this power was tempered by wisdom, tolerance and, above all, the law.

Voltaire thus made a crucial distinction between absolute and arbitrary power, the absolutism of the monarch being legitimised not through divine right but through his ready submission to the rule of law. The absolute monarch must be enlightened and must act within the confines of reason and justice, in other words, be a 'philosopher-king' – a prospect that Voltaire hoped at one stage would materialise in the person of Frederick the Great (see Besterman 1965; Fleischauer 1958).

Despite its bland, unpromising title, *ABC* is one of the most revealing and radical works about power and the State that Voltaire wrote. It was first published towards the end of 1768 at one of the most politically active periods in Voltaire's life and was immediately disowned. It was placed on the Index in 1776. The first edition (with only sixteen conversations) was printed under the title *The A B C. A curious dialogue, translated from the English by Mr Huet*, and Voltaire made great efforts to attribute the work to Mr Huet's mysterious Englishman. It now consists of seventeen conversations between three characters, the boldest and most loquacious being A, an Englishman. B might well be Voltaire himself, and C is a Dutchman.

The conversations focus on subjects that could certainly not be discussed openly in France in a critical way, namely politics, morality and theology; the work was, as he put it in a letter to Mme Du Deffand in 1768, 'an English roast beef, very difficult to digest for the many small stomachs at Paris' (Best. D15387). The first conversation is about the respective merits of Hobbes, Grotius and Montesquieu, and it is soon clear that Montesquieu is the real object of Voltaire's analysis. Much of this conversation is in fact a commentary on Montesquieu's *Spirit of the laws*, about which Voltaire had mixed feelings, despite his view, expressed through B, that the book should be ranked among 'works of genius'.

Voltaire also crosses swords, though not very convincingly, with Hobbes, a 'sad philosopher' with a grim view of human nature, but with the ring of unpalatable truth behind his uncompromising attitudes. Voltaire's objections to Hobbes are emotional rather than intellectual; he found Hobbes uncomfortable rather than wrong (see Thielmann 1959). He has little of substance to say about Grotius here, except to remark that he was a pedant whose compilations have not merited the praise bestowed on them by the ignorant. In conversation 4, Voltaire resumes battle with his old enemy Jean-Jacques Rousseau, whose views on property, man in the state of nature, natural law and natural equality, as expressed in the *Discourse on the origin of inequality among men* (1754) and the *Social contract* (1762), are also attacked in *IR* and other texts.

Conversations 5–9 and 14 range interestingly and provocatively over subjects with a direct bearing on power, the State, and the human implications of the relationship between the two. They also illuminate Voltaire's use of anecdotal skills in the advancement of arguments about freedom, the lessons of ancient history in the consideration of the best forms of government, the political advances of modern Europe, and particularly England, serfdom, and the enslavement of the mind.

Some of the views on power and the State in *ABC* had been voiced in a much earlier, though more circumspect, work with a more open title. *PA* was written in Paris in 1750, published in 1752, and judiciously hidden away in a collective edition of Voltaire's works. In 1750 Voltaire had written a pamphlet called *The voice of the wise man and of the people*, in which, among other things, he had attacked the inequities of the tax system, and in particular the continuing exemption of the Church, which still owned between a quarter and a fifth of the nation's wealth and about 6 per cent of the land (Lough 1960). The pamphlet had caused a furore, and was placed on the Index. On 21 May 1751 it was officially condemned by the government. It was during the composition of this pamphlet that Voltaire started to list his reflections on government and the exercise of power generally. In preparing this work for re-publication in 1756, he cut seven sections, and added nine. Thirteen sections from *The voice of the wise man and of the people* were reprinted as part of the *PA*, although this material was to be deleted later in Kehl. These have been restored, as has the pre-1756 text that Voltaire had himself excised in later editions. Moland printed this work under the title that Voltaire used in the first edition, *Thoughts on government*.

In *PA* Voltaire set out his basic position on freedom: 'Freedom consists in being dependent only on the law.' This definition enabled him to identify those states and city-states in Europe that enjoyed true freedom (e.g. Sweden, Holland, England, Geneva, Hamburg) and those that did not (discreet silence on France, other than a general reference to large Christian countries). Only with the possession of freedom, so defined, could the true significance of what it was to be human emerge. It followed that the best form of government was the one that guaranteed equal protection for all ranks of citizens before the law. France's situation in this context is introduced with a piece of verse by Conyers Middleton, and this leads to a series of reflections on the French monarchy, and the benefits of absolutism *under the law*: 'A king who is not contradicted can hardly be wicked', while conversely a king who does not enjoy absolute power is compelled to assert himself. Thus it is that when Louis XV declared to the Paris *parlement* on 3 March 1766 that he was the sole source of power in the State, causing much public consternation, Voltaire approved strongly of the King's statement (Best. D12331-D12334; Besterman 1965; Perkins 1989 section 3).

There is a hard-nosed pragmatism about Voltaire's thinking on politics, and many of the articles in *DP* offer good examples of this. According to one of Voltaire's secretaries, Collini, the idea for *DP* was born at a supper party hosted by Frederick the Great at Potsdam on 28 September 1752 (see Todd 1980), but Voltaire did not start serious work on the articles for his 'pocket philosophical dictionary' until well after 1760. By this time Diderot's great *Encyclopaedia*, from which Voltaire drew inspiration for his own alphabetical project, had fallen foul of officialdom. The first edition of *DP* appeared in July 1764. It was reissued in 1765 and in 1767, with changes, and again in 1769, after which its history becomes a little confused. The 1769 *DP*, containing 118 articles, was merged with *ABC*, and published under the title *Reason through the alphabet*. Forty-eight of the articles were then combined, expanded and revised in the context of *QE*. This latter work was conceived as a supplement to Diderot's *Encyclopaedia*, and Voltaire assembled no less than 423 articles for it. After his death, the Kehl editors further muddied the waters by adding material from other writings to produce a vast, composite seven-volume work also entitled the *Philosophical dictionary*. The original 1764 *DP* was thus absorbed to the point of invisibility in the first collective edition of Voltaire's works (see Todd 1980 ch. 1). Four texts in this collection are classified as part of *DP* (see Note on the translation).

E(DP) was possibly composed as early as 1757. It contains Voltaire's acid comments on the futility of political theory as an effective means of influencing those who actually wield power, together with comments on the fashion for publishing political 'wills' of five great men: Richelieu, Louvois, Charles V, Duke of Lorraine, Alberoni and Belle-Isle. To these he adds significantly, and not without irony, a sixth, the notorious brigand Louis Mandrin, who had been broken on the wheel in 1755. In so doing, he was reminding his reader of a point that he made frequently, namely that all political power sprang originally from the actions of robbers and the exercise of force. The difference between a Mandrin and a Richelieu was ultimately only the difference between a winner and a loser. The point is illustrated again in *G(QE)*.

The first six sections of *G(QE)* were published in 1771 in the sixth part of *QE*, and the last section appeared in the seventh part in 1774. Section 6 contains a detailed commentary on the merits of the English constitution, and on the historical struggle that England endured over the centuries to achieve freedom under the law, and a state in which each citizen had those natural rights restored to him of which most men living under monarchical systems are deprived. England again shines as a beacon of hope for the future.

D(QE) was first published in the fourth part of *QE* in 1771. In *L(DP)*, Voltaire had written that democracy was superior to all other systems of government, 'because there everyone is equal, and everyone works for the happiness of everyone else'. In *D(QE)* his views are more cautiously formulated. As many commentators have pointed out, Voltaire's views on democracy are at best ambivalent. His respect for the views, and certainly for the potential power, of ordinary people certainly increased in his later years, particularly after his experience of living with the *natifs* of Geneva (see Gay 1988, ch. 4). In *D(QE)* Voltaire's enthusiasm for the people's power is considerably less than his enthusiasm for their rights (see Birchall 1990). Liberty and equality are discussed largely in the context of Athenian history in which the definition of what constituted the 'people' is very specific and restrictive. Republics on Athenian lines certainly resulted in less crime and less injustice, and here Voltaire is thinking almost certainly of the merits of the Genevan Republic, but these considerable advantages are weighed against 'the real vice of a civilised republic', namely the tendency to anarchy and ultimately tyranny. Democracy was at best suitable only for small countries, and even then its success could not be guaranteed, if only because it was operated by fallible human beings on whose qualities and talents it was entirely dependent.

Is a republic better than a monarchy? Voltaire's answer in *D(QE)* is tentative: government is a difficult matter; if the Jews could not succeed with God as their master, what hope is there for the rest of us! For Voltaire history proved conclusively that Montesquieu was wrong about virtue being the dynamic principle of republics. In real life republics have never come into being from acts of virtue, but from acts of ambition, whose motive is merely to alter the balance and source of power (but see Gay 1958).

Voltaire also examines the origins of political power and social organisation in *P(QE)* and in *H(QE)*. The former was published in 1774, and starts with speculation on the pre-social state of man in nature. The picture painted of natural man is very different from that of Rousseau's noble savage, endowed with qualities of natural virtue and happiness. The political aspiration of Voltaire's natural man was to 'equal the animals', that is, to become self-sufficient in the food, clothing and shelter afforded to animals by nature. The essence of primitive existence, and indeed the whole of man's story, is reduced to the pursuit of well-being and the acquisition of defences against omnipresent evil. The climb from the pit of brutality is long, arduous and uncertain, and Voltaire describes in bleak terms the decisive factors in the evolution of political life: the law of kill or be killed; enslave or be enslaved; the alliance between religion and politics to legitimise those acts of brigandage that define the frontiers of modern states, and cement treaties of expediency between competing carnivores.

In the second part of this article Voltaire comes back to the issue of who should govern, the people or the King? In aristocracies power can be abused too easily, and revolutions are always to be feared. The egalitarianism of democracies is in principle 'natural and wise', but in practice such systems are rare and fragile. Voltaire leaves the final judgement on monarchy open as he looks to the future: monarchies fall because individual monarchs are unfit to govern. But it is the ruler who fails, not the system, and 'in ten or twelve centuries, when men are more enlightened', the system might work (see Rivière 1987).

H(QE) was published in the seventh part of *QE* in 1771. Here Voltaire resumes his attack on Rousseau. Society, asserts Voltaire, is natural to man; man's instincts incline him towards social organisation. Contrary to Rousseau's view, Voltaire always thought that life *outside* society was what 'degraded' man, and he compares the need for society to the individual's basic need for the family unit. Without society man has no more resources for survival than an abandoned child. Voltaire ridicules Rousseau's account of the foundation of modern society in terms of the invention of the false notion of property. 'Liberty and property' Voltaire countered in his 1771 article on property in *QE*, 'is the cry of the English ... it is the cry of nature.' The ownership of property was for Voltaire one of the major strands in that bond of shared, enlightened self-interest holding society together.

Man in society is not irredeemably wicked; in the state of nature, so vaunted by the deluded Rousseau, he is a miserable brute. The 1771 text of this article ends after a brief discussion of one of Pascal's *Thoughts* on man. Pascal was an intellectual adversary of longer standing than Rousseau, a 'sublime misanthropist' not without a measure of reluctantly felt appeal for Voltaire, but like the 'mad' Rousseau he had a negative view of human nature and potential. The final paragraph of *H(QE)*, celebrating man's thirty-century-long struggle for enlightenment, and denying once more the anti-social, anti-progressivist Pascal-Rousseauist thesis, was added in 1774.

Freedom and humanity

The nature of Voltaire's long campaign against the abuses of freedom in France is best encapsulated in his memorable slogan: 'Crush the infamous.' The slogan had in fact been suggested to him by Frederick the Great in 1759 (Best. D8304), and it rapidly became his well-repeated battlecry throughout the 1760s, as he engaged the authorities publicly in combat around the notorious breaches of human rights and freedom that were to occur in France with the cases of La Barre, Calas and Sirven (see Bien 1960; Nixon 1961). These three *causes célèbres* were to come to Voltaire's attention between 1762 and 1766, and to preoccupy him for another decade. The enemy, at a political as well as ideological level, was the Church, and in nearly all of Voltaire's political essays, whenever the argument turns to an attack on the cruel abuse of the governed by those who govern arbitrarily and in ignorance and/or defiance of the law, tyrants are seen as the willing accomplices, puppets or co-conspirators of ecclesiastical authorities.

In Voltaire's eyes, the Church legitimised and sanctified often fragile claims to power by means of an infernal bargain whereby rulers conceded some or, in some cases, all of their powers to the ever voracious representatives of Rome. The malignant presence of the Roman Church in the executive and legislative arms of government in Catholic countries constituted for Voltaire the major cause of civil disorder, intolerance, persecution and judicial corruption. This was 'the infamous', and while the main attacks were reserved for Rome, no sect was entirely free of the stains of superstitious intolerance and fanaticism. Superstition might be absurd, its tenets risible, its representatives grotesque, but in eighteenth-century France, and elsewhere, it could deny freedom and obliterate ideals of humanity and brotherhood, as well as torture and kill. In conversation 11 of *ABC* he calls this a 'rabid madness' that has soaked the earth in blood with depressing regularity throughout Jewish and Christian history.

In defence of freedom and humanity, Voltaire felt obliged to wage an unremitting war against religion as an institution of the State, and as a repository of political power. Many of the articles in *DP* are concerned with this issue; it also surfaces in the *IR* and elsewhere in *ABC* (see especially conversations 10, 14–16). It is no coincidence that in *ABC*, as in so many of Voltaire's works, statements on freedom, equality, power, legal codes, kingship, tyranny and economics are intermingled with diversions on religion, the nature of religious belief, the history of Christianity and Judaism, metaphysical systems and superstitions. Such diversions are, in fact, central to Voltaire's understanding of political realities, and of his diagnosis of the political, social and moral ills he witnessed in the world around him. What men believe in, or what they are persuaded to believe in and, more importantly, persuade others to believe in, governs the nature of the institutions they establish. This dynamic, ever-present tension between the spiritual and temporal powers of the State was to Voltaire a vitally important key to any meaningful political analysis.

DH, dated 24 June 1768, was almost certainly inspired by a French government pamphlet issued over the name of C. E. Pfeffel in the same year. Avignon had been sold to Pope Clement VI in 1348 by the Countess of Provence, Joanna I of Naples, and it remained a papal possession until 1791. Pfeffel's quasi-official justification for papal occupation, sub-titled *Historical researches into the rights of the Pope over the city and state of Avignon*, prompted Voltaire to investigate the whole issue of papal involvement in politics, the legitimacy of papal rights to temporal rule, and in particular the pretentions of acquisitive popes such as Alexander VI and Julius II in the dynastic upheavals of Naples, Sicily, Ferrara, Castro and Ronciglione. In the case of Italy, such unholy intrigue unleashed the power of the Borgias. The lesson for France was clear: 'Popes do not possess an inch of land over which they have sovereign power that has not been acquired through civil upheaval or through fraud'. Popes cannot legitimise any action taken in defiance of the law, whatever theologians might say to the contrary. That Avignon is held illegally by the papacy is the inference running through the concluding paragraphs of *DH*.

The unsigned pamphlet *IR* that Voltaire wrote in October or November 1765 (see Gay 1988, Appendix 2), sprang originally from his involvement with the politics of Geneva after he took up residence in Les Délices in the winter of 1754–5. The Genevan context of this work, written and circulated against the tumultuous background of the power struggles between the bourgeois *représentants*, the patrician *négatifs* and the *natifs*, that had been intensifying in that city-state ever since the 1738 settlement, and reached something of a crescendo in the 1760s, should not be forgotten. It is important to retain this perspective in mind when interpreting *IR* as a *bona fide* statement of Voltaire's republicanism and liberalism. The case can also be made that *IR* has a far wider significance than that afforded by the 'Genevan bickerings'. By most criteria *IR* must remain one of Voltaire's most important political pronouncements. It is a powerful defence of freedom and tolerance, and it has an important general point of principle to make about the rule of law and the overmighty role of the clergy in affairs of state (for an excellent analysis, see Gay 1958).

One of the central statements of this work is to be found in sections XI-XII (pp. 197–8). Here Voltaire sharpens the attack on freedom represented by church interference and the Church's manipulation of the forces of superstition. The city of Calvin also had its fanatics, and was also subject to a baleful church influence over the conduct of its affairs. It was thus in a Protestant context that Voltaire formulated one of his most telling treatments of the issue raised by the ecclesiastical abuse of power, also demonstrating once more his skills in drawing out issues of universal importance from the daily ebb and flow of human drama. The case of Robert Covelle, whom the Genevan Consistory had condemned in 1763 to ask God's pardon on his knees for fathering an illegitimate child and who, in refusing to accept the sentence of public genuflection, had caused a public furore. Voltaire had quickly sprung to 'Mr Fornicator's' defence. The case had farcical overtones, but in Voltaire's hands the general principle went to the heart of the controversial nature of the relationship of ecclesiastical authority to civil government.

The Covelle incident reverberates through the *IR* from start to finish. Liberty of thought and speech is the *sine qua non* of civil stability and maturity (see section XXV on p. 201). Only when a nation has finally freed itself of fanaticism, and crushed the infamous, will true humanity and nationhood emerge. Freedom restores to man his natural rights. Perfect government has never been achieved because men have passions, and if they did not have passions they would not need government. In section XLIII (p. 207) Voltaire addresses the question of the franchise, the rights of property-owners and the economic advantages of Protestant republics, returning again to a discussion of Montesquieu's theories. Voltaire was never to express himself in quite such radical terms again.

In a letter written in 1734, he told his friend Argental that he had left France for England in order to enjoy in a free country the greatest benefit, and the finest of human rights, which is to 'depend only on the law and not on men's whims' (Best. D738). The law, based on reason and justice, is emphasised again and again in his political writings as the life-source of civil society. In *PA* he wrote that this was the basis of freedom, and that without it men were simply yoked animals. Six years later, at the end of conversation 13 in *ABC*, he expands on what this meant, coming back to the fundamental condition of freedom that the English experience had taught him (Waldinger 1959; Rowe 1955; Perkins 1962).

Crime and punishment

L(DP) started life in the 1764 edition of *DP*. A new section was added in 1767, and Voltaire expanded it considerably again in 1771 for the first edition of *QE*. The section dealing with the reforms of

Catherine II was sent to the Empress for comment prior to publication (see Best. D17081). Voltaire uses this article to emphasise that while government is a principle of organisation well established in nature, a perfect, uniform and enduring set of laws has never yet been established in any society. Moreover, laws are relative to time, place and need. If pigeons and vultures had law-codes, those codes would differ profoundly. Often laws have been made in the interests of rulers and legislators and have been subjected to the pressures of ignorance, cruelty and superstition. Their evolution through history has owed more to chance than to rationality. The sceptical, somewhat pessimistic, tone that pervades Voltaire's investigation of the origins of law is tempered by the rays of light that shone from the reforms carried out by Catherine II.

Voltaire's approach is again entirely pragmatic. The laws are seen exclusively here in terms of their usefulness, their relevance to society's needs, their basis in reason, good sense, justice and humanity. Men make the law, using abilities given to them by nature. Unfortunately, they do not always make good laws. There is no serious attempt in this article to relate systems of law to abstract concepts of natural law and justice. In fact, Voltaire wrote quite prolifically on the question of natural law (see Gay 1988, Appendix 1). He even wrote a long poem about it, and references to it are scattered throughout his writings. In conversation 4 of *ABC*, a definition of natural law is offered by A, but is received with considerable scepticism by B and C, and the discussion veers away from the issue more than it confronts it. In section 14 in the commentary on Beccaria's treatise on crime and punishment Voltaire refines his view of natural law. Natural laws are 'those laws that nature points to in all ages to all men for the maintenance of that sense of justice which nature, whatever else one might say about it, has engraved in our hearts'. It is on this basis that murder, robbery, violence, perjury, treason are true crimes infringing natural law, and blasphemy and heresy are not. The ramifications are not explored further than this somewhat bland assertion of principle. In conversation 13 in *ABC* he deals with 'basic laws', not quite the same thing, but again this is reduced to a single concrete issue: freedom. Freedom is the 'basic law of all nations; it's the only law against which nothing can be ordained, because it's the law of nature.'

Voltaire was thus no natural law philosopher, and his interest in the subject is tenuous and slightly unconvincing. Natural law belonged to the realm of speculative metaphysics, and like Dr Pangloss' 'cosmolonogonomy', was a distraction from the urgent business of securing justice in the real world in which for Voltaire the need to take action always took precedence over abstract debate. In *L(DP)* the focus is again characteristically on the interface between moral–legal codes and social realities – whether these relate to incest on desert islands, or to crime and punishment in eighteenth-century Russia.

In 1762, on the basis of weak evidence and strong religious prejudice, a jury in Toulouse had found the head of a Protestant family, Jean Calas, guilty of the murder of his son, rumoured to be about to convert to Catholicism, and sentenced Calas to be broken on the wheel and strangled. The event had a profound impact on Voltaire, who fought the subsequent case for the rehabilitation of the Calas family without respite until the name of Calas and the iniquities of the French judicial system were the talk of Europe. The verdict was quashed in 1765.

It was fresh from this epic struggle that Voltaire came to write one of the most important works of these portentous years from the standpoint of public impact. During the course of 1765 he was studying in the original Italian a work by Cesare Beccaria, a relatively obscure Milanese jurist, entitled *Trattato dei delitti e della pene* (On crimes and punishments), which had been published in the previous year, and translated into French by Morellet. Beccaria's treatise was the first attempt by a modern legal expert to formulate a coherent theory of penal policy, and it made a deep impression on Voltaire, who was by now engaged in another public confrontation with the authorities in France. This revolved around the case of the Sirven family who, like Calas, had also been falsely accused of murder and sentenced to horrific punishment. In 1766 Voltaire was to be affected even more violently by a third case of miscarriage of justice, followed by judicial atrocity, when a young, disrespectful teenager, the chevalier de La Barre, failed to observe the courtesies when a religious procession passed by, and was cruelly mutilated and executed in Abbeville in July of that year. Interestingly, a copy of *DP* was found among La Barre's possessions, and a copy had been duly burned with the boy's corpse (see Mason 1982, ch. 8).

Introduction

These three tragic casualties of the 'infamous', Calas, Sirven and La Barre, sharpened Voltaire's interest in the issues of crime and punishment as set out in Beccaria's treatise (see Van Den Heuvel 1975). The result was the publication in 1766 of his own commentary on the treatise, *CLDP*. The issue of crime and punishment stayed with Voltaire for many years, and in 1777, the year before his death, he was still writing on the subject, publishing a complementary work to *CLDP* in the form of *The prize for justice and humanity*, a pretended entry for an essay competition announced in Berne. Part of the text of *CLDP* was reprinted in section 22 of that work.

In sections 1–5 of *CLDP*, Voltaire examines what constitutes a criminal act. Crime for Voltaire was exclusively a secular matter, an act that injures society, not churches. The fact that so much of the penal code was linked to non-secular matters is a further indication to Voltaire of the perversion of legislative codes that had arisen as a consequence of the intrusion of the ecclesiastical powers into areas that are properly the concern of civil governments alone. It was in the context of crime and punishment that the 'infamous' did its bloodiest work, as Voltaire illustrates graphically in sections 8–9.

One of the key parts of *CLDP* is to be found in sections 10–12, which deal with the place of torture and the death penalty in judicial procedures – the epitome of vengeful legal systems. Death, often accompanied by tortures of Gothic extravagance, was the normal penalty (though not always exacted) for a wide range of offences in mid-eighteenth-century France. Voltaire's arguments against it are both humanitarian and utilitarian. The death penalty caused suffering for the victim and brutalised society generally. It was also an economic irrationality. Here Voltaire follows Beccaria and Montesquieu in insisting that severe penalties serve to increase crime levels rather than reduce them. In ancient Rome citizens were condemned to death only when the security of the State was at stake (section 10).

Voltaire also opposed on this basis the laws exacting confiscation of a condemned man's property, a disproportionate punishment that unjustly affected innocent widows and orphans. He calls this penalty in section 21 'state robbery' (see Perkins 1989). He felt so strongly about the confiscation of property issue that section 21 of *CLDP* was reprinted in 1769 in chapter 42 of the *Summary of the age of Louis XV*, and again in 1771 in the article on confiscation in *QE*. Extreme law tends to destroy the law (section 15). Mercy was cost-effective in as much as a living man could do forced labour and benefit society. A dead man was unproductive – an echo of one of the few observations in Rousseau's *Social contract* of which Voltaire approved. Moreover, disproportionate penalties, such as death for petty theft, discouraged victims of theft to bring the culprit to justice. Punishment should be a deterrent, not an instrument of vengeance, and in this of course Voltaire opposed both the spirit and the letter of legislative procedures established in France since the 1670 Criminal Ordinance.

Section 22 contains a lengthy commentary on the interrogation practices prescribed in the 1670 Criminal Ordinance, whereby ill-treated prisoners were kept in ignorance of the charge against them, witnesses were questioned secretly and separately, and if necessary put to the question to extract the 'truth'. The penalties for changing or withdrawing evidence were ferocious. The image of the wretched Calas, lying for months in chained torment, could not have been far from Voltaire's mind when he wrote this angry section on *ancien régime* criminal procedures, and the closing paragraph makes this clear. Voltaire's appeal at the end of his remarkably powerful commentary on Beccaria's treatise is for urgent reform of the French legal system (see Maestro 1942; Foucault 1975). His play for public opinion in his commentary on Beccaria was to bear fruit quickly. The number of death sentences passed in France fell noticeably in the 1780s (Mason 1982, ch. 8), and by 1788 the death sentence was becoming relatively rare in French judicial procedures. The 1670 Criminal Ordinance was abolished by the Revolution, and the 1791 code heralded the reforms to be implemented under the Napoleonic codes of the early nineteenth century.

War and peace

The international order in eighteenth-century Europe was seriously disrupted by two major wars and, as a confidant of kings and a friend of ministers, Voltaire was uniquely placed to observe the workings of the diplomatic machinery that accompanied both. There had also been a War of the Polish Succession in 1733–5, but this had been a relatively minor affair. During the War of the Austrian Succession (1740–8) Voltaire's close relationship with Frederick the Great enabled him to act as an intermediary between Berlin and Paris, although after 1742, when Frederick broke his alliance with France,

Fleury had doubts about Voltaire's trustworthiness as an agent acting on behalf of French interests (see Perkins 1965; Stavan 1986). Voltaire witnessed and actively participated in the international power-brokering that took place not only in the context of France's relations with Prussia, but also in connection with Franco-Dutch affairs, and the French campaign in the Netherlands. In 1756 Voltaire, by then in Geneva, found himself embroiled in the diplomacy surrounding the outbreak of the second great European war, the Seven Years War, during which he again tried to act as an arbitrator between Louis XV and the Prussian king.

The authenticity of so many of his observations on war, peace and the contemporary international scene owes as much to this personal engagement in events as to the many eye-witness accounts and theories that he studied. For international law theorists like Grotius, Pufendorf, Barbeyrac and Wolff, and pacifist thinkers like the *abbé* de Saint-Pierre, he had in fact little time (see Perkins 1961). In *PA* he sneers at Pufendorf as a thinker with the foresight of a composer of 'defective almanachs'. In the early phases of his friendship with Frederick, his admiration for Machiavelli's style and genius gave way to a dislike for his 'poisonous' precepts (Best. D1476, D1506), and he supported Frederick's own plans to refute Machiavellian theory, acting as editor of the Prussian king's work on the subject (see Fleischauer 1958, introduction). The fact that Frederick was to turn out to be the most adept Machiavellian of all undoubtedly contributed to the cynicism and disillusionment at the heart of the portrayal of war, human nature and international relations painted by Voltaire after 1756.

G(DP) was composed for the 1764 edition of *DP*, in the aftermath of the Seven Years War, which had been brought to a humiliating conclusion for France in 1763 with the Treaty of Paris. Voltaire revised the opening paragraphs and expanded the article in 1765, and again in the 1771 *QE*. War for Voltaire was the greatest of all the moral evils, and as *G(DP)* makes clear in a number of Hobbesian observations, conflict is endemic to the human condition. In the case of both the War of the Austrian Succession and the Seven Years War Voltaire locates their cause in the arbitrary whims and ambitions of 'a few men'. The 'genealogical' justification for the warrior prince to raise an army and declare war, is a thinly veiled reference to Frederick's rationale for the invasion of Silesia, which had triggered the general conflagration. Voltaire goes on to describe the *danse macabre* of ever-changing alliances and disagreements between the warring partners. His description of 'the infernal enterprise' closely echoes the sardonically clinical tableaux of battle-scenes between the Abars and the Bulgars portrayed in the third chapter of *Candide* (1759). Voltaire's experience suggested to him that international law and international codes of conduct were illusory concepts without any basis in the realities of human behaviour, again closely echoing Hobbes' analysis in Part 1 of the *Leviathan* (see Thielemann 1959).

P(DP) first appeared in the 1764 edition of *DP*, and was revised and expanded for *QE* in 1771. Here Voltaire explores one of the most emotionally charged issues in the name of which war is often justified: patriotism. Patriotism becomes a diversified form of self-interest. He identifies it first with the notion of ownership and property, which meant that the majority of people would have no homeland. To have a homeland, and to be truly a patriot, meant being a citizen, and that is only possible in that utopian state, a republic. In other political systems patriotism was a spurious sentiment that only meant wishing to advance national self-interest at the expense of other countries, and as such fed the psychology of war that continued to hold the nation-states of Europe in its grip.

War was not subject to rational or honourable justification, as Voltaire's attack on Montesquieu's axiom about the rights of pre-emptive attack at the end of *G(DP)* indicates. *G(DP)* presents the reader with the stark Hobbesian view that war is natural to man, and that for all animals this is in the order of nature: 'each species was born to devour another'. *P(QE)* reinforces that view, even in the face of the evidence of man's progress in other areas. Peace treaties arose from expediency, not good will, and their provisions were contingent and precarious. There were various projects for world peace put forward in the eighteenth century, of which perhaps the *abbé* de Saint-Pierre's *Project for perpetual peace in Europe*, published to coincide with the Treaty of Utrecht in 1713, received the most attention from Voltaire (see Perkins 1961). Voltaire attacked all of them as being hopelessly naive about the causes of war, and the realities of human nature.

In spite of God's gift of reason, war remained irremediably the frightful lot of humanity, together with plague, famine and natural disasters. The opening paragraphs of *G(DP)* confirm Voltaire's close alignment with Hobbes on this point. As B makes clear in conversation 1 in *ABC*, Hobbes is a philosopher for whom society is a 'prison' inhabited by criminals and slaves, and in which man is born the enemy of other men. On the other hand, Voltaire accepts that Hobbes might have had a valid point to make, and he certainly agrees with Hobbes that on the international level the only law is that of national self-interest, in which force rather than reason or morality dictates the outcome of conflict.

G(DP) also underlines the eager willingness with which the masses fight for causes they do not understand in the interest of rulers who are at best indifferent to their welfare. The peasant soldiers are for Voltaire little more than brutalised automata, enthusiastic cannon-fodder driven by greed, superstition and xenophobia, and led by avaricious statesmen and churchmen. In *DH* and *ABC* he comments acidly on the moral vacuum in the hearts of most politicians who know only how to 'cheat at cards', and through whose personal feuds and rivalries thousands of men are persuaded, only too readily, to march off to battle. Papal usurpations in *DH* illustrate the casual, but lethal, volatility of international power games, especially when the Vatican is involved. The emptiness and hypocrisy of international law codes also provide the focus for debate in conversation 11 in *ABC*. In section 6 of *G(QE)* Voltaire sees war as the fundamental fact of life upon which all else is built, and by which all else is conditioned.

The somewhat mechanistic view of human affairs that predominates in Voltaire's writings on international affairs does not mean that he was a pessimist or a determinist, as his unflagging attack on Leibnizian optimism after the 1755 earthquake in Lisbon amply demonstrates. Man's salvation and destiny lay in human hands, and would be realised through human actions. This is why in *ABC* the *Leviathan* must remain in the final analysis a 'prison', and why B would not care to be a citizen of Hobbes' civil commonwealth.

Wealth and poverty

Voltaire was a very young man when a Scotsman named John Law became Comptroller-General in France after the death of Louis XIV, and began to apply his ideas to the economic life of the Regency period. The collapse of Law's financial system in 1720 had long-term repercussions for the French economy, despite the fact that by 1726 the currency had stabilised (see Mason 1982, ch. 1). Contrary to prevailing theory (see Payne 1976; Taylor 1964), Law believed that precious metals did not in themselves constitute wealth, but were rather the means to create wealth. Paper money could therefore be substituted for gold and silver, and Law issued large amounts of paper currency in the belief that this would improve France's prosperity and trading position. The experiment failed, but Law's ideas were recycled in a revised form by Jean-François Melon, and Melon's *Political essay on commerce* (1734) influenced Voltaire greatly (see Kotta 1966, introduction). While Voltaire rejected Law's faith in the beneficial effects of paper money, Melon nevertheless thought that paper money had some use, if the proper restraints were in place. Voltaire agreed with this, and interestingly he never really placed total responsibility for France's financial problems on Law's policies. On the contrary, references to Law in Voltaire's writings are almost always positive and laudatory.

Following Melon's adaptations of Law's views, Voltaire developed a number of theories about national wealth which find their clearest and most engaging exposition in a work published in 1751 in the form of a dialogue between a philosopher and a comptroller-general, *DPC*. In this dialogue the interlocutors are *personae* representing Voltaire himself and Jean-Baptiste Machault d'Arnouville, France's Comptroller-General from 1745 to 1754, whom Voltaire wished to influence. The pamphlet is a direct challenge to orthodox mercantilist theory which had dominated economic philosophies in Europe since the Middle Ages and the collapse of feudalism. The mercantilists believed that the more gold and silver a state possessed, the better placed that state was to pursue its interests at the expense of its neighbours (see Kotta 1966, introduction). The example of Spain, with its ready supply of gold from the South American colonies, was regularly cited by mercantilists as proof of the validity of their theories.

Thus the reference to the Spanish army in *DPC* is not inconsequential. Voltaire concedes the value of gold and silver in the context of balance of trade problems and in times of war (see Perkins 1962; 1965 ch. 8). However, he insists that the true wealth of a state does not reside exclusively in its holdings of precious metals, but rather in produce, industry and labour. The Spanish army might have swords made of gold, but what is the use of that if they have no shirts and no bread? Wealth lies in commodities, and is the creation of a productive labour force and a forward-looking manufacturing sector. At the same time, in *DPC*, with its emphasis on the crucial importance of industry and trade, the groundwork for Voltaire's later disagreements with the physiocrats was also being laid, prefiguring in an interesting way the views of Adam Smith.

The physiocrats were a group of mid-century economists led by Mme de Pompadour's doctor, Quesnay, and his disciple Le Mercier de La Rivière. Their taxation philosophy provides the main satirical target in *LHQE*. In *DPC* an echo of the physiocratic debate is reflected in the discussion of what constitutes net produce, the importance of agriculture and the need for the free circulation of agricultural produce (see Payne 1976). Voltaire comments astringently on the 'shameful and ridiculous' workings of a taxation system that levied duty on produce as it moved from one province to another within France's borders. On this point at least, he agreed with physiocratic arguments, and he was greatly encouraged when Turgot became Comptroller-General in 1774, and enacted reformist legislation to ensure the free circulation of grain and wine.

In *I(QE)*, composed for *QE* in 1771, and expanded in 1774, Voltaire assesses the balance of inequities in economic life. The peasant is right to protest against the system that exploits his labour for the benefit of the few, but the rich lady's lackey is also right: his rich mistress's magnificent court pension is spent on conspicuous consumption of the produce of the labouring class, and is thus returned to society through her extravagant purchases. The circulation of money and goods was a *sine qua non* of national prosperity, and following Melon, Voltaire always maintained that the pursuit of luxury did not necessarily imply decadence and stasis.

By the middle of the eighteenth century fiscal disorder had scaled record heights in France. Voltaire provides a particularly acute analysis of the situation in the third section of *G(QE)* (pp. 52–4). Here he illustrates how the tax policies followed by successive ministers had been merely *ad hoc* responses to immediate issues, short-term improvisation rather than long-term strategy. Mountains of inadequately framed legislation had accumulated over the years, and the result was absurdity, fraud and unnecessary hardship, illustrated in a typically serious-comic Voltairean way with the anecdote of the 'excess drink' tax, accounts of official venality and financial cheating, and a telling exposure of the impotence of a theoretically all-powerful government to do anything about the situation. In a note added in 1774, Voltaire comments that a traveller returning to the same country two years later would have seen some reforms, although if he returned four years later he would have seen the abuses re-established. The reference is to Maupeou's abolition of venal offices in 1771, and to the re-establishment of those offices by Louis XVI when he came to the throne in November 1774, and recalled the *parlements* (see Mason 1982 ch. 1).

E(QE), published in 1771, takes a broader view of the domestic and public sectors of the economy, and further exemplifies the techniques of anecdote and analogy that Voltaire deploys to make the most complex technicalities vivid and readily comprehensible. In the section on public economy Voltaire compares the workings of different national economies, the purchasing power of money in different parts of Europe, and the differing ways of handling national debts. He reviews the effects on France of the policies of different ministers, including the detested Bois-Guillebert, the much admired Colbert, and the 'serious fool' Law. When referring to the state bank in the section on public economy, Voltaire almost certainly has in mind the damage inflicted by Law's abortive attempt to establish such a bank, complete with credit arrangements and paper money, in 1716 – a move resulting in ruin and widespread public disorder.

The soil and its products always return to the centre of Voltaire's considerations on national prosperity. 'Whoever possesses wheat will always lay the law down to those who need bread', he wrote in his article on corn in *QE*. That simple precept informs much of the argument set out in *E(QE)*.

Voltaire's France was a state in which the king ruled as a supreme autocrat by divine right, and was accordingly above the law. The person of the monarch was sacred, and was to remain so throughout most of the century until the execution of Louis XVI in 1793, an event that shocked Europe but marked the birth of modern France. What Voltaire's reaction to regicide would have been, had he lived to witness it, is a matter for tentative speculation and debate. Whatever else might be involved in such a debate, however, it would necessarily have to include a careful assessment of the paradoxes and ambivalences of his position on kings and republics.

The problem of measuring the precise degree to which Voltaire retained faith in monarchism and the *thèse royale* as a pragmatist, and the degree to which his sympathies as an idealist reflect a preference for republicanism in its modern sense has not yet been resolved in a clear-cut fashion, and is possibly unresolvable in simplistic terms. *IR*, with its statement that the most tolerable government of all 'is without any doubt the republican', offers tempting evidence of a republicanism of the most liberal variety (see p. xxii above), but *IR* remains the exception rather than the rule, and was by no means Voltaire's final word on the subject. In one of the last works that he wrote, the *Commentary on the Spirit of the laws* (1777), he reiterated his distrust of republican 'virtue', and scholars remain divided on this very central issue of Voltairean politics.

The ambiguities of Voltaire's position are perhaps nowhere better illustrated than in his description of the utopian state in *Candide*. Eldorado has some virtuous features that are recognisably republican in a vaguely moral way: a happy, fulfilled people, equality before the law, no factions, no privileged power-groups, no poverty, no role for religion in government, and an ethos of *philosophe* rationality. But Eldorado is still a discreetly absolute monarchy, albeit governed under the law on enlightened lines by a philosopher-king. There is no hint of a general franchise, a constituent assembly, or democratic procedures. The Eldoradans are subjects under paternalistic rule, not citizens participating in a collective, egalitarian enterprise. A similar picture emerges in the description of William Penn's Pennsylvania in the *Philosophical Letters*, published a quarter of a century before. Conversely, the republics portrayed in *Candide* are noticeably lacking in virtue.

In spite of his unhappy experience with kings and courts, in spite of his radicalism on moral and social issues, it is difficult on present evidence to align Voltaire unequivocally with republicanism and democracy in the modern sense of these terms. He returns too frequently to the *thèse royale*, and his hostility to Rousseauist notions of a social contract is too consistent. Ironically, all this did not prevent him from becoming, along with Jean-Jacques Rousseau, an icon of the French Revolution, his name and reputation after 1789 associated unreservedly in the popular mind with the mission and aspirations of France's First Republic.

Bibliographical note

There are three great post 1784 collective editions of Voltaire's works: the 'Kehl' edition, edited by Beaumarchais and others in 70 volumes (1785–9); the 'Beuchot' edition, edited by A. J. O. Beuchot in 72 volumes (1829–40); the 'Moland' edition, edited by L. Moland in 52 volumes (1877–85). A new critical edition of Voltaire's *Complete works* is currently in progress under the auspices of the Voltaire Foundation at Oxford, but none of the works relevant to this collection have so far been published. The definitive Besterman edition of the correspondence forms part of this new edition (volumes 85–135). As far as the works are concerned, Moland, with all its defects, remains the vulgate for the time being. Editions of Voltaire's writings are catalogued in G. Bengesco's four-volume bibliography (1882–90), and this is still a valuable work of reference.

DP was first translated into English in 1765 as *The philosophical dictionary for the pocket*, and reprinted in 1767. Between 1793 and 1852 eight further English translations appeared, some of selected articles only. An unabridged selection in English was published by Pioneer Press in 1919, and another selection was translated by H.I. Woolf and published by Allen and Unwin in 1924 (reprinted in 1945). A 'compendium' of articles was translated by W. Baslin and published by Peter Owen in 1962. In the same year Peter Gay's two-volume translation, with a preface by André Maurois, was published by Basic Books in New York. The latest translation, by Theodore Besterman, appeared in 1971 (Penguin).

The best modern edition in French of *DP* is the 1954 edition established by R. Naves, with introduction and notes by J. Benda.

This is based on the 1769 text. The Benda-Naves edition of *DP* explains the development of this complex work, and illuminates clearly the additions and changes, including the revisions for the *QE*. Y. Florenne published an edition of *DP* in 1962 (Club français du livre), and another edition was published in 1964 in the Garnier-Flammarion series, edited by R. Pomeau. René Pomeau also published an anthology of extracts of Voltaire's political writings in 1963 (Colin).

With the exception of *DP*, none of the works in this collection have appeared in separate English translation before.

A good, though lengthy, general introduction is Ira Wade's study of Voltaire's intellectual development (Wade 1969). The first two chapters of Haydn Mason's survey of French writers and their society 1715–1800 offer an excellent assessment of the main socio-political features of eighteenth-century France (Mason 1982). Besterman's biography is a lively, if sometimes tendentious study, and contains an interesting commentary on Voltaire's political thought in chapters 24 and 28 (Besterman 1969). For a more neutral account of Voltaire's life Mason's biography should be consulted (Mason 1981). The most recent biographical study is by a French team of scholars, and three volumes have been published so far (Pomeau 1985, Vaillot 1988, Pomeau and Mervaud 1991).

The most comprehensive study in English of Voltaire's political thought is still Peter Gay's book, now in its second edition (Gay 1988). *IR* is probably the most frequently quoted source in assessments of Voltaire's political ideas, and Gay's substantial article is the best analysis of *IR*'s genesis and import (Gay 1958). R. Waldinger's examination of Voltaire and reform in the light of the Revolution is still very informative (Waldinger 1959), as is the introduction to J. H. Brumfitt's edition of *La philosophie de l'histoire* (Voltaire 1969), which establishes Voltaire's credentials as a political historian.

On constitutional matters, Besterman's article on Voltaire and absolute monarchy is well focussed (Besterman 1965), but should be read in conjunction with chapter 7 of Gay's book. A well-informed and lucid analysis of Voltaire's views on government and society is found in chapter 2 of Fletcher's guide to the *Lettres philosophiques* (Fletcher 1986), and this contains helpful commentaries on the impact of England on Voltaire's political attitudes. On English influence Perry's study is also essential reading (Perry 1977; see also A.

M. Rousseau 1976). Constance Rowe's book on Voltaire and the
State offers a general overview (Rowe 1955). Tate's closely argued
article on Voltaire and the *parlements* is also relevant to a balanced
understanding of Voltaire's criticism of French political institutions
(Tate 1972; see also Rivière 1987).

The most detailed analysis of Voltaire's views on international
affairs is Perkins' full-length study of Voltaire's concept of international order (Perkins 1965). This has very useful chapters on European politics, international law, despotism, war, sovereignty and other
Voltairean concerns. See also Appendix 2 of Perkins' study for a list
of the books in Voltaire's library directly relevant to key aspects of his
political thought. Perkins' articles on war and peace (with particular
reference to the peace project of the *abbé* de Saint-Pierre, Perkins
1961) and on the source of national power (Perkins 1962), are also
valuable contributions. Meyer's study of Voltaire's views on war and
peace should be consulted (Meyer 1976), and Lamm's article on this
subject is also very helpful (Lamm 1978).

On influences, Gay 1988 provides a great deal of information, as
does Perkins 1962, 1965. Of particular relevance to several of the
texts in this collection is Thielemann's study of Hobbes' impact on
Voltaire (Thielemann 1959), and Crocker's more general study of
sources is equally illuminating (Crocker 1983, see also Dzwigala's
article on Voltaire's sources on the Polish question, Dzwigala 1986).
On Voltaire's relations with Frederick the Great, see the introduction
to Fleischauer's edition of Frederick's *Anti-Machiavelli*, which also
throws light on Voltaire's reaction to Machiavelli (Fleischauer 1958,
see also Stavan 1986).

With regard to specific controversies, most scholars have concen-
trated on the Calas case. Bien's book is a good place to start with
regard to this crucial *cause célèbre* (Bien 1960, see also Nixon 1961,
Besterman 1969 chapter 33, Mason 1975 chapter 5, Gay 1988 chapter 6, Van Den Heuvel 1975, Birchall 1990). On issues relating to
freedom, section 3 of Perkins' article on the *philosophes* and human
rights should be consulted (Perkins 1989). Maestro's 1942 study of
Voltaire and Beccaria is still essential reading for an understanding
of Voltaire's thinking on the law and criminal reform, but for a more
up to date analysis of the commentary on Beccaria's treatise, see
Mason 1982 ch. 8, and Besterman 1969 ch. 35. There is an excellent
section on crime and punishment in the introduction to N. Kotta's

study of Voltaire's satirical tale, *LHQE* (Kotta 1966). Michel Foucault's study of punishment opens up other fascinating aspects of eighteenth-century penal philosophy (Foucault 1975).

Relatively little has been written on Voltaire's economic theories. Kotta is a mine of information on Voltaire's views on taxation (particularly Law, Melon and Le Mercier), mercantilism, and the physiocrats. Payne's article on poverty and the aims of enlightened economics also offers valuable insights (Payne 1976, see also Perkins 1989 and Taylor 1964). Vignery has most to say in this area on Voltaire, specifically Vignery 1960. For general background on eighteenth-century economics, see Taylor 1964.

Select bibliography

Beccaria, Cesare, 1963 *On crimes and punishments*, ed. and trans. H. Paolucci (Indianapolis/New York: Bobbs-Merrill)

Besterman, Theodore, 1965 'Voltaire, absolute monarchy, and the enlightened monarch', *Studies on Voltaire and the Eighteenth Century*, 32, pp. 7–21

1969 *Voltaire* (London: Longmans)

Bien, D. D., 1960 *The Calas affair: persecution, toleration and heresy in eighteenth-century Toulouse* (Princeton: Princeton University Press)

Birchall, I. H., 1990 'Voltaire and collective action', *British Journal for Eighteenth-Century Studies*, 13, pp. 19–29

Crocker, Lester G., 1983 'Voltaire and the political philosophers', *Studies on Voltaire and the Eighteenth Century*, 219, pp. 1–17

Dzwigala, W., 1986 'Voltaire's sources on the Polish dissident question', *Studies on Voltaire and the Eighteenth Century*, 241, pp. 187–202

Fleischauer, Charles, 1958 *L'Anti-Machiavel, par Frédéric II, Studies on Voltaire and the Eighteenth Century*, 5

Fletcher, Dennis, 1986 *Voltaire: Lettres philosophiques* (London: Grant & Cutler)

Foucault, Michel, 1975 *Surveiller et punir: naissance de la prison* (Paris: Gallimard)

Gay, Peter, 1958 'Voltaire's *Idées républicaines*: A study in bibliography and interpretation', *Studies on Voltaire and the Eighteenth Century*, 6, pp. 67–105.

1988 *Voltaire's politics: the poet as realist* (New Haven/London: Yale University Press). Second edition

Kotta, Nuçi, 1966 *L'Homme aux quarante écus. A study of Voltairean themes* (The Hague/Paris: Mouton)

Kunstler, C., 1960 *La vie quotidienne sous la régence* (Paris: Hachette)

Lamm, H., 1978 'Voltaire and the idea of peace', *Revue d'Histoire Diplomatique*, 92, pp. 262–74.

Lough, John, 1960 *An introduction to eighteenth-century France* (London: Longmans)

Maestro, Marcello T., 1942 *Voltaire and Beccaria as reformers of criminal law* (New York: Columbia University Press)

Mason, Haydn T., 1975 *Voltaire* (London: Hutchinson)

1981 *Voltaire: a biography* (London: Granada Publishing)

1982 *French writers and their society 1715–1800* (London: Macmillan)

Meyer, H., 1976 'Voltaire on war and peace', *Studies on Voltaire and the Eighteenth Century*, 152, pp. 15–26.

Montesquieu, 1949–51 *Oeuvres complètes*, ed. R. Caillois (Paris: Gallimard). Bibliothèque de la Pléiade.

Nixon, E., 1961 *Voltaire and the Calas case* (London: Gollancz)

Payne, H. C., 1976 ' *Pauvreté, misère* and the aims of enlightened economics', *Studies on Voltaire and the Eighteenth Century*, 154, pp. 1581–92.

Perkins, Merle L., 1961 'Voltaire and the *abbé* de Saint-Pierre on world peace', *Studies on Voltaire and the Eighteenth Century*, 18, pp. 9–34

1962 'Voltaire on the source of national power', *Studies on Voltaire and the Eighteenth Century*, 20, pp. 141–73

1965 *Voltaire's concept of international order, Studies on Voltaire and the Eighteenth Century*, 36

1989 'Six French *philosophes* on human rights, international rivalry and war: their message today', *Studies on Voltaire and the Eighteenth Century*, 260, pp. 44–61

Perry, Norma, 1977 'Voltaire's view of England', *Journal of European Studies*, 7, pp. 77–94

Pomeau, René, 1963 *Politique de Voltaire* (Paris: Colin)

1985 *D'Arouet à Voltaire 1694–1734* (Oxford: The Voltaire Foundation)

Pomeau, René and Mervaud, Christine, 1991 *De la cour au jardin 1750–59* (Oxford: The Voltaire Foundation)

Rivière, Marc S., 1987 'Voltaire and the Fronde', *Nottingham French Studies*, 26, pp. 1–18.

Rousseau, André-Michel, 1976 *L'Angleterre et Voltaire, Studies on Voltaire and the Eighteenth Century*, 145–7

Rousseau, Jean-Jacques, 1962 *Du contrat social, ou principes du droit politique* (Paris: Garnier). This includes the *Discours sur l'origine de l'inégalité parmi les hommes.*

Rowe, Constance, 1955 *Voltaire and the State* (New York: Columbia University Press)

Stavan, H. A., 1986 'Landgraf Frederick II of Hesse-Kassel and Voltaire', *Studies on Voltaire and the Eighteenth Century*, 241, pp. 161–83

Tate, Robert S., 1972 'Voltaire and the *parlements*: a reconsideration', *Studies on Voltaire and the Eighteenth Century*, 90, pp. 1529–43

Taylor, G. V., 1964 'Types of capitalism in eighteenth-century France', *English Historical Review*, 79, pp. 478–97

Thielemann, Leland, 1959 'Voltaire and Hobbism', *Studies on Voltaire and the Eighteenth Century*, 10, pp. 237–58

Todd, Christopher, 1980 *Voltaire: Dictionnaire philosophique* (London: Grant & Cutler)

Trapnell, William H., 1972 *Voltaire and his portable dictionary* (Frankfurt-am-Main). *Analecta romanica*, 32

Vaillot, R., 1988 *Avec Mme Du Châtelet 1734–59* (Oxford: The Voltaire Foundation)

Van Den Heuvel, J., 1975 *L'Affaire Calas et autres affaires* (Paris: Gallimard (Folio 672))

Venturi, Franco, 1971 *Utopia and reform in the Enlightenment* (Cambridge: Cambridge University Press)

Vignery, J. Robert, 1960 'Voltaire's economic ideas', *French Review*, 33, pp. 257–63

Voltaire, François Arouet de, 1877–85 *Oeuvres complètes*, ed. L. Moland (Paris: Garnier)

    1954 *Dictionnaire philosophique, comprenant les 118 articles parus sous ce titre du vivant de Voltaire avec leurs suppléments parus dans les Questions sur l'Encyclopédie*, ed. J. Benda and R. Naves (Paris: Garnier)

    1962 *Philosophical dictionary*, trans. Peter Gay (New York: Basic Books)

    1968–77 *Correspondence and related documents*, ed. Theodore Besterman (Oxford: The Voltaire Foundation)

1968– *The complete works of Voltaire*, ed. W. H. Barber *et al.* (Oxford: The Voltaire Foundation)

1969 *La Philosophie de l'histoire*, ed. J. H. Brumfitt (Toronto: University of Toronto Press). Voltaire 1968, vol. 59

1971 *Philosophical dictionary*, ed. and trans. Theodore Besterman (Harmondsworth: Penguin)

Wade, Ira O., 1969 *The intellectual development of Voltaire* (Princeton: Princeton University Press)

Waldinger, René, 1959 *Voltaire and reform in the light of the French Revolution* (Geneva: Droz/Paris: Minard)

Biographical note

ALBERONI, JULIO (1644–1752).
Spanish cardinal and statesman who became Prime Minister of Spain in 1717. His policies to retrieve Spanish territory lost after the Treaty of Utrecht misfired, and he was dismissed from office by Philip V in 1719.

BARBEYRAC, JEAN DE (1674–1744).
French Professor of jurisprudence who, as a Calvinist, was forced to flee France after the Revocation of the Edict of Nantes in 1684. He is the author of an important commentary on the works of Grotius.

BECCARIA, CESARE BONESANA (1738–94).
Milanese jurist and author of *On crimes and their punishments* (1764). This seminal work on criminal jurisprudence revitalised thinking on penal codes in the eighteenth century, and reflected many of the humanitarian concerns of the period. Beccaria was also one of the first economic theorists to analyse questions relating to capital and the division of labour.

BELLE-ISLE, CHARLES-FOUQUET (1684–1761).
Soldier and military theorist. Belle-Isle became Marshal of France in 1741, and Ambassador to the Diet of Frankfurt. He was largely responsible for the defeat of Austria in the War of Austrian Succession.

BUFFON, GEORGES LOUIS LECLERC (1707–88).
Scientist and economic theorist. Buffon published a magisterial multi-volumed *Natural history* (1749–89), and was the author of

xliii

numerous other works relating to geology and natural history. As an
an economist, he is remembered mainly for his *Essay on moral arithmetic* (1777).

CALAS, JEAN (1698–1762).
Merchant and victim of religious intolerance and judicial error. Calas'
son hanged himself and to avoid the indignities reserved by law for
suicides and their families Calas and his wife denied that the death
resulted from suicide. The family was Calvinist, and Calas was
accused of murder to prevent his son's conversion to Rome. Following sentence by the Toulouse *parlement*, he was broken on the wheel
in March 1762. Voltaire offered shelter to his widow and two of his
children, and eventually succeeded in obtaining the legal annulment
of the Toulouse judgement and the rehabilitation of Calas' name in
1765. The affair led directly to the publication of Voltaire's *Treatise
on tolerance* in the same year.

CHARLES V, DUKE OF LORRAINE (1643–90).
Implacable enemy of Louis XIV who prevented him from ever taking
possession of his dukedom. He became a Field-Marshal in the service of Austria. His son Leopold regained possession of Lorraine in
1697.

COLBERT, JEAN-BAPTISTE (1619–83).
Colbert was Louis XIV's great finance minister, becoming Comptroller-General in 1665. He was responsible, through his reforms of the
financial system and his taxation policies, for building up France's
wealth and prestige during the Sun King's reign. He also left his
mark on the literary and scientific life of France, and was greatly
admired by Voltaire.

COVELLE, ROBERT (dates unknown).
A Genevan watchmaker charged with immoral conduct by the City
Fathers of Geneva in 1763 for fathering a child with an unmarried
woman, Catherine Ferloz. Persons found guilty by the Consistory
Court of Geneva of immorality were obliged to kneel before the court
to be reprimanded. Covelle refused, and was imprisoned. Voltaire
wrote a bawdy epic on the affair, *The civil war of Geneva, or the loves
of Robert Covelle*, thereby deflecting the wrath of the authorities on to
himself. The decree of genuflection was withdrawn in 1769, but the

echoes of the case rumbled on for some time in the bitter controversies about the place of the Church in Genevan judicial procedures and political life.

DIDEROT, DENIS (1713–84).
French philosopher, encyclopaedist, novelist, art critic and playwright. A driving force behind the *philosophes*, Diderot was always at the forefront of the ideological struggles of the French Enlightenment. He was the principal editor of the *Encyclopaedia*. An atheist and philosophical determinist, he was deeply interested in questions of moral relativism, and as a political thinker, was influenced particularly by Locke and Montesquieu. His works include the *Letter on the blind* (1749), which led to his temporary imprisonment, the *Thoughts on the interpretation of nature* (1754), and the *Supplement to Bougainville's voyage* (1772?).

FREDERICK II, KNOWN AS 'THE GREAT' (1712–86).
King of Prussia from 1740, and correspondent of Voltaire, who edited his *Anti-Machiavelli*. In his youth Frederick devoted himself to science and philosophy. On assuming the throne he soon proved himself to be a brilliant strategist in the War of Austrian Succession, and later in the Seven Years War. He pursued successful economic policies as well, and made a major contribution to the growing military and financial power of Prussia.

GROTIUS, HUGO (1583–1645).
Dutch statesman and jurist. Author of *Of the laws of war and peace* (1625), the first great modern attempt to establish the principles of jurisprudence. A victim of theological disputes in Holland and the Low Countries, Grotius eventually took refuge in Paris, where he was given a pension by Louis XII, and finally went to Sweden.

HOBBES, THOMAS (1588–1679).
English philosopher, best known for his *Leviathan*, published in 1651, two years after the execution of Charles I. Hobbes' political analysis was based on a mechanistic psychology of man, civilisation being maintained by fear and the calculation of self-interest. Hobbes defended the absolute powers of the sovereign, without whose iron fist society would degenerate into the lethal anarchy of the state of nature, in which life was 'nasty, brutish and short'.

HUME, DAVID (1711–1776).
Scottish philosopher and historian. He worked as a secretary in the British Embassy in Paris in 1763, and this enabled him to make contact with leading French writers and intellectuals. He exercised a deep influence over Kant and Adam Smith, whom he knew well. His *Treatise on human nature* was published in 1739.

LA BARRE, JEAN-FRANÇOIS LEFEBVRE (1747–66).
Accused of blasphemy and wilful damage to a cross, La Barre was arrested with three other young men for showing insufficient respect as a religious procession passed by. He was condemned by the court at Abbeville to have a hand amputated, his tongue torn out and his body burnt. La Barre appealed to the Paris *parlement*, and his sentence was commuted to decapitation prior to burning. Voltaire's attempts to have the sentence repealed failed, but the La Barre's name was eventually rehabilitated by the Revolutionary Convention in 1793.

LAW, JOHN (1671–1729).
Son of an Edinburgh goldsmith who fled to France after a duelling incident, and quickly gained the favour of the Regent. He persuaded the French government to adopt a system of paper money, and to establish a state bank in 1718. He became Comptroller-General in 1720. His schemes caused widespread financial devastation and public disorder, and he died an impoverished refugee in Venice.

LE MERCIER DE LA RIVIÈRE DE SAINT-MÉDARD, PIERRE-PAUL (1720–92/3).
French economic theorist and Counsellor in the Paris *parlement*. He was the author of the *The natural and essential order of political societies* (1767) in which he defended the concept of legal despotism. He became a close associate of Quesnay and the physiocrats.

LOCKE, JOHN (1632–1704).
An influential English philosopher whose ideas dominated the French Enlightenment. Locke was the author of *Two treatises on government* (1689), and the *Essay concerning human understanding* (1690), and he also wrote on questions of tolerance. He showed in his political writings how freedom was limited by the nature of political organisation, and in his philosophical investigations how human understanding was limited to the world revealed by the senses. His empiricism, com-

bined with epistemological humility, marked the final break with the medieval world-view, and the beginning of modernism. Locke had a deep and lasting influence over Voltaire.

LOUVOIS, FRANÇOIS MICHEL LE TELLIER (1641–91).
Louvois was Louis XIV's great war minister, and Colbert's rival. He was a distinguished military strategist responsible for the complete reorganisation of the French army. He encouraged Louis XIV's war policies, culminating in the devastation of the Palatinate in 1689, and initiated policies of religious intolerance at home. He died in disgrace, having finally alienated Mme de Maintenon.

MABLY, GABRIEL BONNOT (1709–85).
Mably was a diplomat and secretary to Cardinal Tencin. He prepared the draft of the treaty that Voltaire was charged with delivering to Frederick the Great in 1743. An early prophet of the French Revolution, Mably was the author of a number of treatises on government and the moral foundations of international order, including *Public law in Europe . . . since the Peace of Westphalia* (1748).

MACHIAVELLI, NICCOLÒ (1479–1527).
Florentine statesman who idealised the rise to power of Cesare Borgia, and with the support of the Medicis became official historiographer to Florence. He was an influential political theorist whose most celebrated work, *The prince* (1513), contains perceptive psychological and socio-political insights into the exercise of power. The work has given him a reputation for cynicism in the art of government, in view of its clear separation of politics from moral and religious considerations. *The prince* has often been seen as a plea for despotism.

MANDEVILLE, BERNARD (1670–1733).
Dutch doctor and social satirist who lived in England for most of his life. In 1714 he published *The fable of the bees: or private vices, publick benefits*. Using the analogy of a hive of bees, he sought to show that without vices, and their attendant economic benefits, civilisation would wither away. Thus Mandeville portrayed a society in which each man, working for his own interest, with minimum intervention on the part of the State, would be prosperous and happy. He anticipated later *laissez-faire* economists such as Adam Smith, who was greatly influenced by him.

MANDRIN, LOUIS (1724–55).
A celebrated French bandit known as the 'Captain-General of smugglers'. He was the leader of a band of some 200 men bringing tobacco, silk and other goods subject to tax into France illegally. Mandrin gained widespread popularity with the public, particularly as his main victims were the tax-farmers. After his arrest and execution he was feted as a public hero.

MELON, JEAN-FRANÇOIS (1680–1738).
A Bordeaux lawyer who worked in various government departments concerned with financial and economic policy. Melon was an associate of John Law and author of *A political essay on commerce* (1734). A precursor of the physiocrats, he is also considered to be a supporter of mercantilist theory.

MONTESQUIEU, CHARLES-LOUIS DE SECONDAT (1689–1755).
Bordeaux magistrate and important political philosopher. Montesquieu was the author of the *Persian letters* (1721), a novel containing the seeds of many of the ideas to be developed in his masterpiece, the *Spirit of the laws* (1748). His works represent a significant contribution to political theory, jurisprudence and sociology. He is known particularly for his work on climatic influence, for his analysis of different political systems, and for his theory of the separation of powers.

PASCAL, BLAISE (1623–62).
Outstanding French mathematician, mystic and eloquent apologist for Christianity. Pascal fell under the influence of the Port-Royal Jansenists, and made a complete conversion to the Christian faith through a mystical experience on the night of 23 November 1654, from then on devoting himself entirely to religious activities. His *Provincial letters* were published in 1656–57, but his apology for the Christian religion remained unfinished at his death. His notes for this work were first published in 1670 as the *Thoughts*.

PUFENDORF, SAMUEL (1632–94).
German jurist and historian, and Professor of natural and international law. Pufendorf published *On the duty of man and citizen* in 1673 which condensed the main elements of natural law political theory that he had set out in his classic *On the nature of law and nations* in

1672. Pufendorf's views on natural law dominated political thought until Kant.

QUESNAY, FRANÇOIS (1694–1774).
An eminent French surgeon and economic theorist who became personal medical adviser to Mme de Pompadour and Louis XVI. He contributed important articles on economic subjects to Diderot's *Encyclopaedia*. His *Economic tableau* (1758) established him as the leader of the physiocrats, a group of thinkers who became influential in France in the 1760s, developing an economic system based on doctrines of natural order.

RICHELIEU, ARMAND JEAN DUPLESSIS (1582–1642).
Statesman and diplomat. Cardinal Richelieu became chief minister under Louis XIII, and the most powerful figure in France next to the King. He survived a period of great turbulence, rife with plots and plotters such as Cinq-Mars and his friend Thou. He ruined the Protestant cause, consolidated the autocratic status of the monarch, and added territory to France at the expense mainly of Austria. Richelieu was also interested in literature and the arts, and was the founder of the French Academy.

ROUSSEAU, JEAN-JACQUES (1712–78).
Son of a Genevan watchmaker, Rousseau was a deeply influential writer in the fields of philosophy, education, political theory, botany, music, autobiography and pre-Romantic fiction. He suffered from real and imagined persecutions after the condemnation of his educational treatise, *Emile*, and from 1762 on he led a life of wandering and exile. Author also of the *Discourse on the sciences and the arts* (1750), the *Discourse on the origin of inequality among men* (1754), *The social contract* (1762), and many other political treatises. While he shared a hatred of tyranny with other contemporary thinkers, he was an adversary of Enlightenment faith in progress and science, defending fiercely values that he ascribed to nature and to natural man. The enmity between Rousseau and Voltaire was particularly bitter.

SAINT-PIERRE, CHARLES IRÉNÉE CASTEL (1658–1743).
Political writer and diplomat. Saint-Pierre published the *Plan for perpetual peace* in 1715, having assisted Cardinal Polignac during the Peace of Utrecht negotiations in 1712. He is known for his advocacy

of the modern-sounding notion of a league of sovereign heads of state which would impose peace and settle territorial disputes through its own court and congress.

SIRVEN, PIERRE PAUL (1709–77).
A French Protestant whose convent-educated daughter threw herself down a well to avoid a forced conversion to Catholicism in 1762. The circumstances of the case echoed closely the Calas affair. Sirven was accused of her murder and escaped to Switzerland, he and his wife having been condemned to death *in absentia* in 1764. Voltaire persuaded the Toulouse *parlement* to rehabilitate them in 1771.

SMITH, ADAM (1723–90).
Economic theorist and Professor of moral philosophy at the University of Glasgow. Author of the *An inquiry into the nature and causes of the wealth of nations* (1726). Smith was an enemy of the mercantilists, being an advocate of free trade and non-interventionism on the part of the government. In the field of public finance he established what have now been recognised as the classical principles of taxation theory.

Editorial note

Most of the texts in this collection were revised frequently by Voltaire, and numerous editions of each were issued, with or without his permission, during his lifetime. Text added to the original in the interests of clarity has been placed within square brackets. Substantial variants, as in the case of *PA*, have been included, as have Voltaire's own notes, with the exception of minor references. In the case of Voltaire, first editions do not often offer the most appropriate base text for modern editorial and scholarly purposes. However, important areas of text in the first edition of *PA*, *ABC*, *DP* and *QE*, subsequently suppressed by Voltaire, have been identified and restored. In the case of *DP*, articles having their provenance in the 1764, 1765, 1767 or 1769 editions, but which underwent further change and expansion in *QE*, have been listed under *DP*. Only articles appearing for the first time in *QE* have been listed under *QE*. In the case of both alphabetical works, the French title of articles precedes the English title so that the correct sequence can be maintained.

Note on the translation

The most dependable contemporary base text of Voltaire's works is the 1775 quarto collective edition, the so-called 'encadrée', which was published by Cramer and Bardin in Geneva (forty-three volumes).[1] This is the last edition known to have been revised and corrected by Voltaire, and is regarded as definitive. Better known and more widely accessible is the 52-volume edition of Voltaire's works by Louis Moland (Paris: Garnier), published in 1877–85. Moland has defects, but for reasons of practicality and easy reference, readers are referred for general purposes to this edition. The French text in Moland has been checked against the 1775 'encadrée' for any major discrepancies. In the case of *DP* the base text used for the translation is the 1954 Benda-Naves edition.

The translation has benefited from the work of earlier translators, in particular the English translations of *DP* by Peter Gay (1962) and Theodore Besterman (1971). See the Bibliographical note.

A certain number of specialised terms remain in French to avoid confusion arising from literally translated forms, and have simply been italicised. The word *parlement*, for example, cannot be adequately conveyed by the English literal equivalent, *parliament*. Currency terms have also been left untranslated, and readers are referred to the note in Pomeau 1985 (p. vi) for further information on this subject. Titles of French books, essays and pamphlets have been translated.

[1] See S.S.B. Taylor, 1974 'The definitive text of Voltaire's works: the Leningrad *encadrée*', *Studies on Voltaire and the Eighteenth Century*, 124, pp. 7–132.

Pocket philosophical dictionary

Etats, gouvernements. Quel est le meilleur? States, governments. Which is the best?

So far I have not known anyone who has not governed some state. I am not talking about right honourable ministers, who really do govern, some for two or three years, others for six months, others for six weeks; I am talking about all those other men who, over supper or in their study, set out their systems of government, reform the army, the Church, the law and [the world of] finance.

The *abbé* Bourzeis set about governing France around 1645 in the name of Cardinal Richelieu, and wrote that *Political testament*[1] in which he wants to draft the nobility into the cavalry for three years, make the Audit Office and the *parlements* pay taxes, and deprive the king of income from the salt tax. He contends in particular that for the sake of economy a hundred thousand men should be raised in order to wage a campaign with fifty thousand. He maintains that 'Provence alone has more good ports than Spain and Italy put together.'

The *abbé* Bourzeis had done no travelling. Moreover, his work teems with anachronisms and mistakes; he makes Cardinal Richelieu sign in a way that he never signed, just as he made him speak as he never spoke. For the rest, he takes a whole chapter to say that 'reason must be a state's rule of thumb', and to seek to prove this discovery. This work of darkness, this bastard child of the *abbé* Bourzeis, was for a long time taken to be Cardinal Richelieu's legitimate son; and in their inaugural addresses no academician failed to heap excessive praise upon this political masterpiece.

[1] Richelieu's *Political will* (1688) has been attributed to Paul Hay. There is no evidence for Amable de Bourzeis' authorship.

Master Gatien de Courtilz, seeing the success of Richelieu's *Political testament*, printed the *Testament of Colbert* at The Hague, together with a fine letter from Mr Colbert to the King. It is obvious that if this minister had made such a testament, it would have been necessary to suppress it. Several authors have quoted from this book, however. Another rascal, name unknown, promptly brought out the *Testament of Louvois*[2] – even worse, if that is possible, than Colbert's. A certain *abbé* Chevremont also made Charles, Duke of Lorraine, leave a testament.[3] We have had the *Political testaments* of Cardinal Alberoni,[4] of Marshal Belle-Isle[5] and lastly of Mandrin.[6]

Mr Bois-Guillebert, author of the *Detail of France*, printed in 1695, proposed the impractical project of a royal tithe in the name of Marshal Vauban.

In 1720 a starving madman named La Jonchère, put forward a financial project in four volumes, and some idiots have cited this creation as if it were a work by La Jonchère, the Head of the Treasury, under the illusion that a treasurer cannot write a bad book on finance.

But one must agree that wise men, possibly quite worthy to govern, have written on the subject of public administration in France, England and Spain. Their books have done a lot of good. Not that when these books appeared they put the ministers in office right, for a minister does not and cannot mend his ways. He has reached the top of his profession; no more instructions, no more advice; he has no time to listen; the flow of business carries him along; but these good books mould the young men destined for office; they mould princes, and the next generation is educated.

The strengths and weaknesses of all systems of government have been closely examined in recent times. So tell me, all you travellers, who have read a lot and seen a lot, in which state, under which type of government would you like to have been born? I imagine that a great landowner in France would not be displeased to have been born in Germany: he would be a sovereign instead of being a subject.

---

[2] Also by de Courtilz de Sandras. Pub. 1693.
[3] By Theodor Henri de Straatman. Jean-Baptiste Chevremont probably had an editorial role. Pub. 1696.
[4] By Joseph-Marie Durey de Morsan. Pub. 1753.
[5] By François-Antoine Chevrier. Pub. 1761.
[6] By Ange de Goudar. Pub. 1755.

A French peer would be very pleased to have the privileges of the English peerage: he would be a legislator.

The lawyer and the financier would be better off in France than anywhere else.

But what country would a wise and free man, with average means and no prejudices, choose?

A quite learned member of the council of Pondicherry returned overland to Europe with a Brahman who was better educated than your average Brahman. 'What do you think of the government of the Grand Mogul?', asked the councillor. 'It's awful', answered the Brahman. 'How can you expect a state to be well governed by Tartars? Our rajahs, our omras, our nabobs are very happy, but this is hardly the case with the citizens, and these millions of citizens do count.'

The councillor and the Brahman crossed the whole of Upper Asia, engaged in continual discussion. 'On reflection', said the Brahman, 'there isn't a single republic anywhere in this vast part of the world.' 'There was one once in Tyre', said the councillor, 'but it didn't last long. There was another one in the Arabia Petraea area, in a little spot called Palestine, if you can credit with the name of republic a horde of thieves and usurers, governed sometimes by judges, sometimes by kings, sometimes by grand pontiffs, enslaved seven or eight times, and finally thrown out of the country they had usurped.'

'I imagine', said the Brahman, 'that very few republics can be found on earth. Men have rarely deserved to govern themselves. That happiness can only belong to small nations hidden away on islands, or in mountains like rabbits hiding from carnivores; but in the end they are discovered and devoured.'

When the two travellers arrived in Asia Minor, the councillor said to the Brahman: 'Would you believe that a republic was once set up in a remote corner of Italy that lasted for more than five hundred years, and possessed Asia Minor, Asia, Africa, Greece, Gaul, Spain and the whole of Italy?' 'And it turned itself quickly into a monarchy?' asked the Brahman. 'You've guessed right', said the other, 'but that monarchy fell, and every day we compose fine dissertations to discover the causes of its decline and fall.' 'You trouble yourselves too much', said the Indian, 'that empire fell because it existed. Everything must fall; I very much hope that exactly the same thing will happen to the Grand Mogul's empire.' 'Incidentally', said the European, 'do you think that a despotic state needs more honour and a republic more virtue?' The Indian, having had the meaning of honour explained to him, replied that honour was more necessary in a republic, and that virtue was needed much more in a monarchy. 'For', he said, 'a man wishing to be elected by the people won't be if he is dishonoured, whereas at court he will easily be able to obtain an office, according to the maxim of a great prince[7] that for a courtier to succeed, he must have neither honour nor humour. With regard to virtue, you need an awful lot of it to dare to tell the truth at court. The virtuous man is much more at home in a republic. He has nobody to flatter.'

'Do you think', said the man from Europe, 'that laws and religions are made for climates just as furs are needed in Moscow and gauzy material in Delhi?' 'Yes, of course', said the Brahman, 'all physical laws are calculated for the meridian where you live: a German needs only one wife, a Persian needs three or four.

It is the same with religious rites. If I were a Christian, how would you expect me to say mass in my province where there is no bread or wine? As for dogmas, that's a different story; climate has nothing to do with them. Didn't your religion start in Asia, where it was driven out? Doesn't it exist around the Baltic, where it was unknown?'

'In what state, under what sort of rule, would you prefer to live?' asked the councillor. 'Anywhere except my own country', said his companion, 'and I've come across many Siamese, Tongkinese, Persians and Turks who said the same thing.' 'But once again', said the European, 'which state would you choose?' The Brahman replied: 'The one where people obey only the law.' 'That's an old answer', said the councillor. 'None the worse for that', said the Brahman. 'Where is that land?' asked the councillor. The Brahman said: 'We have to look for it.'[8]

---

[7] The reference is to the regent, the Duke of Orleans.
[8] 'See the article "Geneva" in the *Encyclopaedia*' (Voltaire's note).

Guerre. War

Famine, plague and war are the three most famous ingredients of this wretched world. You can include in the famine category all the bad food to which scarcity reduces us to eat with the effect of shortening our lives in the hope of keeping them going.

Under plague I include all contagious diseases, which number two to three thousand. These two gifts come to us from Providence. But war, which combines all these gifts, comes to us from the imaginations of three or four hundred people scattered across the world with the name of princes or ministers; and it is perhaps for that reason that in several dedications they are called the living images of the Divinity.

All animals are perpetually at war with each other; each species was born to devour another. This holds true even for sheep and doves which consume an enormous quantity of tiny, barely visible creatures. The males of the same species fight for the females, like Menelaus and Paris. Air, earth and water are arenas of destruction.

As God has given man reason, you would think that this same reason would warn them not to debase themselves by imitating the animals, especially when nature has not provided them with the weapons to kill their fellow men, nor an instinct to suck their blood.

However, the murderousness of war has been man's horrible lot to such an extent that, with the exception of two or three nations, there are none whose early history is not a picture of armies in conflict. In Canada *man* and *warrior* are synonymous, and we have seen

7

that in our own part of the world *thief* and *soldier* were the same thing. Manicheans, here is your justification.[1]

The most determined sycophant will acknowledge readily that war brings in its wake plague and famine, if he has ever seen German army hospitals, and passed through a few villages where some great feat of arms had taken place.

It is certainly a fine art that lays waste to the countryside, destroys houses and causes, in an average year, forty thousand men to die out of a hundred thousand. This invention was first nurtured by nations assembled for their common good; for example, the Greek diet informed the diet of the Phygians and neighbouring peoples that it intended to set out in a thousand fishing boats to exterminate them if it could.

The assembled Roman people judged it to be in its interest to go and fight the Veians, or the Volscians, before the harvest. And a few years after that all the Romans, angered by the Carthaginians, fought on land and sea for a long time. It is not the same today.

A genealogist proves to a prince that he is a direct descendant of a count whose relatives had made a family pact, three or four hundred years ago, with a house of which not a trace remains in living memory. This house had remote claims to a province whose last owner died of a stroke. The prince and his council conclude without difficulty that this province belongs to him by divine right. This province, which is a few hundred miles away, protests in vain that it does not know him, and that it has no desire to be ruled by him, that to impose laws on people, their consent at least is necessary. These speeches do not even reach the ears of the prince with the incontestable rights. At once he finds a large number of men with nothing to lose; he dresses them up in blue serge at a hundred and ten *sous* a yard, edges their hats with thick white piping, drills them and marches them off to glory.

Other princes, hearing about this escapade, join in as best they can, and occupy a small country with more murderous mercenaries than Genghis-Khan, Tamburlaine and Bajazet ever brought along with them.

---

[1] The above section was published in part 6 (1771) of *QE*, replacing the opening paragraphs of *DP* that precede it here.

People some distance away hear that fighting is going to take place, and that there are five or six *sous* a day to be made if they wish to take part. Immediately they divide up into two groups like harvesters, and off they go to sell their services to anyone who wants to employ them.

These multitudes set upon each other, not only without having any personal interest in the proceedings, but without even knowing what it is all about.

Five or six belligerent powers can be seen at the same moment, sometimes three against three, sometimes two against four, sometimes one against five, all detesting each other equally, fighting in alliance with each other and attacking each other in turn, all agreed on one point, namely to do each other as much harm as possible.

The most wonderful [thing] about this hellish enterprise is that each leader of these murderers has his flags blessed, and solemnly invokes God before going off to exterminate his neighbour. If one leader has the good fortune to butcher only two or three thousand men, he does not give thanks to God; but when there have been about ten thousand exterminated by fire or sword and, the ultimate in God's grace, some town has been totally destroyed, then they sing a rather long song in four parts, composed in a language unknown to the combatants and, what is more, stuffed with barbarisms. The same song is used for marriages and christenings, as well as for murders, which is unforgivable, especially in a nation most renowned for [its] new songs.

On countless occasions natural religion has stopped citizens from committing crimes. A noble soul has no wish to commit them; a tender soul is horrified by them, bearing in mind a just God of vengeance. But artificial religion encourages all those cruelties that people commit together: plots, sedition, robbery, ambushes, surprise attacks on towns, looting, murder. Each man marches cheerfully off to crime under his own particular saint's banner.[2]

Everywhere a certain number of tub-thumpers are paid to celebrate those days of murder: some are dressed in long, black tight-fitting jackets doubled with shortened cloaks; others wear shirts over gowns;

---

[2] The above section was published only in Kehl.

some wear two slings made of some mottled material over their shirts. They all talk at length. They quote what was done a long time ago in Palestine when talking about a battle in Veteravia.

For the rest of the year these people declaim against vices. Making three points and by means of antithesis, they prove that ladies who smear a bit of rouge on their fresh cheeks will be the eternal objects of the eternal vengeance of the Eternal Being; that *Polyeuctus* and *Athaliah* are the works of the Devil; that a man who has two hundred *écus'* worth of fresh fish served at his table in Lent unfailingly ensures his salvation, and that a poor man who eats two and a half *sous'* worth of mutton will go for ever to every devil [there is].

Out of five or six thousand declamations like this, there are three or four at most, composed by a Gaul named Massillon, that an honest man can read without disgust; but in all these speeches there are hardly two in which the orator dares say a word against this crime and scourge of war, which embraces all scourges and all crimes. The wretched tub-thumpers speak unceasingly against love, which is the human race's only consolation, and the only way to keep it going. They say nothing of the abominable efforts that we make to destroy it.

You gave a really bad sermon on impurity, Bourdaloue! But not one on these murders that vary in so many ways, on this pillage, on these acts of brigandry, on this universal madness that lays waste to the world. All the vices from all ages and all places added together will never equal the evils that a single campaign produces.

Miserable soul-doctors, you rail against a few pin-pricks for five quarters of an hour, and say nothing about the sickness which is tearing us into a thousand pieces! Moral philosophers, burn all your books. As long as the whim of a few men causes thousands of our brothers to be loyally butchered, that part of the human race devoted to heroism will be the most frightful thing in the whole of nature.

What does the future of humanity, benevolence, modesty, temperance, gentleness, wisdom and piety matter to me, when half a pound of leadshot fired from six hundred feet shatters my body, and I die at twenty years of age in unspeakable torment with five or six thousand other dying men, when my eyes, opening for the last time, see the town where I was born destroyed by sword and fire, and the last sounds in my ears are the cries of women and children dying in the ruins, the whole thing for the alleged benefit of a man we do not know?

What is worse is that war is an inevitable scourge. If you notice, all men have worshipped the god Mars, Sabbaoth means the God of arms with the Jews, but in Homer Minerva calls Mars a raging, mad, hellish god.

The famous Montesquieu, who is considered to be a humane man, did say, however, that it was a just thing to put one's neighbours to the sword and to the torch to stop them conducting their affairs too well. If that is the spirit of the laws, then it is the spirit of the laws of Borgia and Machiavelli. If, unhappily, what he said is true, we must write against that truth, even though it might be borne out by the facts.

Here is what Montesquieu says: 'Between societies the right of natural defence implies sometimes the need to attack, when a nation sees that to be at peace any longer would place another state in a position to destroy it, and that to attack at that moment is the only way of preventing this destruction.'[3]

How can an attack in peacetime be the only way of preventing this destruction? You would have to be very sure that this neighbour will destroy you if it becomes powerful. To be sure of that, it would have to have made preparations for your ruin. In that case, this would be the State which starts the war, not you. Your assumption is wrong and contradictory.

If there was ever a clearly unjust war, the one that you propose is it. It amounts to killing your neighbour for fear that your neighbour (who is not attacking you) might be in a position to attack you; in other words, you must risk ruining your country in the hope of ruining for no good reason someone else's. That is surely neither honest nor useful because, as you know full well, one is never sure of success.

If your neighbour becomes too powerful in peacetime, who is stopping you from making yourself as powerful as he is? If he has made alliances, make some for yourself. If, because he has fewer prelates, he has more industrialists and soldiers, copy his wise economic policy. If he trains his sailors better, train yours; all that is absolutely right.

---

[3] '*Spirit of the laws*, Book X, chapter 2' (Voltaire's note).

Lois (Des). Laws

In the time of Vespasian and Titus, while the Romans were disembowelling the Jews, a very rich Israelite, who did not wish to be
disembowelled, fled with all the gold he had made from his trade as
a usurer, and took with him his whole family, consisting of his elderly
wife, a son and a daughter, to Eziongaber. In his caravan he had two
eunuchs, one of whom served as the cook, the other was a ploughman
and vine-grower. A good Essenian, who knew the Pentateuch off by
heart, served as his chaplain. All these people embarked at the port
of Eziongaber, crossed the sea called the Red Sea, which is not red
at all, and entered the Persian Gulf in search of the land of Ophir,
not knowing where it was. Believe it or not, a terrible storm blew up
which drove this family of Jews towards the coast of India. The ship
was wrecked on one of the Maldive islands, called Padrabranca today,
which at that time was uninhabited.

The old moneybags and the old woman drowned; the son, the
daughter, the two eunuchs and the chaplain escaped. They dragged
a few provisions from the ship as best they could; little huts were
built on the island, and they lived there quite comfortably. You know
that the island of Padrabranca is five degrees from the equator, and
that you can find there the biggest coconuts and the best pineapples
in the world. Living there at a time when elsewhere the rest of the
chosen people were being slaughtered was very nice, but the Essenian
wept at the thought that perhaps they were the only Jews left in the
world, and that the seed of Abraham was about to come to an
end.

'It's up to you alone to save it', said the young Jew, 'marry my sister.'

'I'd like to very much', said the chaplain, 'but it is against the law. I'm an Essenian; I've taken a vow never to marry; it's the law that vows must be obeyed; let the Jewish race come to an end if it must, but I'll certainly not marry your sister, pretty as she is.'

'My two eunuchs can't give her any children', answered the Jew, 'so I'll give her some, if that's alright with you, and you'll bless the marriage.'

'I'd prefer to be disembowelled by Roman soldiers a hundred times over', said the chaplain, 'than to be the means of letting you commit incest; if she was your half-sister by your father, that would be alright, but she is your sister by your mother and that is an abomination.'

'I quite understand', replied the young man, 'that it would be a crime in Jerusalem, where I would find other girls, but on the island of Padrabranca, where I can see only coconuts, pineapples and oysters, I think that it is permissible.'

So the Jew married his sister, and had a daughter by her, in spite of the protests of the Essenian. It was the only fruit of a marriage that one thought perfectly legitimate and the other an abomination. After forty years the mother died. The father said to the chaplain: 'Have you finally got rid of your old prejudices? Do you want to marry my daughter'? 'May God forbid', said the Essenian. 'Very well. So I'll marry her myself', said the father, 'Whatever happens as a result of this will just have to happen, but I don't want the seed of Abraham to come to nothing.' The Essenian, shocked by this horrible statement, no longer wished to live with a man who acted against the law, and fled. The bridegroom shouted after him in vain: 'Stay, my friend; I'm observing natural law, I'm serving my country, don't abandon your friends!' The other man left him shouting, and with his mind still fixed on the law, swam off to the neighbouring island.

It was the big island of Atoll, well-populated and very civilised: as soon as he got there he was enslaved. He learned to mumble in the Atoll language; he complained very bitterly of the inhospitable way in which he had been welcomed. He was told it was the law, and that ever since the island had been almost taken by surprise by the inhabitants of the island of Addu, it had been the wise rule that all foreigners arriving on Atoll should be enslaved. 'That can't be the law', said the Essenian, 'for it's not in the Pentateuch.' He was told in reply that it was in the country's Book of Laws, and he stayed a slave. Fortunately, he had a very good, very rich master who treated him well, and to whom he became very attached.

One day some assassins came to murder the master and steal his treasures; they asked the slaves if he was at home, and if he had a lot of money. 'We swear to you', said the slaves, 'that he has no money and is not at home.' But the Essenian said: 'The law does not allow me to lie; I swear to you that he's at home, and that he's got a lot of money.' So the master was robbed and killed. The slaves accused the Essenian before the judges of having betrayed his master. The Essenian said that he had no wish to lie, and that nothing in the world would make him lie, and he was hanged.

I was told this story, and many other similar ones, on the last trip that I made from India back to France. When I arrived, I went to Versailles on business. I saw a beautiful woman pass by, followed by other beautiful women. 'Who's that beautiful woman?' I asked my lawyer, who had come with me, for I had a case [going on] in the Paris *parlement* over the clothing made for me in India, and I never went anywhere without my lawyer at my side. 'That's the King's daughter', he said, 'she's charming and kind; it's a real shame that in no circumstances can she ever be Queen of France.' 'What!', I said to him, 'so if she was unfortunate enough to lose her parents and the princes of the blood (which God forbid), she couldn't inherit her father's kingdom?' 'No', said the lawyer, 'Salic law is explicitly opposed to it.' 'And who made this Salic law?' I asked the lawyer. 'I've no idea', he said, 'but it's claimed that an ancient people called the Salians, who could neither read nor write, had a written law that said that on Salic territory a daughter could not inherit a freehold, and this law was adopted in non-Salic lands.' 'And I for one', I told him, 'would break it; you've assured me that this princess is charming and kind: thus she would have an unquestionable right to the crown if the unhappy situation arose that she was the only one left of the royal blood. My mother inherited from her father; I want this princess to inherit from hers.'

The next day my case was heard in one of the courts of the *parlement*, and I lost everything by one vote. My lawyer told me I would have won everything by one vote in another court. 'That's very funny', I said to him, 'What it amounts to is: one law for one court, a different law for another.' 'Yes', he said, 'there are twenty-five commentaries on legal procedures in Paris, that's to say, it's been proved twenty-five times that the Paris procedure is equivocal, and if there were twenty-five judge's chambers, there would be twenty-five different jurisprudences. Fifteen miles from Paris', he continued, 'we've a province called Normandy where you would have had a completely different judgement to the one you had here.' That made me want to see Normandy. I went there with one of my brothers. At the first inn we met a young man in despair. I asked him what his trouble was. He answered that it was the fact that he had an elder brother. 'What's so bad about having a brother?' I asked him, 'My brother is older than I am, and we get on very well together.' 'Alas', he said, 'here the law gives everything to the eldest and nothing to younger ones.' 'You're right to be upset', I said to him. 'Where I come from, things are divided up equally, and sometimes brothers don't like each other any more for all that.'

These little adventures made me think deeply about the law, and I can see that as with our clothes so it is with our laws. In Constantinople I had to wear a dolman, and in Paris a jacket.

If all human laws are laws of convention, I said, all that is left [to do] is to make the best of them. The citizens of Delhi and Agra say that they had a very bad deal with Tamburlaine; the citizens of London congratulate themselves on having reached a very good agreement with King William of Orange. A London citizen once said to me: 'Necessity makes the laws, and force ensures that they are kept.' I asked him whether force also made the laws sometimes, and whether William the Bastard or the Conqueror had not given the English their orders without having reached an agreement with them. 'Yes', he said, 'then we were cattle. William put a yoke on us and goaded us along. Since then we have changed into men, but we still have horns, and we strike anyone down who wants us to work the fields for their own benefit and not for ours.'

Full of all these reflections, I took pleasure in the thought that there is a natural law independent of all human conventions: the fruit of my labour must belong to me; I must honour my father and my mother; I have no rights over my neighbour's life, and my neighbour has none over mine, etc. But when I thought that, from Chodorlahomor down to the Hussar Colonel Menzel, everyone loyally kills and robs his neighbour, with a licence to do so in his pocket, I was very upset.

I have been told that there are laws among thieves, and that there are also laws of war. I asked what these laws of war were. 'These', I was told, 'are about hanging brave officers who hold out in a bad position, without any cannon, against a royal army; about hanging a prisoner if they have hanged one of your [men]; about putting villages to the sword and to the torch who do not surrender all their possessions on the appointed day in accordance with the order of the local gracious sovereign.' 'Great', I said, 'there's the *Spirit of the laws* for you.'

After having been well instructed on the matter, I discovered that there are wise laws by which a shepherd is condemned to nine years galley service for having given a little foreign salt to his sheep. My neighbour was ruined in a court case involving two oak trees which belonged to him, and which he had cut down in his own wood, because he had not observed a formality which he could not have known about: his wife died in misery, and his son ekes out a life worse than death. I admit that these laws are just, although their implementation is a little harsh; but I take strong exception to laws that authorise a hundred thousand men to loyally go and cut the throats of a hundred thousand of their neighbours. It seems to me that most men have received from nature enough common sense to pass laws, but that not everybody has enough sense of what is just to make good laws.

Bring together simple, peaceful farmers from all over the world; they will all agree readily that selling one's surplus corn to one's neighbour must be permitted; that a law to the contrary is inhuman and absurd; that the currency representing the value of produce must be no more rotten than the fruits of the earth; that a father must be master in his own house; that religion must bring men together to unite them, not to make fanatics and persecutors out of them; that those who work must not deprive themselves of the fruits of their labour in order to finance superstition and idleness. In an hour they would make thirty laws like this, all of them useful to the human race.

But let Tamburlaine arrive on the scene and enslave India, then you will see nothing but arbitrary laws. One will oppress a province in order to enrich one of Tamburlaine's tax-gatherers; another will make it a crime of *lèse-majesté* to have spoken ill of the mistress of the first man-servant of a Rajah; a third will rob a farmer of half of his crop, and challenge his right to the rest of it. There will in the end be laws by which some Tartar official will come along and take your children from their cradles, make the stronger one into a soldier, and the weaker into a eunuch, leaving their mother and father without support or consolation.

Now, which is better – to be one of Tamburlaine's dogs or one of his subjects? Clearly his dog is much better off.

Sheep live together very peacefully; by nature they are supposed to be very meek because we cannot see the enormous quantity of living creatures that they devour. It is even assumed that they eat them innocently and unconsciously, just like we do [when we eat] a Sassenage cheese. The republic of sheep is a true image of the Golden Age.

A hen-house is clearly the most perfect monarchical state. There is no king comparable to a cock. If he walks proudly among his people, it is not because of vanity. If the enemy approaches, he does not order his subjects to go and get themselves killed for him by virtue of his certain knowledge and absolute power. He goes himself, lines up his hens behind him, and fights to the death. If he is the victor, he is the one who sings the *Te Deum*. In civil society there is nothing so gallant, so honourable, so free from self-interest. He has all the virtues. If he has a grain of corn in his royal beak, or a little worm, then he gives it to the first of his subjects to present herself. In a word, Solomon in his harem has nothing on a farmyard cock.

If it is true that bees are ruled by a queen to whom all of her subjects make love, then that is an even more perfect form of government.

Ants are regarded as having an excellent democracy. It is superior to all other states because there everyone is equal, and everyone works for the happiness of everyone else.

The beaver republic is even better than that of the ants, at least judging by their work as builders.

Monkeys are more like knockabout comedians than a civilised people, and they do not seem to be united under a system of fixed, fundamental laws, like the species mentioned above.

With respect to our gift for imitation, the superficiality of our ideas, and our fickleness, which have never allowed us to have uniform, lasting laws, we are more like monkeys than any other animal.

When Nature created our species, she gave us a few instincts: self-love for our survival, benevolence for the survival of others, love which is common to all species, and the inexplicable gift of combining more ideas than the rest of the other animals [put] together. Having thus assigned to us our lot, she said to us: Get on with it as best you can.

There is no good code of laws in any country. The reason for this is obvious: the laws have been made as we went along in accordance with time, place, and needs, etc.

When needs changed, the laws which remained became ridiculous. Thus the law which forbade the eating of pork and the drinking of wine was quite reasonable in Arabia where pork and wine are harmful. It is ridiculous in Constantinople.

The law which gives the whole fiefdom to the eldest son is very good in times of anarchy and looting. Then the eldest son is captain of the castle which will be attacked sooner or later by brigands. The younger sons will be the chief officers, the ploughmen the soldiers. All that there is to be feared is that the younger son might murder or poison his elder brother, the Salic lord, to become in his turn the master of the hovel. But these cases are rare because nature has combined our instincts and passions in such a way that we feel more horror at the thought of murdering our elder brother than desire to take his place. Now this law, which suited the dungeon-owners in the time of Chilperic, is hateful when it comes to the division of income in a town.

To men's shame, we know that the laws of gambling are everywhere the only ones that are fair, clear, unbreakable, and observed. Why is the Indian who gave us the rules of chess obeyed cheerfully throughout the whole world, while the decretals of popes, for example, are today objects of horror and scorn? It is because the inventor of chess put everything together with precision for the satisfaction of the players, while popes with their decretals had eyes only for their own advantage. The Indian wished to exercise men's minds on an equal basis, and give them pleasure; popes wished to brutalise men's minds. Thus the basis of the game of chess has survived in the same form for five thousand years; all the world has it in common; and the decretals are recognised only in Spoleto, Orvieto and Loretto where the skinniest little jurist secretly detests and despises them.[1]

[1] The above section was added to *DP* in 1767.

It is difficult to find a single nation living under good laws. It is not just because they are the creation of men, for men have done some very good things; and the people who invented and perfected the arts could think up a reasonable system of laws. But in nearly all states the laws were established by the self-interest of the legislator, short-term need, ignorance and superstition. People made them up as they went along, haphazardly, irregularly, just like they built towns. Look at the Halles district in Paris, at Saint-Pierre-aux-Boeufs, at Brise-Miche Street, at Pet-au-Diable street, in contrast to the Louvre and the Tuileries: there is the image of our laws.

London only became worth living in since it was reduced to ashes. Since that time, its streets have been widened and straightened. Being burnt down made a city out of London. If you want to have good laws, burn what you have, and create new ones.

The Romans were three hundred years without any fixed laws. They were obliged to go and ask the Athenians for some. They gave them such bad ones that nearly all of them were soon revoked. How could Athens itself have had good legislation? They were obliged to abolish Draco's legislative code, and Solon's was short-lived.

Your procedure in Paris has been interpreted differently in twenty-four commentaries; it has thus been proved twenty-four times that it is ill-conceived. It contradicts a hundred and forty other ways of doing things, all having the force of law behind them in the same country, and all mutually contradictory. In a single European province, between the Alps and the Pyrenees, there are therefore more than a hundred and forty small nations whose people call each other *compatriots*, but who are really foreign to each other, just as people in Tonkin are to those in Cochin-China.

It is the same with all of Spain's provinces. It is much worse in Germany: there nobody knows what either the leader's rights are, or those of the ordinary citizen. The only thing that the man who lives on the banks of the Elbe has in common with the Swabian farmer is the fact that they speak more or less the same, albeit crude, language.

The English nation has more uniformity about it; but having only emerged from barbarity and servitude through intermittent upheavals, and having in their freedom retained several of the laws once promulgated by great tyrants disputing the throne, or by little tyrants invading prelacies, it has developed out of all that quite a robust body on which you can still see a lot of bandaged wounds.

The spirit of Europe has made greater progress over the last hundred years than the whole world has made since the time of Brama, Fohi, Zoroastra, and the Theaetetus of Egypt. How is it that the spirit of the laws has made so little?

We were all savages from the fifth century on. This is how the world goes round: brigands who loot, farmers who are looted, that is what the human race consisted of, from the far reaches of the Baltic Sea to the Straits of Gibraltar, and when the Arabs appeared in the south the desolation caused by these upheavals was world-wide.

In our corner of Europe, the minority being made up of bold, ignorant conquerors, armed to the teeth, and the majority of unarmed, ignorant slaves, who were almost totally illiterate, even Charlemagne, it came about quite naturally that the Roman Church, with its pens and its ceremonies, should rule those who spent their lives on horseback, with their lances up and their visors down.

The descendants of the Sicambri, of the Burgundians, of the Ostrogoths, the Visigoths, the Lombards, the Heruli, etc., felt that they needed something like laws. They looked in places where they had them. The bishops of Rome knew how to make them in Latin. The barbarians adopted them all the more respectfully for not understanding them. The decretals of popes, some genuine, others blatantly fabricated, became the code for the new kings, lords and barons who had divided up the land. They were wolves who allowed themselves to be chained by foxes. They retained their ferocity, but it was subdued by credulity, and by the fear produced by credulity. Gradually, Europe, except for Greece and what still belonged to the Empire of the East, found itself under the sway of Rome; so that one could say for the second time:

Romanos rerum dominos gentemque togatam[2]

As nearly all agreements were accompanied by the sign of the cross and by an oath often made on relics, everything was under the jurisdiction of the Church. Rome, as the capital see, was the supreme judge in the trials of the Cimbrian Chersonese and in the trials in Gascony. After a thousand feudal lords had made their practices fit in with canon law, the result was this monstrous system of laws of which so many traces still remain.[3]

[2] Virgil, *Aeneid*, I. 281.
[3] 'See the article "Abuse" ' (Voltaire's note).

What would have been best: to have no laws at all or to have had ones like these?

It has been to the advantage of one empire vaster than the Roman Empire to be in chaos for a long time; for as everything was yet to be created, it was easier to erect a building than to repair one whose ruins would still be respected.

North Thesmophoria brought together in 1767 deputies from every province with an area of about twelve hundred thousand square miles. There were pagans, Muslims from Ali, Muslims from Omar, Christians from about twelve different sects. Each law was put to this new synod, and if it seemed to suit the interests of each province, it was sanctioned by the sovereign and by the nation.

The first law to be passed was that of tolerance, so that the Greek priest would never forget that the Roman priest is a man; so that the Muslim would tolerate his pagan brother, and so that the Catholic priest would not be tempted to sacrifice his Presbyterian brother.

The sovereign wrote in her own hand in this great legislative council: 'Among so many different faiths, the most harmful offence would be intolerance.'

They agreed unanimously that there was only one power,[4] that it was always necessary to say civil *power* but ecclesiastical *discipline*, and that the allegory of the two swords was the dogma of discord.

She started by freeing the serfs on her personal estate.

She freed all those on Church estates: in this way she created men.

Prelates and monks were paid from the [state] Treasury.

Punishments were made to fit crimes, and the punishments were useful; the guilty, for the most part, were sentenced to [community] work projects, in view of the fact that dead men are useless.

Torture was abolished, because it was punishment before the truth was established, and because it is absurd to punish in order to establish the truth; because the Romans only tortured slaves; because torture is the way to spare the guilty, and ruin the innocent.

Things were at that state when Mustapha III, the son of Mahmoud, forced the Empress to interrupt her law-making in order to fight.[5]

I have tried to discover some ray of light in the mythological age of China before Fohi, and I tried in vain.

[4] 'See the article "Power" ' (Voltaire's note).
[5] The above section was published in part 7 (1771) of *QE*.

But confining myself to Fohi, who lived about three thousand years before our own vulgar modern era in the northern part of the western world, already I can see mild, wise laws being established by a benevolent king. The ancient Books of the Five Kings, sanctified by so many centuries of respect, tell us about his institutes of agriculture, about rural economy, domestic economy, about simple astronomy marking off the seasons, about music calling men to their various duties [with the use of] different notes. It is beyond dispute that this Fohi lived five thousand years ago. Judge how ancient this huge nation must have been, educated by its emperor in everything that could make them happy. I can see nothing in those laws that is not mild, useful and pleasing.

I am then shown the code of laws of a little nation from a frightful desert on the banks of the Jordan which, two thousand years later, arrives in a country hemmed in by, and bristling with, mountains. Its laws have come down to us; they are presented to us every day as a model of wisdom. Here are a few of them:

'Never eat ocreatae, or charadridae, or griffin, or ixion, or eel, or hare because hare eats grass, and does not have cloven feet.'

'Never sleep with your wife when she is having a period under pain of death for both of you.'

'Exterminate without mercy all the poor inhabitants of the land of Canaan, who did not know these laws; cut their throats, massacre the whole lot, men, women, old people, children, animals, for the greater glory of God.'

'Sacrifice to the Lord everyone whom you have cursed in the name of the Lord, and kill them without giving any thought to their redemption.'

'Burn those widows who cannot be remarried to their brothers-in-law, and might have found consolation with some other Jew in the middle of the street or somewhere, etc., etc.'[6]

A Jesuit, who was once a missionary with the cannibals in the days when Canada still belonged to the King of France, once told me

[6] 'this is what happened to Tamar who, having been raped, slept on the open road with Juda her stepfather, who did not recognise her. She became pregnant. Juda condemned her to be burnt. The sentence was all the more cruel because, had it been implemented, our Saviour, who descends directly from this Juda and Tamar, would not have been born, unless the order of all world events had been re-arranged' (Voltaire's note).

that as he was explaining these laws to his neophytes, a rash little Frenchman, who was present during the catechism, took it into his head to shout out: 'But those are cannibal laws!' One of the citizens replied: 'Look, you little idiot, you should know that we are honourable people: we have never had laws like that. And if we were not respectable people, we would give you the Canaan treatment to teach you to mind your tongue.'

From a comparison of the first Chinese code of laws with the Jewish code, it appears that laws follow the customs of the people who have made them. If vultures and pigeons had laws, they would no doubt be different.[7]

---

[7] The above section was added to *QE* in 1774.

Patrie. Homeland

We shall limit ourselves here, as is our custom, to posing a few questions that we cannot resolve.

Has a Jew got a homeland? If he has been born in Coïmbra it is among a herd of ignorant fools who would argue with him, and to whom, if he dared reply at all, he would give foolish answers. He is watched by inquisitors who will have him burnt if they learn that he does not eat bacon, and all that he owns will belong to them. Is Coïmbra his homeland? Can he love Coïmbra dearly? Can he say, as in Pierre Corneille's *Horace*:

> Alba, my dear country and my first love . . .
> To die for one's country is such a worthy fate
> That crowds would clamour for such a fine death.[1]

Rubbish!

Is his homeland Jerusalem? He has heard vague talk that once upon a time his ancestors, whoever they were, lived in that stony, sterile land, bounded by an awful desert, but that today the Turks are masters of that little country, from which they get almost nothing. Jerusalem is not his homeland. He has none; there is not a square foot of land anywhere on earth that belongs to him.

Can the Ghebr, who is more ancient and a hundred times more respectable than the Jew, a slave of either the Turks or the Persians or the Grand Mogul, count on a few altar-pyres that he raises secretly on mountain-tops as being a sign of his homeland?

---

[1] Act I, scene 1; act II, scene 3.

25

Can the Banian and the Armenian, who spend their lives wandering all over the East practising the art of broking, say 'My dear, dear country'? They have no country apart from their stock exchange and their ledgers.

Among our European nations, do all those murderers who hire out their services, and sell their blood to the first king who wants to pay them, have a homeland? They have no more homeland than a bird of prey returning each evening to the craggy hollow where its mother used to nest.

Would monks dare to say that they have a homeland? They say it is in Heaven; good luck to them, but I do not know where their homeland is in this world.

Would this word *homeland* be suitable in the mouth of a Greek, who is unaware that there was ever a Miltiades or an Agesilaus, and who only knows that he is a janissary's slave, who is the slave of an agha, who is the slave of a pasha, who is the slave of a vizir, who is the slave of a Padishah, whom we call in Paris the *Great Turk*?

So what is the homeland? Would it not be by any chance a good field whose owner, comfortably set up in a well-kept house, could say: This field I am cultivating and this house that I have built are mine. I live there under the protection of laws that no tyrant can transgress? When people like me, who own fields and houses, gather together in pursuit of their common interests, I have a vote in that assembly. I am part of the whole, a part of the community, a part of the sovereign power: that is my country. Apart from where men live, is it not the case that everywhere else tends to be a stable run by a groom who whips the horses when he feels like it? You have a country under a good king; you do not have one under a bad king.

A young apprentice pastry-cook, who had been to college, and who still knew a few sentences from Cicero, was preening himself on loving his homeland. 'What do you mean by your homeland?' asked a neighbour, 'is it your oven? Is it the village where you were born, and which you have never seen again since? Is it the street where your mother and father lived, who were ruined and who have reduced you to stuffing little pies for a living? Is it the Town Hall where you will never be a quarter-master's clerk? Is it the church of Our Lady where you have never been able to make it as a choirboy, while a ridiculous fool is archbishop and duke, with an income of twenty thousand gold *louis?*'

The apprentice pastry-cook did not know what to say in reply. A thinker, listening to this conversation, concluded that in a country spread over a fairly large area there were often several million people with no homeland.

You pleasure-loving Parisian, you say you love your homeland! You, who have travelled only as far as Dieppe for fresh fish, who know only your painted townhouse, your pretty country house, your box at the Opera, where the rest of Europe persists in getting bored, who speak your mother-tongue so nicely because you don't know any other language, that's what you love, and you love even more the girls you entertain, the champagne you get from Reims, and the pension the Town Hall pays you every six months.

In all conscience, does a financier truly love his homeland?

Do the officer and the soldier, who will lay waste to their winter quarters if they are allowed to, feel a tender love for the peasants they ruin?

Where was the homeland of the Duke of Guise, old scar-face? Was it Nancy, Paris, Madrid, Rome?

What homelands did you have, Cardinals La Balue, Duprat, Lorraine and Mazarin?

Where was Attila's homeland, and that of a hundred heros of that ilk who, always rushing about, never diverged from their path?

I would really like someone to tell me which was Abraham's homeland.

The first to write that the homeland is the place where one feels at home is, I believe, Euripides in his *Phaethon*:

Ὡς πανταχοῦ γε πατρις η βόσχοθσαγῆ.[2]

But the first man to leave his birthplace to look for somewhere else to feel at home said it before he [did].[3]

A homeland is made up of several families; and just as you normally stand by your family out of pride, when there is no conflicting interest,

[2] 'As if everywhere was the homeland on which [one's] herds graze.'
[3] The above two sections were published in part 8 (1771) of *QE*.

because of that same pride you support your town or your village, which you call your homeland. The larger that homeland becomes, the less you love it, for a love that is divided is a love that is weakened. It is impossible to love a family dearly that is too large and whom you hardly know.

The man who burns with ambition to be an Aedile, a Tribune, a Praetor, a Consul, a dictator, declares that he loves his country, but he loves only himself. We all want to be sure of being able to sleep in our own beds without someone else arrogating to himself the right to tell us to sleep elsewhere. Everybody wants to be sure of his wealth and his life. With everyone thus having the same desires, it works out that private interest becomes the general interest: when we express our hopes for ourselves, we are expressing them for the Republic.

It is impossible for any state on earth not to have been governed first of all as a republic; it is the natural way forward for human nature. First a few families got together against the bears and the wolves. The family which had grain traded it with the family which had only wood.

When we discovered America, we found all the little tribes there divided into republics. There were only two kingdoms in the whole of that part of the world. Of a thousand nations we found only two that were enslaved.

It was the same with the ancient world. Everything was a republic in Europe before the time of the petty kings of Etruria and Rome. You can still see republics today in Africa. Tripoli, Tunis, Algeria, towards the North where we live, are republics of brigands. The Hottentots in the South still live as we are told people used to live in the earliest ages of man: free, equal, without masters, without subjects, without money, without needs almost. Meat from their sheep fed them, their skins clothed them, huts of wood and earth provided them with shelter. They stink worse than any other men, but are not aware of it; they live and die more peacefully than we [do].

In our Europe there remain eight republics with no monarchs: Venice, Holland, Switzerland, Genoa, Lucca, Ragusa, Geneva and San Marino.[4] Poland, Sweden and England can be considered repub-

---

[4] 'This was written in 1764' (Voltaire's note).

lics under a king, but Poland is the only one to call itself a republic.

Now, is it better for your homeland to be a monarchical state or a republican state? People have been worrying away at that question for four thousand years. If you ask the rich for a solution, they will all prefer an aristocratic system; ask the people, and they will want democracy. Only kings prefer monarchies. How is it possible, therefore, for almost the entire world to be ruled by monarchs? Ask the rats who proposed to bell the cat.[5] But in truth the real reason is, as has been said before, that men are very rarely fit to rule themselves.

It is sad that in order to be a good patriot one is very often the enemy of the rest of mankind. The elder Cato, that good citizen, always said when speaking in the senate: 'That's what I think, and let Carthage go hang.' To be a good patriot is to want one's city to prosper through trade and be powerful through arms. Clearly, one country cannot win without another losing, and it cannot conquer without making some people unhappy.

So that is the human condition: to want your own country to be great is to wish your neighbours ill. The man who would want his homeland never to be larger, or smaller, or richer or poorer would be a citizen of the world.

---

[5] La Fontaine, *Fables*, II ('The council of the rats').

Questions on the Encyclopaedia

Démocratie. Democracy

The worst of all states is the popular state.[1]

Thus Cinna justifies himself to Augustus. But Maximus also maintains that the worst of all states is the monarchical state. Bayle, having more than once in his *Dictionary* argued for and against this, paints in his article on Pericles a quite hideous picture of democracy, particularly of the one in Athens.

A great republican enthusiast for democracy, one of our askers of questions, sends us his refutation of Bayle and his defence of Athens. We shall make his arguments public. It is the privilege of every writer to judge the living and the dead; but one is judged oneself by others, who are judged in their turn, and from one century to the next the judgements passed are revised.

So Bayle, after a few banalities, says specifically: 'That you would look in vain in the history of Macedonia for as much tyranny as there is in the history of Athens.'

Perhaps Bayle was unhappy with Holland when he wrote like that, and probably my republican, who refutes what he says, is pleased with his little democratic city *at the moment.*

It is difficult to weigh accurately in the scales the iniquities of the Athenian Republic against those of the Macedonian court. We still reproach the Athenians today with the banishment of Cimon, Aristides, Themistocles, Alcibiades, the death sentences pronounced on Phocion and Socrates, judgements similar to those passed by a few of our own cruel, absurd courts.

[1] Corneille, *Cinna*, act II, scene 1.

33

Ultimately, what people do not forgive the Athenians for is the death of their six victorious generals, who were condemned for not having had the time to bury their dead after victory, and for having been prevented from doing so by a storm. This judgement is so ridiculous, and at the same time so barbaric, it is marked so much by superstition and ingratitude, that the judgements of the Inquisition made on Urbain Grandier and Marshal Ancre, on Morin, and on so many witches, etc., are no worse as examples of atrocious follies.

In order to excuse the Athenians it has been said in vain that they believed, according to Homer, that the souls of the dead always wandered unless they received the honour of burial or the stake: absurdity is no excuse for barbarity. What a terrible thing for the souls of a few Greeks to have to do, to take walks by the seaside for a week or two! What is terrible is to deliver up living people to executioners, and moreover living people who have won a battle for you, and whom you ought to be thanking on your knees.

Here we have the Athenians then, convicted of being the most stupid and barbaric judges on earth.

But you must now weigh in the scales the crimes of the Macedonian court; you will see that this court beats Athens hands down for tyranny and villainy.

Normally, there is no comparison to be made between the crimes of great men, who are always ambitious, and the crimes of the people, who never want, and cannot ever want, anything other than liberty and equality. These two sentiments *liberty* and *equality* do not lead directly to calumny, plunder, murder, poisoning, the devastation of one's neighbour's territory, etc. But ambitious grandeur and the mania for power have precipitated all these crimes in every place and every era.

In Macedonia, whose virtue Bayle contrasts with that of Athens, you see nothing but a string of horrible crimes for two hundred successive years.

We have Ptolemy, Alexander the Great's uncle, murdering Alexander, his brother, to usurp the kingdom.

We have Philip, his brother, spending his life in deception and rape, and ending up by being stabbed by Pausanias.

Olympias has Queen Cleopatra and her son thrown into a vat of molten bronze. She murders Aridai.

Antigonus murders Eumenes.

Antigonus Gonatas, his son, poisons the governor of the citadel of Corinth, marries his widow, gets rid of her, and takes possession of the citadel.

Philip, his grandson, poisons Demetrius, and stains the whole of Macedonia with murder.

Perseus kills his wife with his own hands, and poisons his brother.

These perfidies and barbarities are famous historical events.

Thus, for two centuries, the fury of despotism turned Macedonia into a theatre of every crime; and over the same period of time you see the popular government of Athens stained with only five or six judicial iniquities, five or six atrocious judgements, for which the people always showed repentance, and for which it made honourable amends. It asked pardon of Socrates after his death, and erected the little temple of the *Socrateion* to him. It asked pardon of Phocion, and raised a statue to him. It asked pardon of the six generals, condemned so absurdly, and executed so shamefully. They imprisoned the main prosecutor, who only just escaped vengeance at the hands of the people. Thus the natural goodness of the Athenian people matched their rashness. In what despotic state has the injustice of ill-advised judgements been lamented like this?

Thus this time Bayle was wrong; my republican is therefore right. Popular government is in itself less iniquitous, less abominable than tyrannical power.

The great vice of democracy is certainly not tyranny and cruelty; there have been some fierce and savage mountain republics, but it was not the republican spirit that made them thus: it was nature. The whole of North America was made up of republics. Republics of bears.

The real vice of a civilised republic is to be found in the Turkish tale of the dragon with several heads and the dragon with several tails. The large number of heads harmed each other, and the large number of tails obeyed a single head which ate everything up.

Democracy seems to suit only very small countries, and even then the country has to be favourably situated. Small as it is, it will still make many mistakes, because it is composed of men. Discord will reign there just as it does in a monastery; but there will be no Saint Bartholomew Day, no Irish massacres, no Sicilian Vespers, no

Inquisition, no sending of people to the galleys for having taken water from the sea without paying, unless you presume that this republic is composed of devils and is located in some corner of Hell.

After having sided with my Swiss against the ambidextrous Bayle, I will add:

That the Athenians were as warrior-like as the Swiss, and as refined as the Parisians [were] under Louis XIV;

That they excelled in all the arts requiring skill of mind and hand, like the Florentines in the time of the Medicis;

That they could teach the Romans, even those in the time of Cicero, a thing or two about the sciences and about oratory;

That this little nation, with scarcely any territory, and which today is nothing more than a bunch of ignorant slaves, a hundred times less numerous than the Jews, and having lost everything apart from its name, has nevertheless surpassed the Roman Empire with the victory of its ancient reputation over time and over slavery.

Europe has seen a republic,[2] ten times smaller than Athens, attract attention for a hundred and fifty years, with its name placed alongside that of Rome, at a time when Rome was giving kings their orders, condemning Henry, sovereign King of France, absolving and chastising another Henry, the number one man of his age; at a time when Venice still retained its ancient splendour, when the new republic of the seven United Provinces astonished Europe and India with its institutions and its trade.

This nearly invisible anthill could not be crushed by the Demon King of the Midi,[3] and ruler of two worlds, nor by the plots of the Vatican which pulled the strings of half of Europe. It fought back with words and weapons, and with the help of a Picard who wrote, and a small number of Swiss who fought, it became stronger; it triumphed. It could say *Rome and I*. It had the spirit of all those people who had been divided up by the rich pontiffs who succeeded the Scipios, *Romanos rerum dominos*,[4] and of those poor inhabitants of a little spot no-one had ever heard of in the land of poverty and goitres.

---

[2] Geneva.
[3] The reference is to Philip II.
[4] Virgil, *Aeneid*, I. 286.

Then the issue at stake was what Europe would think about questions that nobody understood. It was a time of war for the human mind. They had [people like] Calvin, Bèze, Turretin for their Demosthenes, their Plato and their Aristotle.

When the absurdity of most of the controversial issues that gripped Europe had finally been recognised, the little republic turned to what appeared to be more solidly based, the acquisition of wealth. Law's system, more fantastic and no less deadly than those of the supralapsaries and the infralapsaries, occupied with arithmetical problems those unable to make a name for themselves in theo-morianics. They became rich and nothing more.

People think that today there are republics only in Europe. If I am not mistaken, and I have said this elsewhere, that would be a very big lapse of memory. In America the Spanish found a very well-established republic of Tlaxcala. Everything that has not been enslaved in that part of the world is still a republic. In the whole of that continent there were only two kingdoms when it was discovered; and that might well prove that republican government is the most natural. One would have had to become very advanced, and to have been through many testing trials, in order to submit oneself willingly to government by a single person.

In Africa the Hottentots, the Kaffirs, and several black nations are democracies. It is claimed that those countries where the most negroes are sold are ruled by kings. Tripoli, Tunis, Algeria are republics of soldiers and pirates. There are similar ones today in India: the Maharashtra, several hordes of Pathans, the Sikhs, have no kings; they elect their leaders when they go off plundering.

Several Tartar societies are like this too. The Turkish Empire itself was for a long time a republic of janissaries who would often strangle their sultan when their sultan did not make them decimate [other countries].

People ask every day whether a republican government is preferable to government by a king. The argument always ends with agreement that men are very difficult to govern. The Jews had God himself as their master. Look what happened to them as a result: they have almost always been beaten and enslaved, and today they make a fine spectacle, don't you think?

Economie. Economy

This word means in its normally accepted sense the way in which one manages one's wealth; the father of a family has it in common with the Comptroller-General of a kingdom. Different systems of government, the chicanery of families and courts, unjust and badly conducted wars, the sword of Themis placed in the hands of executioners to bring death to the innocent, internal quarrels, are all irrelevant to the economy.

This is not about those pronouncements of politicians who rule the State by pamphlet from their offices.

Domestic economy

The primary economy, the one through which all the rest survive, is the rural economy. It is this that provides the only three things which men really need: food, clothing, shelter. There is no fourth need, unless it is warmth in cold countries. All three, when they are well-managed, keep [people] healthy, and without that there is nothing.

Sometimes country life is called a *patriarchal way of life*; but in our climate the patriarchal way of life would be impractical, and would cause us to die of cold, hunger and poverty.

Abraham travels from Chaldea to the land of Shechem; from there he has to take a long journey through arid desert land to Memphis to buy grain. I put to one side, with my usual respect, as I should, everything that is holy about the story of Abraham and his children; I am looking here only at Abraham's rural economy. I cannot see a single house in it; he leaves the most fertile country in the world, and cities where there are comfortable houses, to go wandering off to countries whose language he does not understand.

He goes from Sodom into the Gerar [Negev] desert without set-tling anywhere. When he sends Hagar away, together with the child he had with her, it is still into a desert, and for their only sustenance he just gives them a bit of bread and a jug of water. When he goes off to sacrifice his son to the Lord, it is still in a desert. He cuts the wood for burning the victim himself, and loads it on to the back of the son who is to be sacrificed.

His wife dies in a place called [*Kirjath-*]*Arba* or *Hebron*; he has not even got six feet of earth to bury her in; he is obliged to purchase a cave for his wife, and that is the only piece of ground he ever possessed.

Yet he had many children because, in addition to Isaac and his line, he had with his other wife, Cethura, at the age of a hundred and forty, according to accepted calculations, five male children who went off to Arabia.

It is not said that Isaac possessed a single plot of land in the country where his father died; on the contrary, he goes off into the Gerar desert with his wife Rebecca to the country belonging to Abimelech, the very same King of Gerar, who had been in love with his mother.

This king of the desert also falls in love with Isaac's wife Rebecca, whom her husband passes off as his sister, just like Abraham had passed his wife Sarah off as his sister to this same King Abimelech forty years previously. It is somewhat surprising that people are always passing their wives off as their sisters in this family in order to gain something; but as these are consecrated facts, we must remain respectfully silent.

The Scriptures say that he became rich in this awful land, which became fertile for him, and that he became extremely powerful. But it is also said that he did not have any water to drink, that he had a great quarrel with the pastors of this petty King of Gerar over a well, and it is not clear whether or not he possessed a house in his own right.

His children, Esau and Jacob, had no more of a home than their father. Jacob was obliged to seek his fortune in Mesopotamia, which his father had left. He was in service [there] for seven years in order to obtain [the hand of] one of the daughters of Laban, and served for another seven to obtain [the hand of] the second daughter. He escaped with Rachel and the herds belonging to his father-in-law, who pursued him. There was nothing there to assure him of a secure future.

Esau is represented as being as much of a wanderer as Jacob. None of the twelve patriarchs, the children of Jacob, had a fixed abode, or owned a plot of land. They slept only in tents, like the bedouin Arabs.

It is clear that this patriarchal way of life would in no way be suited to our temperatures. A good farmer, like the Pignoux of the Auvergne, needs a solid house facing east, huge barns, equally large stables, clean and well-maintained cowsheds. And the whole lot can come to at least fifty thousand *francs* in today's money. Each year he must sow a hundred acres of corn, turn as many again into good pasture land, have a few acres of vineyards, and about fifty acres for other kinds of grain and vegetables; about thirty acres of woodland, fields for mulberry trees, for silkworms, for beehives. If all these assets are well-managed, he will be able to provide a large family with the best of everything. His land will improve day by day. He will cope fearlessly with the upsets of the different seasons, and with the burden of taxes, because one good year makes up for the losses of two bad ones. In his domains he will enjoy real sovereignty, subject only to the law. That is the most natural state for man, the most peaceful, the happiest, and unfortunately the rarest.

The son of this venerable patriarch, when he sees that he is rich, soon gets fed up with paying the humiliating tithe tax. Unfortunately, he has learned a little Latin; he rushes to the city, buys a public office which exempts him from this tax, and confers noble status on his son after a period of twenty years. He sells his land to pay for his vanity. A girl brought up in luxury marries him, dishonours him, and ruins him. He dies a beggar, and his son wears a servant's livery in Paris.

Such is the difference between a rural economy and the illusions of city life.

The economy of the city is quite different. If you live on your own land, you buy almost nothing: the earth produces everything for you; you can feed nearly sixty people almost without noticing it. Take the same income to the city, you buy everything at a high price, and you can barely feed five or six servants. A family man living on his own land with an income of twelve thousand *livres* will need to be very careful if he wants to live in Paris at the same standard with an income of forty thousand. This has always been the ratio between a rural economy and the economy of capital cities. One should always refer to the strange letter from Madame de Maintenon to her sister-in-law, Madame d'Aubigny, which people have talked so much about. It cannot be placed before one's eyes too often:

'You'll readily believe that I know Paris better than you [do]; sharing that view, my dear sister, here is a budget that I would put into effect if I lived outside the court. There are twelve of you: Sir and Madam, three females servants, four lackeys, two coachmen and a valet.

Fifteen pounds of meat @ five *sous* per pound	3 *liv.*	15*sous*
Two joints	2	10
Bread	1	10
Wine	2	10
Wood	2	0
Fruit	1	0
Wax candles	0	10
Tallow candles	0	8
	14 *liv.*	13 *sous*

'I am allowing for four *sous* in wine for your four lackeys and your two coachmen: that's what Madame de Montespan gives to hers. If you had wine in your cellar, it would not cost you three *sous*. I estimate six *sous* for your valet, and twenty for you two who drink more than enough for three.

'I estimate a pound of tallow candles a day, although only half a pound is necessary. I estimate ten *sous* for wax candles; you get six in a pound, which costs one *livre* and two *sous*, and which lasts for three days.

'I estimate two *livres* for wood; but you only burn it for three months in the year, and you only need two fires.

'I estimate one *livre* and ten *sous* for fruit; sugar costs only eleven *sous* a pound, and you need only a quarter to make stewed fruit.

'I estimate two joints; one can be saved when Sir and Madam have dinner or supper out; but I've also forgotten boiled fowl for the soup. We understand housekeeping. Without spending more than fifteen *livres*, you can very easily have an *entrée*, sometimes of sausages, sometimes of sheep's tongue or calves crow, and leg of mutton – the eternal pyramid, and the stewed fruit that you like so much.[1]

'On these assumptions, and from what I learn at court, my dear child, your expenditure should not exceed a hundred *livres* a week: that's four hundred *livres* a month. Let's assume five hundred, so that the trifles that I've forgotten cannot complain that I've not done them justice. Five hundred *livres* a month will make a total of:

Expenses on food	6,000 *liv.*
On your clothes	1,000
On rent	1,000
On servants' wages and dress	1,000
On Sir's clothes, the opera and Sir's little luxuries[2]	3,000
	12,000 *liv.*

'Isn't that all quite straightforward?' etc.

At that time, the value of money was about half that of today's legal tender. All of the absolutely essential items were about half as dear, and normal luxury items, which have become necessities, no longer luxuries, were three or four times less expensive than they are today.

Thus for his income of twelve thousand *livres*, which in Paris disappear without trace, Count d'Aubigny could have lived like a prince on his own land.

In Paris there are three or four hundred families in public service who have worked in the magistracy for a century, and whose wealth is in the form of pensions from the city. I presume that each one would receive an income of twenty thousand *livres*. Those twenty thousand *livres* used to be worth twice what they are today; thus in reality they have less than half of their former income. From that half you can cut another half during the unimaginable time when

---

[1] 'In those days, the most brilliant of Louis XIV's reign, side-dishes were served only during formal meals on grand occasions' (Voltaire's note).

[2] 'Madame de Maintenon has counted in two coachmen, but has forgotten four horses, which in those days, together with the maintenance of the coaches, must have cost about 2000 *francs* a year' (Voltaire's note).

Law's system was in operation. Thus these families only really enjoy a quarter of the income that they had when Louis XIV came to the throne. And as luxury items have risen in price by three quarters, they have almost nothing left, unless they have made up for their ruination through rich marriages, legacies, or clandestine activities; and that is what they have done.

In every country every ordinary person living on an annuity in a capital city who does not increase his wealth, loses it in the long run. Landowners maintain their position because, when currency values rise with inflation, income from their land rises in proportion. But they are vulnerable to another misfortune, and that misfortune is in themselves. Their love of luxury and their carelessness, no less dangerous, leads them to ruin. They sell their land to financiers who amass it, and whose children, in their turn, fritter the lot away. It is a never-ending circle of advancement and decline; the whole business results from the absence of a rational economy, which consists solely in not spending more than you earn.

On the public economy

The economy of a state is just like that of a large family. That is what persuaded the Duke of Sully to call his memoirs *Economies*. All other branches of government are more like obstacles than aids to the management of the public purse. Treaties that sometimes have to be concluded with a price [paid] in gold, [and] unsuccessful wars, ruin a state for a long time. Even successful wars exhaust it. Trade that is interrupted and badly managed impoverish it further; excessive taxes complete the misery.

What is a rich, well-organised state? It is a state where every working man is sure of having a reward commensurate with his condition, from king to labourer.

As an example, let us take England, the state where the management of financial affairs is the most complicated. The King is almost certain to have a million pounds sterling per year to spend on his household, his table, his ambassadors, and his pleasures. The whole of that million is returned to the people through consumption, for if ambassadors spend their emoluments elsewhere, foreign ministers get through their money in London. All landowners are secure in the enjoyment of their income, except for taxes levied by their representatives in Parliament, that is to say, by themselves.

The businessman pits his wits against the whole world almost, and for a long while is unsure of whether he will be marrying his daughter off to a peer of the realm, or whether he will be dying in the workhouse.

Those people who are not businessmen, and invest their fragile wealth in big commercial companies, are exactly like those idle people in France who buy royal bonds whose fate depends on the fortunes or misfortunes of the government.

Those whose only job is to sell and buy promissory notes on the basis of any good or bad news going around, of trading on fears and hopes, are in a minor way like shareholders. They are all gamblers, except for the farmer, who provides the wherewithal to gamble with.

A war comes along; the government has to borrow cash, for fleets and armies are not paid with promises. The House of Commons dreams up taxes on beer, coal, fireplaces, windows, acres of corn and pasture land, imports, etc.

What this tax will generate is calculated in round figures; the whole nation is informed; an act of Parliament tells the citizenry: Those who wish to lend to the country will get four per cent back on their money over ten years, at the end of which they will be repaid in full.

This same government establishes a sinking-fund from the surplus of what these taxes yield. This fund is to be used to pay back creditors. When the time for payment falls due, they are told: Do you want your money back, or would you like to leave it there at three per cent? The creditors, who think that what is owed to them is safe, for the most part leave their money in the government's hands.

A new war, new loans, new debts: the sinking-fund is empty; nobody gets anything back.

In the end this heap of paper symbolising non-existent silver has risen to one hundred and thirty million pounds sterling, amounting to a hundred and twenty-seven million guineas in the year 1770 of our vulgar era.

It must be said in passing that France is more or less in the same position; it owes to lenders about a hundred and twenty-seven million gold *louis*. Now these two sums, amounting to two hundred and fifty-four million gold *louis*, cannot be found in the whole of Europe.

How are they going to be paid off? Let us take the case of England first.

If everyone asked for his investment back, the whole business becomes clearly impossible without the philosopher's stone, or some such miracle of multiplication. What is to be done? One part of the nation has lent to the whole nation. England owes to England a hundred and thirty million pounds sterling at three per cent interest; thus it is paying out with that very reasonable interest alone three million nine hundred thousand pounds sterling every year. Taxes amount to about seven million.[3] Three million one hundred thousand pounds sterling are left over to meet the cost of the State's responsibilities, out of which, by making savings, some of the public debt can be gradually wiped out.

The state bank, while producing immense advantages for its directors, is useful to the nation because it provides increased prestige, its transactions are understood, and because it cannot make more banknotes than necessary without losing that prestige and ruining itself. That is the great advantage of a trading nation, where everything is done by virtue of positive law, where no transactions are hidden, where confidence is established on the basis of calculations made by representatives of the State, subject to public scrutiny. Whatever one might say, England thus sees that its wealth is safe as long as it has fertile land, plenty of herds of cattle, and a favourable balance of trade.

If it should happen that other countries have no more need for its grain, and tip the balance of trade against it, then a great upheaval in individual wealth might take place; but the land will remain, industry will remain, and England, which would then be less rich in cash terms, always stays rich in terms of the valuable, renewable produce of the soil. It reverts to the same position it was in during the sixteenth century.

It is absolutely the same case with a whole kingdom as with an individual's land: if the basic soil is good, the land will never be ruined. The family that made money out of it might be reduced to penury, but the soil will flourish under another family.

There are other kingdoms that will never be rich, whatever efforts are made. They are those which, located in harsh climates, can only

---

[3] 'This was written in 1770' (Voltaire's note).

possess at most the bare necessities. There citizens can only enjoy the comforts of life by importing them from abroad at what is for them an excessive cost. Give to Siberia and Kamchatka, now united and with four times the area of Germany, a Cyrus for a sovereign, and a Solon for a legislator, a Duke of Sully or a Colbert for a comptroller-general, a Duke of Choiseul for a minister of defence, an Anson for an admiral, and they would starve to death there, for all their genius.

On the other hand, if you were to have France ruled by a serious madman like Law, by an agreeable fool like Cardinal Dubois, by some of the ministers we have seen now and again, you could say of them what a Venetian senator said of his colleagues to King Louis XII, according to anecdotal sources. An angry Louis XII threatened to ruin the Republic: 'I defy you to', said the senator, 'it doesn't seem possible. For five years my colleagues have made every imaginable effort to destroy it, and they haven't been able to finish it off.'

There has perhaps never been anything more outrageous than the founding of the imaginary Mississippi Company, which was to have given a return of a hundred to one for every participant, to triple immediately the nominal value of money, to pay off in fancy paper the State's debts and responsibilities, and to culminate in the prohibition of all citizens from holding more than five hundred *francs* in gold or silver coinage. As this height of folly was unparalleled, the general upheaval was as big as it deserved to be. Everyone screamed that it was the finish of France for ever. After ten years, that would appear not to be the case.

A good country always recovers by itself, however poorly governed it might be; a bad state can only grow rich by means of intensive and successful ingenuity.

The so-called proportional relationship between Spain, France, England and Sweden will always be the same. Twenty million inhabitants is the usual number calculated for France; that is perhaps a little too much; Ustariz accepts only seven for Spain; Nichols gives eight to England; less than five are attributed to Sweden. The Spaniard on average has the equivalent of eighty of our *livres* to spend a year; the Frenchman, being a better farmer, has a hundred and twenty *livres*; the Englishman a hundred and eighty; the Swede fifty. If we wished to speak of the Dutchman, we would find that he only has what he can earn, because it is not his land that feeds and clothes him: Holland is always a marketplace where nobody gets rich except through his own, and his father's, hard work.

What an enormous disproportion there is in people's wealth! An Englishman with an income of seven thousand guineas uses up what a thousand people are worth. At first glance, that calculation is shocking, but at the end of the year he has distributed his seven thousand guineas throughout the state, and everyone has had more or less his share.

In general, man costs nature very little. In India, where the rajahs and nabobs amass so much wealth, the common people live on two *sous* a day at most.

Those Americans who are not subjugated, having nothing more than their bare hands, spend nothing. Half of Africa has always lived in the same way, and what makes us superior to all those people is just forty *écus* a year; but those forty *écus* make a huge difference; that is what covers the earth with fine cities and the sea with ships.

It is with our forty *écus* that Louis XIV acquired two hundred ships and built Versailles; and as long as each individual on average can be assumed to enjoy an income of forty *écus*, the state can flourish.

Obviously, the more people and the more wealth there is in a state, the more abuses there are to be seen. Friction in big machines is so great that they nearly always break down. These upsets make such an impression on people's minds that in England, where every citizen is allowed to say what he thinks, every month there is some theorist who kindly gives his compatriots a warning that all is lost, that the nation is ruined, and has no further resources. As there is less permission to think in France, people smuggle their complaints in like contraband. Books are printed secretly, but often, saying that never in the reign of Clotaire's children, nor in the time of King John, Charles VI, in the days of the Battle of Pavia, of civil war, and of the Saint Bartholomew massacre, have the people been as poor and wretched as [they are] today.

If these laments are answered with a warrant for arrest, which is not a very legitimate reason, but which is unanswerable, the plaintiff flees protesting to the police that it will take him six weeks to pay, and that, thank God, they will die of hunger like everyone else before them.

Bois-Guillebert, who attributed so impudently his *Royal tithe* to Marshal Vauban, claimed in his *Detail of France* that the great minister Colbert had already impoverished the State to the tune of fifteen hundred million, and that he expected the situation was worse than that.

A modern-day theorist,[4] with the best intentions in the world apparently, although he is very keen on everyone getting drunk after mass, claims that the bills and securities of France, which are recovering their value, and which constitute the nation's income, only amount to about four hundred million. In that he appears to have mistakenly undervalued the currency only by about sixteen to twenty hundred million, the rate of conversion to cash being forty-nine *livres* and ten *sous*. And he assures us that tax revenue to pay for the State's responsibilities might only be seventy-five million, at a time when it is in the order of three hundred million, which is not enough, by a long way, to pay off annual debts.

A single error in all of this speculation, and there is a very large number of them, is like those made in those earth-based calculations in astronomy. Two coordinates correspond to immense [volumes of] space in the sky.

It is in France and in England that the national economy is most complicated. The rest of the world, from the Atlas mountains to Japan, has no concept of that kind of administrative system. It was barely a hundred and thirty years ago when this art of making one half of the nation indebted to the other half started, the art of passing wealth by means of bits of paper from hand to hand, of turning the State into the State's creditor, of creating chaos out of what should be subject to consistent regulation. This system has spread to England and to Holland. It has been refined to the point where a game of chance is set up between the sovereign and his subjects: this game is called a lottery. Your stake is hard cash; if you win, you get banknotes or bonds; the losers are not badly hurt. The government normally takes ten per cent for its trouble. These lotteries are made as elaborate as possible in order to baffle and tempt the public. All these methods have been adopted in Germany and Holland; nearly every state in turn has been forced into deep debt. That is not too clever, but who is clever? Children, who do not have the power to ruin themselves, are.

[4] John Law.

Gouvernement. Government

Government must be a very great pleasure, since so many people want to get involved in it. We have many more books on government than there are princes in the world. God forbid that I should educate kings, their esteemed ministers, their esteemed manservants, their esteemed confessors, and their esteemed tax-collectors! I understand nothing about it, I respect them all. It is only for Mr Wilkes to weigh in the balance of his English scales those at the head of the human race. Moreover, it would be very strange that with three or four thousand volumes on government, with Machiavelli, and Bossuet's *Politics of holy scripture*, with the *Financier-citizen*, the *Financial guide*, the *Means of enriching the State*, etc., there should be anyone left who does not fully understand the duties of kings and the art of being a leader.

Professor Pufendorf, or Baron Pufendorf, said that King David, having sworn never to threaten the life of Semein, his privy counsellor, did not betray his oath when (according to Jewish history) he ordered his son Solomon to have Semein murdered 'because David had committed only himself not to kill Semein'. The Baron, who disapproves so loftily of the mental reservations of the Jesuits, allows David, the anointed, to have one here that would not be to the taste of privy counsellors.

Weigh carefully the words of Bossuet in his *Politics of holy scripture* dedicated to my Lord, the *Dauphin*: 'see how royalty is thus connected by direct line of succession to the house of David and Solomon, and how the throne of David is confirmed for ever (though this little stool called a *throne* is relatively new). By virtue of this law, the

49

eldest was to succeed, placing his brothers at a disadvantage: that is why Adonias, who was the eldest, said to Bathsheba, Solomon's mother: "You know that the kingdom belonged to me, and that the whole of Israel recognised me; but the Lord has transferred my kingdom to my brother Solomon." ' Adonias' right was irrefutable; Bossuet says as much at the end of this article. *The Lord has transferred* is just an everyday expression meaning: I have lost my possessions, my possessions have been taken away from me. Adonias was the offspring of a legitimate wife; the birth of his younger brother was just the fruit of a double crime.

'Thus', says Bossuet, 'unless something extraordinary happened, the eldest would succeed.' Now that extraordinary something was the fact that Solomon, born of a marriage based on a double act of adultery and on a murder, had his elder brother, his legitimate king, whose rights were confirmed by Pontiff Abiathar and General Joab, murdered at the foot of an altar. After that, let us acknowledge that it is more difficult than people think to take lessons on the rights of people and governments from Holy Scripture, handed down to the Jews, and then to us, for more sublime purposes.

'Let the supreme law be the security of the people'; this is the fundamental maxim of nations; but the security of the people is made to consist in all civil wars of the slaughter of one group of citizens. In all foreign wars a people's security lies in killing its neighbours, and taking over their possessions. It is difficult to find in all that a right that is very beneficial to the people, and a way of governing likely to advance the art of thinking and the smooth-running of society.

There are very regular geometrical figures that are perfect in their own way; arithmetic is perfect; many professions are practised in ways that are always uniform and always good; but as far as the government of men is concerned, can there ever be a good system when they are all based on conflicting passions?

No community of monks has ever existed without discord; it is thus impossible for there not to be any discord in kingdoms. All governments are similar not only to monasteries, but also to households. There are none which do not have quarrels in them, and quarrels between nations, between princes, have always been bloody. Those that have taken place between subjects and their sovereign have sometimes been just as lethal. How must we proceed? Either by taking a risk, or by hiding ourselves away.

. . .

More than one nation wants a new constitution. The English would like to change ministers every week, but they would not like to change their form of government.

Modern Romans are all proud of Saint Peter's Church and their ancient Greek statues, but the people would like to be better fed and better dressed, even if they had to be less rich in the way of blessings. Fathers of families would like the Church to have less gold, and their granaries to contain more corn. They long for the time when apostles walked, and Roman citizens were carried in litters from palace to palace.

People never stop singing the praises of those fine Greek republics to us. What is sure is that the Greeks would prefer government by Pericles and Demosthenes to government by a pasha; but in times of the greatest prosperity they always complained. Discord and hatred existed externally between cities, and internally within individual cities. They gave laws to the ancient Romans, who did not yet have any, but their own were so bad that they changed them continually.

What kind of government [was it] that banished the just Aristides, put Phocion to death, condemned Socrates to drink hemlock after having been mocked by Aristophanes, that witnessed the Amphiction-ies stupidly surrendering Greece to Philippus because the Phocaeans had ploughed a field that was part of Apollo's domain? But the gov-ernment of neighbouring monarchies was worse.

Pufendorf promises to examine which form of government is best; he tells you that 'some people are in favour of monarchy and others, on the contrary, rage furiously against kings', and that it is outside [the scope of] his subject to examine the latter's reasons.

Should any bright reader expect anyone here to tell him more than Pufendorf he will be making a big mistake.

A Swiss, a Dutchman, a Venetian nobleman, an English peer, a cardinal, and an imperial count were arguing, while travelling together one day, about their reasons for preferring their own systems of government. Nobody understood anybody else, everyone stuck to his own view without having any view about which they were very sure, and they went home without having reached any conclusion, vanity making each one praise his own country, and sentiment making them complain about it.

What a destiny then for the human race! Almost no great nation is ruled by itself.

Let us start with the East on a world tour: Japan has closed its ports to foreigners, rightly fearing a terrible revolution.

China has had this revolution; it owes obedience to Tartars who are half Manchurian and half Hun. India owes obedience to Tartar Moguls. The Euphrates, the Nile, the Orontes, Greece and Epirus are still under the yoke of the Turks. A race of English does not rule in England, but a German family which succeeded a Dutch prince, and he succeeded a Scottish family which had succeeded a family from Anjou, which had replaced a Norman family, which had driven out a family of Saxon usurpers. Spain owes obedience to a French family, which succeeded a race of Austrians; these Austrians succeeded families that boasted that they were Visigoths. For a long time these Visigoths had been hounded by Arabs, after having succeeded the Romans, who had driven off the Carthaginians.

Gaul obeyed the Franks, after having obeyed Roman prefects.

The same banks of the Danube have belonged to Teutons, Romans, Abars, Slavs, Bulgars, Huns and twenty other families, nearly all foreign.

And has anyone seen anything stranger in Rome than so many emperors born in barbaric provinces, and so many popes born in provinces that are just as barbaric? Let whoever can govern, govern. And when one has succeeded in becoming the master, one governs as best one can.[1]

What follows was told by a traveller in 1769:

I have seen on my travels quite a large and well-populated country in which all public offices are bought, not in secret and to cheat the law, but in public to conform to the law. The right to be the sovereign judge of the honour, fortune and life of citizens is auctioned off, in the same way that you sell a few acres of land.[2] There are very important army commissions given only to the one who bids the most. The main mystery of their religion is celebrated for three sesterces, and if the celebrant does not get this fee, he stays as idle as an unemployed labourer.

[1] 'See the article "Laws" ' (Voltaire's note).

[2] 'If this traveller had passed through the country just two weeks later, he would have seen that that famous custom had been abolished, and four years later he would have seen it re-established' (Voltaire's note, added in 1774).

Fortunes in this country are not the prize of agriculture; they are the result of a game of chance that several people play by signing their names, and by passing these names around. If they lose, they return to the gutter whence they came; they disappear. If they win, they get to enter directly into the public service, they marry their daughters off to mandarins, and their sons become mandarins of one sort or another.

A considerable number of citizens have all their assets drawn against an institution that has not got any; and for a hundred thousand *écus* each a hundred people have the right to receive and pay out money due to these citizens against the security of this imaginary mansion, a right that they never make use of, being blissfully unaware of what is supposed to have passed through their hands.

Sometimes you hear the streets ring with a proposal aimed at anyone with a bit of gold in his piggy-bank with a view to dispossessing him of it in exchange for a wonderful bit of paper which will allow you to lead a happy, comfortable, problem-free life. The next day they shout out an order to you obliging you to change this bit of paper for another, much better one. The day after that you are deafened with another piece of paper that cancels out the first two. You are ruined; but sharp minds console you by assuring you that within a fortnight the city's pedlars will be shouting more attractive propositions [in your ear].

You travel around one province in this empire, and you buy there the things necessary to clothe yourself, to eat, to drink, to sleep. If you go to the next province, you have to pay duty on all of those items, as if you had come from Africa. You ask the reason, you get no answer; or, if they deign to give you [an answer], they reply that you come from a province *deemed to be foreign*, and that therefore you must pay the service costs of the transaction. You try in vain to understand how the kingdom's provinces can be foreign to the kingdom.

A little while ago, when I was changing horses, and feeling weak with tiredness, I asked the staging-post superintendent for a glass of wine. 'I can't give you one', he said, 'the thirst-tax collectors, who are very numerous and very sober, would make me pay *excess drink duty*, which would ruin me.'

'It's not excess drinking', I said to him, 'to keep up my strength with a glass of wine; and what difference does it make whether it's you or me who swallowed this glassful?'

'Sir', he replied, 'our laws on drink are much more subtle than you think. As soon as we have got the harvest in, the landlords of the kingdom appoint doctors to come and visit our wine-cellars. They put to one side as much wine as they judge appropriate to let us drink to keep us healthy. They come back at the end of the year, and if they judge that we have exceeded the prescription by one bottle, they sentence us to pay a heavy fine; and if ever we are disobedient, we are sent to Toulon to drink sea-water. If I gave you the wine you are asking for, they would not fail to accuse me of having drunk too much. You see what I would risk with our health-inspectors.'

I admired that regime, but I was nonetheless surprised to meet a plaintiff in despair who told me that he had just lost the same case on the other side of the stream that he had won the day before on this side. I learned from him that the country had as many different law-codes as it had villages. His conversation pricked my curiosity. 'Our country is so wise', he said, 'that nothing has been regulated there. Laws, customs, the rights and privileges of public bodies, rank, seniority, everything is arbitrary, everything is left to the wisdom of the nation.'

I was still in the country when the people had a war with a few neighbours. They called this war the *ridiculous war*, because there was a lot to lose and nothing to gain. I went off somewhere else, and only returned after the peace. On my return, the nation seemed to be in the utmost misery; it had lost its money, its soldiers, its fleet, its trade. I said: 'Its final hour has come; everything must pass away; here is a nation that has been obliterated; it's a pity because many of the people were likeable, industrious and very cheerful, after having once been crude, superstitious and barbaric.'

I was totally astonished that within two months its capital and its main towns seemed to me to be more opulent than ever; luxury had increased, and one breathed in only the scent of pleasure. I could not understand this miracle. I saw the reason for it only when I examined the system of government of its neighbours; I realised that they were all just as badly governed as this country, but that it was more industrious than all of them.

A man from the provinces in this country I am talking about complained bitterly one day about all the harassment he was experiencing. He knew his history quite well; he was asked if he thought he would have been happier a hundred years ago when, in his then barbaric country, a citizen would be sentenced to be hanged for eating meat on a feast-day. He shook his head. 'Would you prefer the age of civil wars that started with the death of Francis II, or the time of the defeats of Saint-Quentin and Pavia, or the prolonged disasters of the wars against the English, or the age of feudal anarchy and the horrors of the second race, and the barbarities of the first?' With each question he was seized with horror. The rule of the Romans seemed to him to be the most intolerable of all. 'There's nothing worse', he said, 'than belonging to foreign masters'. We came finally to the question of the druids. 'Ah!' he cried, 'I was mistaken; it's even more horrible to be ruled by blood-thirsty priests.' In the end, he came to the conclusion, in spite of himself, that the times in which he lived were the least odious of any, all things considered.

An eagle ruled over all the birds in the land of Ornithia. Admittedly, he had no right other than the right derived from beak and talons. But in the end, when he had made provision for his meals and his pleasures, he ruled as well as any other bird of prey.

In his old age, he was attacked by starving vultures from the far North, who came and laid waste to all the eagle's provinces. Then a tawny owl appeared, who had been born in one of the scraggiest thickets in the empire, called for a long time *lucifugax*. He was crafty; he joined forces with the bats, and while the vultures fought against the eagle, our owl and his gang entered the area under dispute as peacemakers.

The eagle and the vultures, after having fought a pretty long war, finally referred the matter to the owl who, with his solemn features, knew how to impose his authority on the two sides.

He persuaded the eagle and the vultures to have their nails trimmed and the tip of their beaks cut off, the better to reach agreement. Before that the owl had always told the birds: 'Obey the eagle.' After that he said: 'Obey the vultures.' Soon he said: 'Obey me and no-one else.' The poor birds did not know who to listen to; they had their feathers plucked by the eagle, the vulture, the tawny owl and the bats. *Qui habet aures audiat.*[3]

'I have a large number of ancient Roman catapults and ballistas, admittedly worm-eaten, but which could still be used for display. I

---

[3] Matthew, XI.15.

have a lot of water-clocks, half of which are broken; tomb lamps, and an old copper model of a quinquereme. I also have togas, praetexta, lead laticlaves, and my predecessors set up a community of tailors who make robes, not very well, copied from these ancient monuments. For the sake of [all] these causes, of this moving sense of our [national] identity, and having listened to our head antiquary's report, we command all these venerable customs to be kept up for ever, and command everybody throughout the length and breadth of our states to wear shoes and to think thoughts exactly like people who wore shoes and thought thoughts in the time of Cnidus Rufillus, Propraetor of the province that has come down to us by right of all that is proper, etc.'

It was put to the wax-warmer, employed by his ministry to stamp [a seal] on this edict, that all the devices specified in it had become useless;

that men's minds and the arts are improving from one day to the next;

that men have to be led by the bridles they wear today, and not by those they wore in days gone by;

that nobody would set foot on his Serene Highness's quinquereme;

that his tailors make laticlaves in vain: nobody would buy a single one; and that it befitted His Highness to make some concession towards the views that the good people of his country hold today.

The wax-warmer promised to take the matter up with a clerk, who promised to explain the matter to the Chief Clerk, who promised to have a word with His Serene Highness, when the opportunity arose.

It is strange to see how a government is established. I shall not be talking here about the great Tamburlaine, or Timurleng, because I do not know exactly what the mystery of the Grand Mogul's government is. But we can see things more clearly in the way England is administered, and I prefer to examine that system more than the one in India, given the fact that I am told there are men in England, and not slaves, and that in India you find, so it is claimed, a lot of slaves and very few men.

First, let us look at a Norman bastard who took it into his head to become king of England. He had as much right to that as Saint Louis had later to Greater Cairo. But Saint Louis had the misfortune not to start by having Egypt legally bestowed upon him in the court of Rome, and William the Bastard did not fail to lend sacred legitimacy to his cause by obtaining from Pope Alexander II a decree assuring him of his proper rights without having heard the other side, and simply by virtue of these words: 'Every knot that you tie on earth will be tied in Heaven.' With his rival, Harold, the legitimate king, thus tied up with a decree emanating from Heaven, William added to this virtue from the centre of the universe a rather stronger virtue, namely victory at the Battle of Hastings. He thus ruled by the most powerful right of all, as did Pépin and Clovis in France, the Goths and the Lombards in Italy, the Visigoths and then the Arabs in Spain, the Vandals in Africa, and all kings in this world in their turn.

It must be further admitted that our bastard had a legal claim that was just as valid as that of the Saxons and the Danes, who had one just as valid as that of the Romans. And the legal entitlement of all these heroes was the one enjoyed by *highway robbers* or, if you like, by foxes and ferrets when they make their farmyard conquests.

All these great men were such perfect highway robbers that, from Romulus down to the buccaneers, the story has just been one of rich profits, plunder, looting, and cattle stolen by force of arms. In the fable, Mercury steals cows from Apollo, and in the Old Testament the prophet Isiah gives the name of *thief* to the son his wife is to give birth to, and who is to be a major typical example. He calls him Maher-salal-has-bas, *divide the spoils up quick*. We have already noted that the names of *soldier* and *thief* were often synonyms.

Soon we have William, king by the grace of God. William the Red, who usurped his elder brother's crown, also became king by the grace of God without any difficulty; and this same grace of God belonged after him to Henry, the third usurper.

The Norman barons, who had come together at their own expense to invade England, wanted rewards; it was very necessary to give them some, to make them Grand Vassals, Grand Officers of the Crown; they were given the finest territory. Clearly, William would have preferred to have kept everything for himself, and to have turned all these lords into his guards [and attendants], but he would have risked too much. He saw that he was obliged to share.

As far as the Anglo-Saxon lords were concerned, he had no way of killing them all, or even of reducing them all to slavery. They were left in their own lands with the dignity of being seigneurial lords.

They were answerable to Norman Grand Vassals, who were answerable to William.

In that way, everything balanced well until the first quarrel. And what became of the rest of the nation? The same thing that befell almost all the peoples of Europe: they became serfs, villeins.

Finally, after the madness of the crusades, the princes, who were ruined, sold the feudal serfs, who through work and trade had made a bit of money, their freedom; towns were liberated; commoners were given privileges; men's rights were reborn out of anarchy itself.

Everywhere the barons were at loggerheads with the king, and with each other. A dispute became a little internal war, made up of a hundred civil wars. It was out of that dark, horrible chaos that a feeble glow came that gave light to the commoners, and improved their lot.

The kings of England, who were themselves Grand Vassals of France for Normandy, and then for Guyenne and other provinces, readily adopted the practices of the kings to whom they were answerable. For a long time, the States-General was composed, as in France, of barons and bishops.

The English Chancellory court was an imitation of the Council of State presided over by the Chancellor of France. The court of the King's Bench was modelled on the *parlement* founded by Philippe *le Bel*. The sittings of the Commons were like the court of justice in Paris. The Exchequer court was like the Comptroller-General's department, which became the Excise Board in France.

The maxim that the royal domains were inalienable was another clear imitation of the French system of government.

The right of the King of England to have his ransom paid by his subjects if he was taken prisoner of war, the right to demand a subsidy for the marriage of his eldest daughter, and when knighting his son, are all reminiscent of the ancient customs of a kingdom whose first vassal was William.

Philippe *le Bel* had only just called the commons to the meeting of the States-General when Edward, the King of England, did the same thing in order to counterbalance the great power of the barons, for it was during the reign of that prince that the convening of the House of Commons is clearly recorded.

So we see that, up until the fourteenth century, the English system of government followed closely that of France. The two churches are exactly the same, with the same subservience to Rome, the same extortions that people complained about, but always ended up paying to that greedy court, the same fairly serious quarrels, the same excommunications, the same donations to monks, the same chaos, the same mixture of holy pillage, superstitions and barbarity.

As France and England were therefore administered so long in accordance with the same principles, or more precisely, in accordance with no principle at all but just in accordance with entirely similar customs, how is it that these two governments became in the end as different from one another as those of Morocco and Venice?

Is it not because, given the fact that England is an island, the king has no need to always maintain one of those large land armies, used as much against the homeland itself as against foreigners?

Is it not because in general the English have something more solid, more thoughtful, more obstinate about their spirit than certain other peoples?

Is it not for this reason, namely that having always complained about the court of Rome, they have entirely thrown off that shameful yoke, while a less serious people has carried it, all the time pretending to laugh about it while they were dancing in chains?

Also has the location of their country, which makes sea-faring a necessity for them, not given them tougher customs?

Has this toughness in their customs, which has made their island into a theatre of so many blood-soaked tragedies, not also helped to inspire them with a noble honesty?

Is it not their mixture of contradictory qualities that has led to the spilling of so much royal blood in battles and on scaffolds, and which has never allowed them to use poison in their civil disorders, whereas elsewhere, under a priestly government, poison has been such a common weapon?

As they became more enlightened and more wealthy, has not love of freedom become their dominant characteristic? All citizens cannot be equally powerful, but they can all be equally free, and this is what the English have gained in the end by their steadfastness.

Freedom means being dependent only on the law. The English have therefore loved laws as fathers love their children, because they have created them, or believe they have created them.

Such a system of government could only be created at a fairly late stage because for a long time it was necessary to fight powerful forces that were respected: the power of the Pope, the most terrible of all since it was based on prejudice and ignorance; royal power, always ready to be abused, and which had to be kept within its limits; the power of the barons, which was anarchy; the power of the bishops who, by always mixing the profane with the sacred, wanted to triumph over barons and kings [alike].

Gradually the House of Commons became the dam that held back all these torrential forces.

The House of Commons is truly the nation because the King, who is its head, acts only for himself, and for what is called *his prerogative*; because the peers are only in Parliament for themselves; because the bishops similarly are only there for themselves; but the House of Commons is there for the people, because each member is the deputy of the people. Now the ratio of this people to the king is about eight million to one. To the peers and bishops it is at most eight million to two hundred. And the eight million free citizens are represented in the lower house.

This institution, compared to which Plato's republic is but a dream, and which seems to be the invention of Locke, Newton, Halley or Archimedes, has given birth to the most frightful abuses that have ever made human nature shudder. The inevitable grinding friction in this vast machine almost destroyed it in the time of Fairfax and Cromwell. Foolish fanaticism had invaded this vast structure like a raging fire devours a fine building made only of wood.

In the age of William of Orange it was rebuilt in stone. Philosophy destroyed the fanaticism that shakes the most solid of states. It can be assumed that a constitution that has regulated the rights of the king, of the nobility and of the people, and in which everyone finds security, will last as long as human affairs can last.

It can also be assumed that any state not based on such principles will experience revolutions.

In the end this is what English legislation has achieved: the restoration to all men of all those natural rights of which nearly every monarchy deprives them. These rights are: total freedom in matters affecting one's person and one's possessions; the right to speak to the nation through the medium of one's pen; to be judged in criminal matters only by a *jury* of independent men; to be judged in all cases only in accordance with the precise wording of the law; to follow peacefully any religion one wishes, eschewing posts available only to anglicans. Those are called prerogatives. And in fact it is a very great and very happy prerogative, beyond the reach of so many nations, to be sure when you go to bed that you will wake up the next day with the same wealth that you had the day before; that you will not be torn from the arms of your wife and children in the middle of the night, to be taken off to some dungeon or into some desert; that on waking up you will be able to publish what you think; that if you are put on trial, either for having behaved offensively, or spoken offensively, or written offensively, you will be judged only in accordance with the law. That prerogative extends to everyone arriving in England. A foreigner enjoys the same freedom in his possessions and in his person; and if he is put on trial, he can request half of the jury to be made up of foreigners.

I venture to say that if the human race were to be assembled to make laws, people would make them like that for the sake of their security. Why then are these laws not followed in other countries? Is that not the same as asking why coconuts flourish in India, but do not do very well in Rome? You answer that coconuts have not always flourished in England, that they have only been grown there in relatively recent times, that following England's example Sweden grew some for a few years, and they did not do well; if only you could bring those fruits to other provinces, Bosnia and Serbia, for example. So try to plant some.

And above all, poor man, if you are a pasha, an effendi or a mullah, do not be so stupidly barbaric as to tighten the chains of your nation. Remember that the heavier you make the yoke, the more your children, who will not all be pashas, will be enslaved. What! You wretches! For the pleasure of being a petty tyrant for a few days you will cause all those who come after you to groan in chains! Oh, how far apart are an Englishman and a Bosnian today!

You know, dear reader, that in Spain, near the Malaga coast, a little nation was discovered in the time of Philip II, unknown until then, hidden in the Alpujarras mountains. You know that this chain of inaccessible rocks is intersected with delightful valleys. You will not be unaware that today those valleys are still cultivated by the descendants of the Moors, who were forced into Christianity to make them happy, or at least into the appearance of Christianity.

As I was saying, among these Moors there was a tiny nation in the reign of Philip II that lived in a valley which could only be reached through caves. This valley is between Pitos and Portugos; the inhabitants of this remote spot were almost unknown to the Moors themselves; they spoke a language that was neither Spanish nor Arabic, and was thought to be derived from an ancient [form of] Carthaginian.

This tribe had not increased very much. The reason for this, it was claimed, was that their neighbours the Arabs, and before them the Africans, used to come and take the girls away from this little canton.

This feeble, but happy, little people had never heard of the Christian religion, nor the Jewish; they had a vague knowledge of Mohammed's and did not make much of it. From time immemorial they had made offerings of milk and fruit to a statue of Hercules: that was their whole religion. For the rest, these little-known people lived in indolence and innocence. In the end, they were discovered by a friend of the inquisition. The Grand Inquisitor burned the lot of them: this was the only event in their history.

The sacred reasons for their condemnation were that they had never paid any taxes, to be expected in view of the fact that nobody had ever asked them for any, and they had no knowledge of money; that they had no Bible, seeing that they knew no Latin; and that nobody had taken the trouble to baptise them. They were declared to be witches and heretics; they were all dressed in penitential robes, and ceremonially roasted.

Clearly that is how people should be governed; nothing contributes more to the sweet life of society.

Homme. Man

To understand the physical make-up of the human species, you must read works on anatomy, Mr Venel's articles in the *Encyclopaedic dictionary* or, better still, take a course in anatomy.

To understand what is called *moral* man, more than anything else it is necessary to have experienced life and to have reflected on it.

Are not all books on morality summed up in these words of Job: 'Homo natus de muliere, brevi vivens tempore, repletur multis miseriis; qui quasi flos egreditur et conteritur, et fugit velut umbra.' *Man that is born of woman does not live long; he is full of woe; he is like a flower that opens, withers and is crushed; he passes like a shadow.*

We have already seen that mankind has a life-span of only about twenty-two years, including those who die at their wet-nurse's breast and those who drag out what is left of their foolish, miserable lives for anything up to a hundred years.

That old story of the first man, who was destined at first to live a maximum of twenty years, is a fine parable. This came down to five years, taking the average life as the basis to the calculation. Man was in despair; close by was a caterpillar, a butterfly, a peacock, a horse, a fox and a monkey.

'Prolong my life', he said to Jupiter, 'I'm better than all those animals; it's only right that I and my children should live a very long time in order to become the masters of all these beasts.' 'With pleasure', said Jupiter, 'but I've only got a certain number of days to share out among all the beings to whom I've given life. I can only give to you by taking from others. For don't think that just because I'm

Jupiter I'm infinite and omnipotent. I've got my own nature and limitations. Now, I'm very willing to give you a few more years, by taking those years from these six creatures you are jealous of, on condition that you take on their life-forms in turn. Man shall first be a caterpillar, crawling around [like a caterpillar] in early childhood. Up to fifteen he will be as fragile as a butterfly; as a youth he will have the vanity of a peacock. In adulthood he will have to work like a horse. In his fifties he will have the cunning of a fox; and in old age he will be as ugly and ridiculous as a monkey.' That just about sums up the destiny of man.

Note also that, in spite of Jupiter's kindness, this animal, even when all the compensations have been made, and with a maximum of twenty-two to twenty-three years of life, taking the human race as a whole, you have to take away a third of that for sleep, during which you are dead; fifteen or so years remain; of those fifteen, take off at least eight for early childhood, which is, as has been said, the hallway to life. The net yield will be seven years; of those seven years at least half will be taken up with various forms of suffering. Assume three and half years for work, boredom and frustration, and how many people have never had any of that! So there we are, poor little animal, are you still able to give yourself airs?

Unfortunately, in that parable, God forgot to dress this animal as he had dressed the monkey, the fox, the horse, the peacock, right down to the caterpillar. The human race only had its bare skin which, being continually exposed to sun, rain and hail, became cracked, burnt and blotchy. On our continent the male was disfigured by sparse body hair that made him hideous, without covering him. His face was hidden under his hair. His chin became a piece of bumpy ground with a forest of tiny stalks with roots on top and branches underneath. It was in this state, and taking his own appearance as the model, that this animal dared to portray God when, in the course of time, he learned to paint.

The female, being weaker, became even more disgusting and horrible in old age; the most hideous thing on earth is a senile old woman. So, without the help of tailors and dressmakers, the human race would never have dared to show itself in public. But before acquiring clothes, before even learning how to speak, many centuries had to pass. That is a proven fact, but it has to be reiterated frequently.

This uncivilised animal, left to himself, must have been the dirtiest and poorest of all the animals.

> Adam, my dear glutton, my good father,
> What did you do in the Garden of Eden?
> Did you work for this foolish human race?
> Did you caress my mother, Mrs Eve?
> Confess to me that both of you had
> Long nails, rather black and dirty,
> Hair that was pretty untidy,
> A dark complexion, your skin ruddy and tanned.
> Without cleanliness, the happiest love
> Is no love at all, just shameful need.
> Soon, weary of their wonderful adventure,
> They dined in fine style beneath an oak
> On water, birdseed and nuts.
> When they had eaten, they slept in the open.
> There is the state of pure nature for you.[1]

It is a little strange that a very respectable contemporary philosopher, the good, innocent Helvétius, has been harassed, reviled, hunted down for having said that if men did not have hands they would not have been able to build houses, or work high-warp tapestry. Apparently, those who condemned this proposition have the secret how to cut stone and wood, and do needlework with their feet.

I liked the author of the book called *On the mind*. That man worth more than all his enemies put together; but I have never approved of either the errors in his book or the trivial truths that he utters rather ponderously. I took his side openly when silly people condemned him for those [very same] truths.

I cannot put into words the depth of my contempt for those people who, for example, wanted to legally outlaw this proposition: 'The Turks can be regarded as deists.' Come on, you ill-bred pedants, how do you want us to regard them? As atheists, because they worship only one God?

You also condemn this proposition: 'An intelligent man knows that men are what they must be; that all hatred for them is unjust; that a fool produces foolishness like wild stock produces bitter fruits.'

Oh! You wild stock of the schools, you persecute a man because he does not hate you.

---

[1] *Le mondain* (The man of the world) (1736) is Voltaire's apology for luxury.

Let us leave the schools there, and continue.

Reason, busy hands, a mind capable of forming ideas, a tongue supple enough to express them: these are the great benefits granted to man by the Supreme Being, to the exclusion of all other animals.

In general, the male lives for a slightly shorter time than the female.

He is always taller, relatively speaking. The tallest man is normally two or three inches taller than the tallest female.

His strength is almost always superior; he is more agile, and because his organs are all stronger, he is more capable of concentration. All the arts were invented by him, and not by woman. It should be noted that it is not the fire of imagination, but perseverance of thought processes and the combination of ideas that caused the arts to be invented, in the same way as machinery, gunpowder, printing, clock-making, etc.

The human species is the only one that knows that it must die, and it knows it only through experience. A child raised in solitude, and transported to a desert island, would have no more certain knowledge of it than a plant or a cat.

A man with a few eccentricities[2] published a book saying that the human body is a fruit that stays green until old age, and that death is the moment of maturity. Rot and dust, that is a strange maturity! It is that philosopher's mind that was not mature. How the mania for saying something new makes people say wild things!

The main preoccupations of our species are shelter, food and clothing; all the rest are incidental, and it is these wretched, incidental things that have produced so much murder and devastation.

On the different races of men

We have seen elsewhere how this world has in it different races of men, and how surprised the first negro and the first white man must have been when they met each other.

It is even quite probable that several species of men and animals that were too weak have perished. Thus no more murex are to be found; this species was probably devoured by other animals appearing after several centuries on the river banks inhabited by this little shellfish.

---

[2] 'Maupertuis' (Voltaire's note).

Saint Jerome, in his *History of the desert fathers*, speaks of a centaur which had a conversation with Saint Anthony, the hermit. He then gives an account of a conversation that is much longer than [the one that] this same Anthony had with a satyr.

Saint Augustine, in his thirty-third sermon, entitled *To his brothers in the desert*, says things that are just as extraordinary as those that Saint Jerome said: 'I was already the Bishop of Hippo when I went to Ethiopia with a few servants of Christ to preach the Gospel. We saw in that country a lot of men and women without heads, with two big eyes in their chests. In countries even further to the south we saw a people who had only one eye in their foreheads' etc.

It would appear that Augustine and Jerome were speaking at the time in terms of husbandry: they were increasing the works of creation to show to better advantage the works of God. They wished to astonish men with fables so that they could make them more submissive to the yoke of faith.[3]

We can be very good Christians without believing in centaurs, in headless people, in people with only one eye or one leg, etc. But we cannot doubt that the insides of a negro are different to those of a white man, since the network of mucous or fatty membranes is white in one and black in the other. I have already told you that, but you are deaf.

The Albinos and the Darians, the first from Africa, the second from central America, are as different from us as negroes are. There are yellow, red and grey races. We have already seen that all Americans are beardless and have no body hair, except on their eyebrows and their heads. All are equally men, but in the same way as a pine tree, an oak and a pear tree are all equally trees. The pear tree does not come from the pine, and the pine does not come from the oak.

But how is it that in the middle of the Pacific Ocean, on an island called Tahiti, men have beards? That is like asking why we are bearded, while Peruvians, Mexicans and Canadians are not. It is like asking why monkeys have tails, and why nature has refused us this ornament, which is, to say the least, extremely rare among us [humans].

Men's inclinations and natures differ as much as their climates and their governments. It has never been possible to make up a

---

[3] 'See the article "Economy" ' (Voltaire's note).

regiment from Laplanders and Samoyeds, whereas their neighbours, the Siberians, make fearless soldiers.

You will have no more success in making a good grenadier out of a poor Darian or an Albino. It is not because they have tawny eyes; it is not because their hair and eyebrows are of the finest, whitest silky texture; but it is because their bodies, and hence their courage, are extremely weak. Only a blind man, and an obstinate blind man at that, could deny the reality of all these different species. It is as great and as varied as the monkeys.

That all races of men have always lived in society

All people discovered in the most frightful and uncultivated countries live in society, as do beavers, ants, bees and several other animal species.

The country has not been seen where people live separately from one another, where the male mates with the female only by chance, and leaves her out of disgust a moment later; where a mother cannot recognise the children she has reared, where people live without families and without any form of society. A few practical jokers have abused their minds to the point of advancing the astonishing paradox that man was created originally to live alone like a lynx, and that it is society that has depraved his nature. It would be just as valid to say that in the sea herrings were created originally to swim alone, and that it is because of an excess of corruption that they swim in shoals from the polar sea to our coasts; that long ago cranes flew through the air apart from one another, and that through a violation of natural law they decided to travel together.

Each animal has its own instinct; and the instinct of man, strengthened by reason, inclines him towards society, as [it does] towards eating and drinking. The need for society has far from degraded man; it is when he moves away from society that he is degraded. Whoever wants to live completely alone would soon lose his reasoning powers and his ability to express himself; he would be a burden to himself; he would succeed only in changing himself into an animal. Excess of impotent pride, which clashes with the pride of others, can incline a melancholy soul to flee the company of men. In that case, it is that soul that is depraved. It punishes itself for this; its pride becomes its torture; in solitude the secret resentment at being scorned and forgotten gnaws away at it; in order to be free it has enslaved itself in the most horrible way.

Some people have gone so far beyond their normal foolishness as to say that 'it is not natural for a man to stay with a woman during the nine months of her pregnancy. Once their sexual appetite has been satisfied', says the author of these paradoxes,[4] 'the man no longer needs such a woman, nor the woman such a man. The latter has not the slightest concern, nor perhaps the slightest idea, of the consequences of his action. One goes one way, the other goes another, and it would appear that at the end of nine months they have no memory of ever having known each other ... Why should he help her after the birth? Why should he help her raise a child whom he does not even know belongs to him?'

All that is revolting, but fortunately, nothing is more wrong. If this barbaric indifference was a true natural instinct, the human species would have always exhibited it. Instinct is unchangeable; its inconsistencies are very rare. Fathers would have always abandoned mothers, mothers would have abandoned their children, and there would be far less people in the world than there are carnivores; for wild beasts, better equipped and better armed, have a readier instinct, more certain means, and a more certain food-supply, than the human race.

Our nature is very different to the frightful piece of make-believe that this tub-thumper has made out of it. Except for a few barbaric and entirely brutalised souls, or except perhaps for an even more brutalised philosopher, the sternest of men loves, by an overwhelming instinct, the child that has not yet been born, the womb that bears it, and the mother whose love is redoubled for the one from whom she has received in her innermost being the seed of a being similar to herself.

The instinct of the charcoal-burners of the Black Forest speaks to them as loudly, and motivates them as strongly towards their children, as the instinct of pigeons and of nightingales does towards the feeding of their young. People have really wasted their time therefore writing this abominable twaddle.

Is not the great fault of all of these paradoxical books to assume always that human nature is different to what it is? If the satires on men and women that Boileau wrote were not jokes, they would fall

---

[4] Jean-Jacques Rousseau, *Discourse on the origin and foundation of inequality among men* (1754).

into this basic error of presuming all men to be mad, and all women to be wanton.

The same author, an enemy of society, who is like the fox without a tail, who wants all his fellow foxes to cut their tails off, expresses himself thus in magisterial style: 'The first person who, having enclosed a piece of land, ventured to say: *This is mine*, and found people simple-minded enough to believe him, was the true founder of civil society. What crimes, what wars, what murders, what misery and horror would have been spared the human race if, tearing up the stakes and filling in the ditches, someone had said to his fellow men: Take care not to listen to this imposter; you are lost if you forget that the fruits of the earth are for everyone, and that the earth belongs to no-one.'

Thus, according to this fine philosopher, a thief, a destroyer, would have been the human race's benefactor; and it would have been necessary to punish the honest man who might have said to his children: Let us imitate our neighbour; he has fenced off his field, the animals will no longer come and play havoc with it, his land will become more fertile; let us work ours like he has worked his. He will help us, and we will help him. With every family cultivating their own plot, we will be better fed, healthier, more peaceful, less unhappy. We will try to set up laws of distributive justice for the consolation of our poor species, and we will be worth more than the foxes and the ferrets, which this extremist wishes us to resemble.

Would that speech not be more sensible and honest than that of the wild lunatic who wished to destroy the fellow's orchard?

So what kind of a philosophy is it that makes people say things that common sense rejects from deepest China to Canada? Is it not the philosophy of a tramp who wants all the rich to be robbed by the poor in order to reinforce brotherly union among men?

It is true that if all the hedgerows, all the forests, all the plains, were covered with delicious nourishing fruits, it would be impossible, unjust and ridiculous to keep them for oneself.

If there are some islands where nature makes food, and all that is necessary to life, plentiful without any problem, let us all go and live there, away from the hotchpotch of our laws. But as soon as we have filled them with people, we will have to get back to the law of what is mine and what is yours, to those laws which are often very bad, but which we cannot do without.

Was man born wicked?

Does it not seem to have been proved that man was not born depraved and the child of the Devil? If his nature was like that, he would be committing dark, barbaric deeds as soon as he could walk. He would use the first knife he could find to wound whoever displeased him. He would necessarily resemble little wolf-cubs or foxes, who bite as soon as they are able to.

On the contrary, everywhere in the world his nature is like a lamb's while he is a child. So why and how does he so often turn into a wolf and a fox? Is it not because, having been born neither good nor wicked, education, example, the system of government into which he finds he has been tossed, and ultimately opportunity, determine whether he will follow the path of virtue or crime?

Perhaps human nature could not be otherwise. Man could not always have thoughts that were always wrong, nor thoughts that were always right, feelings that were always tender, nor feelings that were always cruel.

It appears to have been proved that women are better than men; you can see around you a hundred *brotherly enemies* for every one *Clytemnestra.*

There are professions which necessarily make the soul pitiless: that of the soldier, the butcher, the policeman, the jailer and all those jobs based on other people's misery.

The watchman, the henchman, the jailer, for example, are happy only in as much as they make others unhappy. They are, it is true, necessary to combat evil-doers, and in that way are useful to society; but out of a thousand men of that ilk, there is not one whose acts are motivated by the public interest, or who even understands how he serves the public interest.

It is particularly strange to hear them talk about their feats of valour, how they count up their number of victims, the tricks they use to trap them, the pain they make them suffer, and the money they make out of them.

Whoever has got down to examining the minor detail of the business of the bar; whoever has just listened to prosecutors arguing informally among themselves, and congratulating each other on the misfortunes of their clients, might have a very poor opinion of human nature.

There are professions that are even more ghastly, yet which are prized like canonries.

There are some which change an honest man into a rogue, and which accustom him, in spite of himself, to lying and deceiving almost without his noticing it; to putting on blindfolds; to deluding himself by self-interest and by the vanity of status, to plunge without remorse the human race into the depths of blind stupidity.

Women, who are continually occupied with the education of their children, and who are enclosed in [a world of] domestic duties, are excluded from all of these professions which pervert human nature, and make it atrocious. Everywhere they are less barbaric than men.

Physical factors combine with moral factors to distance them from great crimes; their blood is milder; they have less of a liking for strong liquor, which inspires savagery. An obvious proof of this is that out of a thousand victims of the law, a thousand executed murderers, you can scarcely count four women, as we have proved elsewhere. I do not believe that in Asia there are two examples of women being condemned to a public execution.

It appears, therefore, that it is our customs and practices that have made the male species very wicked.

If that was a general truth without any exceptions to it, that species would be more horrible than spiders, wolves and ferrets are to us. But fortunately those professions that harden the heart, and fill it with ugly passions, are few and far between. Note that in a country of about twenty million people, there are at most two hundred thousand soldiers. That is one soldier for every two hundred individuals. Those two hundred thousand soldiers are under the strictest control. Among them are very respectable people who go back to their villages to live out their old age as good fathers and husbands.

Other trades that are dangerous to morality are not numerous.

Ploughmen, artisans, and artists are too busy to get involved in crime very often.

There will always be detestable, wicked men in the world. Books always exaggerate their number which, while it is too big, is less than people say.

If the human race had been under the sway of the devil, there would be nobody left in the world.

Let us take consolation; fine men have been seen, and always will be seen, from Peking to La Rochelle, and whatever the academics and theologians might say, people like Titus, Trajan, the Antonines and Pierre Bayle, were very decent.

On man in the state of nature

What would man be like in the state of what is called *nature*? An animal far less advanced than the first Iroquois found in North America.

He would be far inferior to those Iroquois, since the latter knew how to ignite fire and to make themselves arrows. Centuries are needed to get to the stage of those two arts.

Man left in the state of nature would have as his only language a few badly articulated sounds; the species would be reduced to very small numbers through food problems and lack of shelter, at least in some of our more desolate parts of the world. There would be no more knowledge of God and of the soul than there would be of mathematics; man's ideas would be focussed on the concern to feed himself. The beavers would be preferable as a species.

That is when man would be just a sturdy child, nothing more nothing less. Many people have been seen in a state not much better than that.

The Laplanders, the Samoyeds, the inhabitants of Kamchatka, the Kaffirs, the Hottentots are to man in the state of nature what the courts of Cyrus and Semiramis once were compared to the inhabitants of the Cevennes Mountains. And yet those inhabitants of Kamchatka and today's Hottentots, who are so superior to true savages, are animals living for six months of the year in caves, where they eat with their bare hands the vermin by which they are themselves eaten.

In general, the human race is only by two or three notches more civilised than the people of Kamchatka. The multitude of dumb animals called *men*, compared to the small number of those who think, is in the ratio of at least a hundred to one in many countries.

It is amusing to consider on one side Father Malebranche, who is on such intimate terms with the Word, and on the other side those millions of animals like him who have never heard of the Word, and who do not have a single metaphysical thought in their heads.

Between men of pure instinct and men of genius float that huge number who are preoccupied exclusively with survival.

That survival costs such an enormously painful effort that often in North America an image of God has to run five or six miles to find something for supper, and in our country the image of God sprinkles the earth with [drops of] his sweat the whole year round to get bread.

If you add to that bread, or its equivalent, a hovel and a wretched garment, there you have man as he is generally throughout the world. And it is only over many, many centuries that he has been able to reach such a high level.

Finally, after a few more centuries, things have reached the stage we see them now. Here a musical tragedy is performed; there in another part of the world people are killing each other at sea with thousands of bits of bronze. An opera and a ship of the line always stretch my imagination. I doubt that one can go further than that on any planet where land is cultivated. Yet more than half of the habitable world is still populated with two-footed animals living in that horrible state near to nature, with barely enough to live on or to clothe themselves, barely enjoying the gift of speech, barely noticing that they are unhappy, living and dying almost without knowing it.

An examination of one of Pascal's thoughts on man

'I can conceive of a man without hands, without feet, and I would conceive of one without a head, if experience did not tell me that it is with this head that he thinks. Thus it is thought that constitutes the essence of man, and without it he could not be conceived of.'[5]

How can you conceive of a man without feet, without hands and without a head? That would be a being as different from a man as from a pumpkin.

If all men were headless, how would your head conceive of the fact that they were animals like you, as they would have nothing of what mainly constitutes your essence? A head counts for something, the five senses are to be found there; thought also. An animal that looked like a man from the nape of the neck downwards, or like one of those monkeys called *orang-utan* or forest-men, would no more resemble a man than a monkey or a bear [would] with its head and tail cut off.

---

[5] Pascal, *Thoughts*, no. III.

'Thus it is thought that constitutes the essence of man,' etc. In that case, thought would be his essence in the same way that mass and density are the essence of matter. It would be part of the essence of man to be thinking continually, just as matter always has mass and density. He would be thinking when in a deep, dreamless sleep, in a faint, in a state of lethargy, in his mother's womb. I know full well that I have never thought in any of those states. I am often conscious of this, and I suspect that other people are like me.

If thought was of the essence of man, as mass is of matter, it would follow that God was not able to deprive this animal of understanding, since he cannot deprive matter of mass: for then it would no longer be matter. Now, if understanding is of the essence of man, he is therefore a thinking being by virtue of his nature, just like God is God by virtue of *his* nature.

If I wished to try and define God, in as much as feeble creatures like ourselves can define him, I would say that thought is his being, his essence; but man!

We have the faculty of thinking, of walking, of speaking, of eating, of sleeping; but we are not continually making use of these faculties; that is not part of our nature.

Is not thought an attribute with us? And so much of an attribute that it is sometimes weak, sometimes strong, sometimes reasonable, sometimes foolish? It conceals itself, it reveals itself; it goes away, it comes back; it is non-existent; it revives. Essence is something else; it never varies; it does not experience any increase or decrease.

What is this headless animal postulated by Pascal supposed to be? A creature of reason. He might just as well have postulated a tree which God had imbued with thought, like they say the Gods had given a voice to the trees of Dodona.

A general reflection on man

Twenty years are needed to bring a man from the state of a plant in which he exists in his mother's womb, to the purely animal state, which is the lot of early childhood, to the state at which mature reason dawns. Thirty centuries were needed to gain some understanding of how he is constructed. An eternity would be needed to understand something of his soul. Just an instant is needed to kill him.

Impôt. Tax

So many philosophical works have been written on the nature of taxation that I shall have to say a few words about it here. It is true that nothing is less philosophical than this subject, but it can be included under moral philosophy when suggesting to a comptroller-general or to a Turkish teftardar that it is not part of the universal laws of morality to take money from one's neighbour, and that all tax-collectors, customs officials, and excisemen are cursed in the Gospel.

Yet however cursed they might be, it must be admitted that it is impossible for a society to survive without each member paying something towards its cost; and because everyone must pay, it is necessary to have a tax-collector. One cannot see why that tax-collector is cursed, and regarded as an idolater. There is certainly no idolatry about receiving money from fellow guests to pay for their supper.

In republics, and in those states which, with the name of *kingdom*, are in effect republics, each individual is taxed according to his means and in accordance with the needs of society.

In despotic kingdoms or, to put it more politely, in monarchical states, it is not quite the same situation. The nation is taxed without being consulted. A farmer with an income of twelve hundred *livres* is astonished to receive a demand for four hundred. There are even some who are forced to pay more than half of what they earn.

What is all this money used for? The most decent use that can be made of it is to give it to other citizens.

The farmer asks why half of his wealth is taken away to pay for soldiers, when a hundredth would suffice; he gets the answer that over and above soldiers the arts and luxury have to be paid for, that nothing is lost, that in the case of the Persians towns and villages are assigned to the Queen to pay for her sash, her slippers and her hairpins.

He responds that he knows nothing of the history of Persia, and that he is very angry that half of his wealth is taken for the sake of a sash, hairpins and shoes; that he could supply these things much more cheaply, and that the whole thing is daylight robbery.

He is made to listen to reason by being put in a dungeon, and having his possessions sold off. If he resists the extorters damned by the New Testament, he is hanged, and that makes all his neighbours highly co-operative.

If all this money was used by the sovereign only to import spices from India, Mocha coffee, English and Arabian horses, silks from the Levant, baubles from China, it is clear that within a few years not a *sou* would be left in the kingdom. So it is necessary for taxation to be used for the support of industry, and that what has been paid into the prince's coffers should return to the farmers. They suffer; they complain; but at the end of the year everyone turns out to have worked and has lived well or badly.

If a man from the country happens to go to the capital he might look with astonishment on some fine lady dressed in a silken robe with gold brocade, in a magnificent carriage drawn by two prize horses, followed by four servants dressed in material costing twenty *francs* a yard; he might go up to one of this fine lady's servants and say: 'Sir, where does this lady get so much money from to buy such expensive things?' 'My friend', says the servant, 'the King grants her a pension of forty thousand *livres*.' 'Alas!', says the rustic, 'my village is paying for that pension.' 'Yes', says the servant, 'the silk that you have harvested and sold is used in the material in which she is dressed; the material for my clothing is made in part out of the wool from your sheep; my baker has made my bread from your wheat; you have sold in the market the fowl that we eat; in this way, my lady's pension is returned to you and to your comrades.'

The peasant does not quite agree with all the maxims [emanating] from this servant-philosopher, but a proof that there is some truth in his reply lies in the fact that the village survives, that people are having children there who, even while complaining, will also have children, who will still complain.

- - -

If we were obliged to possess all the tax edicts, and all the books written opposing them, that would be the harshest tax of all.

We know well enough that taxes are necessary, and that the curse laid in the Gospel on the tax-gatherers affects only those who abuse their position in order to harass the people. Perhaps the transcriber left out a word like the epithet *pravus*. He could have said *pravus publicanus*; this word was all the more necessary because the general curse formally contradicts the words put into Christ's mouth: *Give unto Caesar what belongs to Caesar*. Certainly, the person who collects what is rightfully Caesar's should not be held in horror; that would be an insult to the order of Roman knights, and to the Emperor himself: nothing would have been more ill-advised.

In all civilised countries taxes are very high because the responsibilities of the State are very heavy. In Spain, the goods for export sent to Cadiz, and from there to America, pay for more than thirty per cent before your bill is calculated.

In England, all taxes on imports are very high; yet people pay them without complaint; people even take pride in paying them. A businessman will boast of adding four to five thousand guineas a year to the Treasury.

The richer a country is, the heavier the taxes. Some speculators would like taxes to fall only on agricultural produce. What! I grow a field of flax which brings me in two hundred *écus*, and some big manufacturer earns two hundred thousand *écus* by converting my flax into lace. That manufacturer pays nothing, and my land pays for everything because everything comes from the land! The wife of that manufacturer will supply the Queen and the princesses with fine Alençon point; she will receive protection; her son will become a high official in the law, the police or the Treasury, and will increase my taxes in my old age! Ah! you speculators, your sums do not add up; you are unjust.

The central issue is that a whole nation should not be robbed by an army of alguazils so that twenty or more bloodsuckers at court or in the city can slake their thirst on its blood.

The Duke of Sully tells in his *Political economies* that in 1585 there were just twenty lords with an interest in farming leases, to whom the government contractors gave three million, two hundred and forty-eight thousand *écus*.

It was even worse under Charles IX and Francis I; it became worse still under Louis XIII; during Louis XIV's minority the level of pillaging was just as high. In spite of all its wounds, France still lives. Yes, but if she had not received those wounds, she would be in a better state of health. The same is true of several other states.

It is right for those enjoying state privileges to bear the costs. Churchmen and monks, who possess great wealth, should for that reason make tax contributions, like any other citizens.

In those days that we call *barbaric*, the great livings and abbeys in France paid a third of their income in tax.

By means of a decree in the year 1188, Philip-Augustus taxed a tenth of the income from all livings.

Philip *le Bel* made the clergy pay a fifth, then a fiftieth and then a twentieth of their income in tax.

King John, with a decree of 12 March 1355, took in tax a tenth of the income from the livings and inherited property of bishops, *abbés*, chapters and all churchmen in general.

The same prince confirmed that tax with two other decrees, one on 3 March, the other on 8 December, 1358.

In the letters patent of Charles V, 22 June 1372, it is stipulated that churchmen will pay tithes and other property and personal taxes.

These letters patent were renewed in 1390 by Charles VI.

How is it that these laws have been abolished, while so many monstrous customs and blood-soaked decrees have been kept?

In truth, the clergy do pay a tax called the *tree gift* and, as everybody knows, it is mainly the most useful and the most impoverished part of the Church, the parish priests, who pay that tax. But why is there this difference and this inequality in tax contributions between citizens in the same state? Why do those who enjoy the greatest privileges, but who are sometimes useless as far as the public good is concerned, pay less than a ploughman, who is so necessary?

The Republic of Venice has just made rules in this area which seem to serve as an example to the other states of Europe.

Not only do churchmen claim exemption from taxation, they have even found the means in a number of provinces of imposing taxes on the people, and to make people pay them as if they had the legal right.

In some countries, as monks had taken over the tithes at the expense of the parish priests, the peasants were obliged to tax themselves to provide for the upkeep of their pastors; and so in a number of villages, especially in Franche-Comté, apart from the tithe that parishioners paid to monks and chapters, in addition they paid through religious ardour three or four measures of corn to their parish priests.

This tax is called the *harvest tax* in some provinces, and *the bushel tax* in others.

It is no doubt right for parish priests to be well-paid; but it would be much better to give them back part of the tithe that the monks had taken from them than to place a surcharge on the poor peasants.

Since the King of France fixed the appropriate level of emoluments for the clergy with his decree of May 1768, and made the tithe-owners responsible for paying them, it seems that peasants should no longer be required to pay a second tithe to their parish priests, a tax that they had paid only on a voluntary basis, and at a time when the influence and violence of monks had taken away pastors' livelihoods.

The King abolished this second tithe in the province of Poitiers by letters patent in July 1769, registered with the Paris *parlement* on the eleventh day of the same month.

It would be very worthy of the justice and benevolence of His Majesty to pass a similar law for the other provinces that are in the same position as Poitiers, such as Franche-Comté, etc.

(By Mr Christin, *a lawyer from Besançon*)

Politique. Politics

The politics of man consists first of all in trying to equal the animals, to whom nature has given food, clothing and shelter.

These preliminaries are long and difficult.

How can we secure our welfare and find shelter from evil? That is the story of man in a nutshell.

Evil is everywhere. The four elements conspire in its creation. The barrenness of a quarter of the planet, diseases, the large number of hostile animals, everything forces us to work unceasingly to keep evil at bay.

No man [acting] alone can protect himself from evil and secure his welfare; he needs help. Society is thus as old as the world.

There are sometimes too many societies, sometimes they are too few and far between. Upheavals on this planet have often destroyed whole races of men and other animals in many countries, and caused them to multiply in others.

For a species to multiply, climate and soil must be tolerable, and even with these advantages a species can still be reduced to walking around naked, suffering from hunger, lacking in everything, and perishing miserably.

Men are not like beavers, bees or silk-worms; they have no sure instinct to secure for themselves what they need.

Out of a hundred males you could barely find one with any genius; barely one out of five-hundred in the case of females.

It is only with genius that the arts are invented, which in the long run secure some of that [sense of] well-being that is the sole purpose of politics.

To pursue these arts, support is needed, hands to help you, minds that are reasonably open to understand you, and sufficiently docile to obey you. Before finding and assembling all that, thousands of centuries flow past in ignorance and barbarism; thousands of attempts prove abortive. Finally an art form takes shape, and still more thousands of centuries are needed to perfect it.

External politics

When a nation discovers metallurgy, it will inevitably fight its neighbours, and enslave them.

You have arrows and swords, and you have been born in a climate that has made you strong; we are weak; we have only clubs and stones; you kill us; and if you spare our lives it's only for ploughing your fields, building your houses; we sing you a few crude songs when you are bored, if we have good voices, or we blow down a few pipes to get clothing and bread from you. If our wives and daughters are pretty, you take them for yourselves. His Lordship, your son, takes advantage of this well-tried policy; he adds new discoveries to this nascent art. His servants cut off my children's testicles; he gives them the honour of guarding his wives and mistresses. In most of Asia this was, and still is, politics; the great art of making men serve your welfare.

When several little tribes have subjugated in this way several other little tribes, the victors fight each other with swords over the distribution of the spoils. Every little nation keeps soldiers in its pay. To encourage and control these soldiers, each one has its gods, its oracles, its prophecies; each one keeps soothsayers and sacrificial butchers in its pay. These soothsayers start by prophesying for the benefit of the nation's leaders; then they prophesy for themselves, and share in government. In the end the strongest and cleverest subjugate the rest after centuries of bloodshed that make you tremble, and roguery that makes you laugh: that complements politics.

While these scenes of brigandage and fraud are played out in one part of the world, other little tribes, who have withdrawn into mountain caves, or into areas surrounded by impassable marshland, or into some small habitable territory in the middle of sandy deserts, or peninsulas, or islands, defend themselves against the mainland tyrants. In the end, when every man has more or less the same weaponry as the next, blood flows from one end of the world to the other.

People cannot go on killing for ever; they make peace with their neighbour, until they believe themselves to be strong enough to start the war all over again. Those who can write draft these peace treaties. The leaders of each people call as witness the gods they have made for themselves, the better to deceive their enemies. Oaths are invented; one promises you in the name of *Sammonocodom*, another in the name of *Jupiter*, to live always in close harmony with you; and at the first opportunity they slaughter you in the name of *Jupiter* or *Sammonocodom*.

In the most civilised of times, Aesop's lion makes a treaty with three neighbouring animals. It's all about dividing up a prey into four equal parts. The lion, for good reasons that he will explain at a time and in a place yet to be determined, takes three parts for himself and threatens to strangle whoever dares to touch the fourth part. That is politics at its most sublime.

Internal politics

This is all about having as much power, as many honours and as many pleasures as you can get. To succeed in that, you need a lot of money.

All that is very difficult in a democracy; each citizen is your rival. A democracy can only survive in a small territory. There is no use in your getting rich through your illicit business, or through your grandfather's; your wealth will make a lot of people jealous, and very few will act as your yes-men. If a rich family does govern in some democracy, it will not be for long.

In an aristocracy you can more easily obtain honours, pleasures, power and money for yourself; but great discretion is needed to do it. If you abuse your position too much, revolutions are always to be feared.

Thus, in a democracy all citizens are equal. This type of government today is rare and feeble, albeit natural and wise.

In an aristocracy inequality and class-consciousness make themselves felt; but the less arrogant it is, the more secure is its [sense of] well-being.

That leaves monarchy. This is where all men have been created for the benefit of one. He accumulates all the honours he wishes to pin on himself, savours all the pleasures he wants to enjoy, exercises absolute power; he does all that provided he has plenty of money. If he lacks money, he will be unsuccessful in domestic and in foreign policy. He will soon lose power, pleasures, honours, and possibly his life.

While this man has money, not only does he enjoy life, but also his relatives and his chief servants enjoy life too. And a crowd of mercenaries work all year round for them in the futile hope of one day enjoying in their little cottages the same life of ease that their sultan and their pashas seem to enjoy in their seraglios. But here is roughly what happens.

A big fat farmer once possessed a huge piece of land made up of fields, meadows, vineyards, orchards and forests. A hundred labourers worked the land for him; he dined with his family, drank and went to bed. His chief servants, who robbed him, dined in their turn, and ate almost everything. The labourers came and ate very poorly. They grumbled, complained and lost patience. In the end they ate the master's dinner, and kicked him out of the house. The master said that these rascals were rebellious children who had struck their father. The labourers said that they had followed the sacred law of nature that the other man had violated. In the end, they consulted a neighbouring soothsayer who was reputed to be an inspired man. This holy man took the farm over for himself, and starved the servants and the former master to death until he himself was thrown out in his turn. That's internal politics.

We have seen this happen more than once, and some of the effects of these politics still survive and are still going strong. We must hope that in another ten or twelve centuries, when men are more enlightened, the great landowners, having become more politically minded, will treat their labourers better, and not allow themselves to be subjugated by soothsayers and wizards.

The A B C, or Dialogues between A B C,
translated from the English by Mr Huet

First conversation.
On Hobbes, Grotius and Montesquieu

A

So you've read Grotius, Hobbes and Montesquieu. What do you think of these three famous men?

B

I was often bored by Grotius; but he is very learned; apparently he loves reason and virtue; but reason and virtue don't affect you very much when they are boring. What's more, he sometimes seems to me to be very bad at arguing. Montesquieu is very imaginative on a subject that only appears to require judgement: he is too often mistaken about the facts; but I believe he also makes mistakes in his arguments. Hobbes is very tough, as is his style, but I fear his toughness often stems from truth. In short, Grotius is an utter pedant, Hobbes a sad philosopher and Montesquieu a fine wit.

C

I agree to some extent. Life is too short, and we have too much to do to learn from Grotius that, according to Tertullian, 'cruelty, fraud and injustice are the companions of war'; that 'Carnaedes defended error as much as truth'; that Horace said in a satire: 'Nature cannot tell the just from the unjust';[1] that, according to Plutarch, 'children

---

[1] '*Nec natura potest justo secernere iniquum.* This cruel line is to be found in the third satire. Horace wants to prove, against the views of the Stoics, that not all crimes are equal. The punishment, he says, must be proportionate to the offence. *Adsit/Regula, peccatis quae poenas irroget aequas.* (I, satire 3, lines 117–18.)

have compassion'; that Chryssipus said 'the origin of the law is in Jupiter'; that, if Florentine is to be believed, 'nature has established a kind of kinship between men'; that Carnaedes said that 'usefulness is the mother of justice'.

I confess that Grotius gives me great pleasure when he says, at the start of his first chapter in the first book, that 'Jewish law did not bind foreigners.' Like him, I don't think Alexander and Aristotle are damned for having kept their foreskins, and for not having used the sabbath for doing nothing. Gallant theologians have opposed him with their usual absurdities; but as someone who is not, thank God, a theologian, I for one think that Grotius is a very good man.

I accept that he doesn't know what he's talking about when he claims that the Jews had taught circumcision to other nations. It's recognised fairly widely nowadays that the little Jewish hordes had taken all their ridiculous customs from the powerful nations sur-

It is reason, natural law, that teaches this justice; nature thus knows what justice and injustice are. It is perfectly obvious that nature teaches all mothers that it is better to correct their children than kill them; that it is better to give a child bread than poke his eye out; that it is more just to help a father than leave him to be devoured by a ferocious beast, and more just to keep one's promise than to break it.

Before this line with such a bad example, *Nec natura potest justo secernere iniquum – nature cannot distinguish between what is just and what is unjust*, there is another line in Horace which seems to say exactly the opposite: *Jura inventa metu injusti fataere necesse est – it must be acknowledged that laws have been invented only through fear of injustice* (line 111).

Nature had thus distinguished between what is just and what is unjust before there were laws. Why should he have a different view to that of Cicero and all the moralists who accept natural law? Horace was a lecher who recommended prostitutes and little boys, I agree; who made fun of poor old women, agreed; whose cowardly flattery of Octavius exceeded the cruelty of his attacks on ordinary citizens, that is true; who often changed his views, which is annoying; but I suspect that here he said exactly the opposite to what he is made to say. *I* read: *Et natura potest secernere iniquum*. Let others put a *nec* instead of an *et* if that is their wish. I find the sense of the word *et* more straightforward as well as being more grammatically correct: *et natura potest, etc.*

If nature did not distinguish between what is just and what is unjust, there would be no moral difference between our actions; it would then seem that the Stoics are right to maintain that all crimes against society are equal. What is very strange is that Saint James seems to take the Stoic position to extremes when he said in his epistle (chapter 2, line 10): "Whoever should keep the law, and yet break it in one point, is guilty of having broken it in all points." Saint Augustine, in a letter to Saint Jerome, gives a little boost to Saint James the apostle, and then excuses him by saying that whoever is guilty of one transgression is guilty of all because he is lacking in charity, which covers everything. Oh Augustine! How has a man who has got drunk, who has fornicated, transgressed the rule of charity? You are always abusing words, you old African sophist! Horace had a finer mind, and one that was more just than yours' (Voltaire's note).

rounding them. But what has circumcision to do with 'the laws of war and peace'?[2]

A

You're right. Grotius's compilations didn't deserve the respect that the forces of ignorance paid to them. Quoting pros and cons from the thoughts of ancient authors isn't the same as thinking. Thus he makes a very bad mistake in his book on *The truth of Christianity* by copying Christian authors who said that their Jewish predecessors taught the world, whereas the little Jewish nation itself had never made this insolent claim; whereas, locked away behind the cliffs of Palestine and its own ignorance, it hadn't even recognised the immortality of the soul, accepted by all its neighbours.

Thus it is that he proves the truth of Christianity by means of Hystaspes and the Sibyls, and of the adventure of the whale who swallowed Jonah with a passage [taken] from Lycophron. Pedantry and intellectual rigour are incompatible.

Montesquieu isn't pedantic. What do you think of his *Spirit of the laws*?

B

It's given me great pleasure because there are a lot of jokes in it, a lot of bold, hard-hitting truths, and whole chapters worthy of the *Persian letters*. Chapter 26 of Book XIX is a portrayal of your England, drawn in the style of Paolo Veronese. I can see bright colours, skillful brush strokes, and a few errors in costume. The portrayal of the Inquisition and of negro slaves, is greatly superior to Callot. Everywhere he fights despotism, depicts financiers as being odious, courtiers despicable, monks ridiculous. Thus those who are neither monks, financiers or public servants, or with no aspirations to be, have been enchanted, especially in France.

I find it annoying that this book is a labyrinth with no route [through it], and no method [in it]. I'm even more surprised that a man who writes about the laws should say in his preface that 'no

---

[2] The reference is to Grotius' *De jure belli et pacis* (1624), translated into French by Barbeyrac.

flashes of wit will be found in his work', and it's stranger still that the book should be a collection of witticisms. It's Michel Montaigne as legislator; and what's more, he was from Michel Montaigne's part of the country.

I can't help laughing when I skip through more than a hundred chapters containing less than a dozen lines, and several with only two. The author always seems to have wanted to play with the reader when dealing with the most serious subject-matter.

You don't think that you're reading a serious work when, after having quoted Grecian and Roman law, he talks about the laws of Bantam, Cochin-China, Tonkin, Acham, Borneo, Jakarta, Formosa as if he had accurate information on the governments of all those countries. He mixes up truth and error too frequently in physics, morality and history. He tells you, following Pufendorf, that in the age of King Charles IX there were twenty million people in France. Pufendorf even goes as far as to say twenty-nine million: he was speaking very much off the top of his head. Nobody has ever taken a count of the population in France. People were too ignorant then to even suspect that you could estimate the number of inhabitants by the number of births and deaths. In those days, France didn't possess Lorraine, Alsace, Franche-Comté, Roussillon, Artois, the area around Cambrai, half of Flanders; and today, when she possesses all these provinces, it has been proved, from the fairly accurate count of homesteads taken in 1751, that she only has about twenty million souls at the most.

The same author assures us, on the strength of Chardin's word, that the only navigable river in Persia is the little river Cyrus. Chardin did not make that blunder. He says in chapter 1, volume II, that 'there is no river open to boats in the central part of the kingdom'; but excluding the Euphrates, the Tigris and the Indus, all the frontier provinces are awash with rivers which help to facilitate trade and make the land fertile. The Zin crosses Isfahan; the Aras joins the Kura, etc. And then what connection can there be between the *Spirit of the laws* and the rivers of Persia?

The reasons that he gives for the founding of the great empires of Asia, and for the multitude of small powers in Europe, seem as wrong as his statements on the rivers of Persia. 'In Europe', he says, 'great empires have never been able to survive.' Roman power survived there, however, for more than five hundred years; and, he continued, 'the reason for the duration of these great empires lies in the fact that there are great plains'. It did not occur to him that Persia is interspersed with mountains; he did not remember the Caucasus, the Taurus mountains, Mount Ararat, the Himalayas, Mount Sharon, whose branches cover Asia. One must neither give reasons for things that don't exist, nor wrong reasons for the things that do exist.

His theory of so-called climatic influence on religion is taken from Chardin, and is no truer for that. The Mohammedan religion, born in the hot, arid earth of Mecca, flourishes today in the beautiful lands of Asia minor, Syria, Egypt, Thrace, Mysia, North Africa, Serbia, Bosnia, Dalmatia, Epirus, Greece. It has held sway in Spain. It only just failed to reach Rome. The Christian religion was born in the stony earth of Jerusalem, and in a land of lepers where pork was an almost lethal food, forbidden by law. Jesus never ate pork, yet it's eaten by Christians. Today their religion is dominant in countries with lots of mud and dirt where people live on pork alone, as in Westphalia. You would never get to the end if you wanted to examine this sort of error with which this book is littered.

What's still more shocking to a reasonably well-educated reader is that nearly all the quotations are wrong. He almost always mistakes his imagination for his memory.

He claims that in the *Testament* attributed to Cardinal Richelieu it is said that 'if among the people there is some unfortunate who is an honest man, you must never use him; which only goes to prove that virtue is not the motivating force of monarchic government'.

The wretched *Testament*, falsely attributed to Cardinal Richelieu, says precisely the opposite. Here are its words in chapter 4: 'You can be as bold as to say that of two people of equal merit, the one who is more comfortably off is preferable to the other, in the certainty that a poor magistrate will need to have a very strongly tempered moral conscience if it is not to be weakened by considerations of self-interest. Thus experience teaches us that rich men are less likely to misappropriate public funds than poor men, and that poverty compels an officer to pay careful attention to the income [to be gained] from looting a town.'

It must be said that Montesquieu is no better at quoting Greek authors than French. Often he makes them say the opposite to what they did say.

Talking about the condition of women under various systems of government, or rather, promising to talk about it, he puts forward the view that with the Greeks 'love took only one form whose name one dare not speak'. He doesn't hesitate to take Plutarch as his authority. He makes Plutarch say that 'women have no part to play in true love'. He doesn't pause to reflect that Plutarch is putting words into the mouths of several interlocutors: there is Protogenes who rails against women, but Daphneus who takes their side. Plutarch decides in favour of Daphneus; he composes a very fine eulogy of celestial love and conjugal love; he concludes by recording several examples of the faithfulness and courage of women. It is in this dialogue even that the story of Camma is to be found, as well as that of Epponina, Sabinus' wife, whose virtues have been used for themes in plays.

In short, it's clear that in the *Spirit of the laws* Montesquieu has slandered the spirit of Greece by taking an objection that Plutarch refutes for a law that Plutarch recommends.

'Cadis maintained that the Grand Sultan did not have to keep his word or his oath when, in so doing, he would restrict his authority.'

Ricaut, who is referred to at this point, just says on page 18 of the 1671 Amsterdam edition: 'There are even some people there who maintain that the Grand Sultan can set aside promises made on oath when, in order to fulfil them, limits must be placed on his authority.'

These words are very vague. The Sultan of the Turks can only make promises to his subjects or to neighbouring states. If they are promises made to his subjects, no oath is involved; if they are peace treaties, he has to keep them like any other prince, or make war. The Koran says nowhere that one's oath can be broken, and says in a hundred places that it must be kept. It's possible that, to wage an unjust war, as nearly all of them are, the Great Turk might assemble a council to guide his conscience, as several Christian princes have done, in order to do evil in good conscience. It's possible that some Muslim scholars have imitated those Catholic scholars who said that one's word of honour need not be kept either with infidels or with heretics, but whether the Turks have this philosophy of law has yet to be ascertained.

The author of the *Spirit of the laws* offers this alleged decision by the Cadis as proof of the Sultan's despotism. It would appear, on the contrary, to be proof that he is subject to the laws, since he would have to consult scholars in order to put himself above the laws. We are neighbours of the Turks, and we do not know them. Count Marsigli, who lived so long among them, says that no author has displayed true knowledge of either their empire or their laws. We did not even have a tolerable translation of the Koran until the Englishman Sale gave us one in 1734. Nearly everything that has been said about their religion and their system of laws is wrong, and the conclusions that are drawn every day to their detriment are too ill-founded. When examining laws only laws that are understood should be referred to.

'With the Greeks all low commerce was vile.' I don't know what Montesquieu means by low commerce, but I do know that in Athens every citizen engaged in trade, that Plato sold oil, and that the father of the demagogue Demosthenes was an ironmonger. The majority of workers were foreigners or slaves. It's important for us to note that a trade was not incompatible with high rank in the Greek republics, except in the case of the Spartans, who did not have commercial interests.

'Several times I have heard people deplore', he says, 'the lack of vision on the part of Francis I's Council, which rebuffed Christopher Columbus, who had proposed the India project to it.' You will note that Francis I hadn't been born when Columbus discovered the islands of America.

Since the subject here is commerce, let's note that the author condemns an order issued by the Council of Spain forbidding the use of gold and silver in gilding. 'Such a decree', he says, 'would resemble one made by the Dutch states if they were to forbid the use of cinnamon.' It doesn't occur to him that the Spanish, having no factories, would have bought gold braid and dress material from abroad, and that the Dutch could not buy cinnamon. What was quite reasonable in Spain would have been quite ridiculous in Holland.

If a king votes in matters of criminal procedure, 'he would lose the finest attribute of his sovereignty, namely that of granting mercy. It would be sheer madness for him to make and unmake his judgements. He would not wish to be at odds with himself. Apart from the fact that this would overturn accepted theory, you would not know whether a man was being acquitted or whether he was receiving mercy.'

All that is clearly mistaken. Who would stop the sovereign from granting mercy after having been himself among the judges? How is one at odds with oneself by judging according to the law, and granting pardons in accordance with one's sense of leniency? In what way would accepted theory be overturned? How could you be unaware that the King had publicly pardoned the man after he had been convicted?

In the trial of a French peer, the Duke of Alençon, in 1458, the *parlement*, which the King had consulted in order to ascertain whether he had the right to be present at the trial and judgement of a peer of France, replied that it had discovered from its records that not only did the kings of France have this right, but that their presence was necessary in their capacity as first peers [of the realm].

This practice has been retained in England. The kings of England delegate their seat on these occasions to a Grand *Steward*, who represents them. The Emperor can be present at the trial of a prince of the Empire. No doubt it's much better for a sovereign not to be present at criminal trials: men are too weak and too cowardly. The breath of the prince alone would be enough to tip the scales.

'The English, to encourage liberty, have removed all the intermediary powers that made up their monarchy.'

It's accepted that the opposite is the case. They have made their House of Commons into an intermediary power balancing that of the Lords. They never stop undermining the power of the Church, which ought to be an organisation that prays, edifies and exhorts, and not one that wields power.

'It is not enough for a monarchy to have intermediary ranks. A repository of the laws is also needed. ... The natural ignorance of the nobility, its negligent ways, its contempt for civil government necessitate the existence of a body that continually makes laws emerge from the dust in which they would otherwise be buried.'

However, the repository of the Empire's laws is in the hands of princes at the Diet of Regensberg; in England this repository is in the Upper Chamber; in Sweden it's in the Senate which is composed of nobles; and last but not least Empress Catherine II locates this repository, under her new code, in the Senate, made up of the greatest people in her empire.

Shouldn't we distinguish between political laws and distributive justice? Shouldn't political laws have as their guardians the most important members of the State? The laws of what is *mine* and what is *yours*, [and] the [1670] decree on criminal procedure, need only to be well formulated and well printed; the repository for them should be with booksellers. Judges must conform with them, and when the laws are bad, as is very often the case, then judges must protest to the supreme authority in order to have them changed.

The same author claims that in Tonkin all magistrates and senior military officers are eunuchs, and in the case of the Lamas the law allows women to have several husbands. Even if these stories were true, so what? Would our magistrates want to become eunuchs, and be only the fourth or fifth husband in line for the good lady councillors?

Why waste time making errors about the fleets that Solomon is supposed to have sent from Ezion-geber to Africa, and about the fanciful voyages from the Red Sea to the Sea of Bayonne, and about the even more fanciful treasures of Sofala? What is the link between these erroneous digressions and the *Spirit of the laws*?

I expected to see how the *Decretals* changed the whole jurisprudence of the old Roman code, with what laws Charlemagne governed his empire, and by what anarchical process feudal government overthrew it, by what art and what boldness Gregory VII and his successors crushed the laws of kingdoms and great fiefdoms beneath the fisherman's ring, the upheavals that succeeded in destroying papal legislation. I hoped to see the origin of the bailiff's courts that dispensed justice almost everywhere from the time of the Ottonians, and the origin of the tribunals called *parlements*, or of *hearings*, or of the *King's bench*, or *exchequer*. I wanted to know the history of the laws under which our forefathers and their children lived, the reasons for their introduction, neglect, destruction and renewal. Unfortunately, I found only cleverness, witticisms, fantasies and errors.

How was it that the Gauls, conquered and plundered by the Romans, continued to live under Roman law when they were reconquered and plundered by a horde of Francs? What exactly were the laws and customs of these new brigands?

What rights did the Gallic bishops arrogate to themselves when the Francs became their masters? Did they not occasionally have a part to play in public administration before the rebel Pépin made room for them in the nation's parliament?

Were there hereditary fiefdoms before Charlemagne? A host of such questions spring to mind. Montesquieu does not resolve any of them.

What was this abominable law court set up by Charlemagne in Westphalia, a tribunal stained in blood called the Vehmic Council, a court even more horrible than the Inquisition, composed of unknown judges who condemned people to death on the reports of its spies alone, and whose executioner was the youngest councillor in this little senate of murderers. Good Grief! Montesquieu talks to me about the laws of Bantam, and he doesn't know the laws of Charlemagne; he takes him to be a good legislator!

I looked for a guide on a difficult road. I found a travelling companion who was hardly any better informed than I was. I found the spirit of the author, who has plenty, and rarely the spirit of the laws. He hops rather than walks; he shines more often than he illuminates; sometimes he satirises more than he assesses, and he makes you wish that such a fine genius had made more attempt to instruct rather than to surprise.

This highly defective book is full of admirable things from which detestable copies have been made. Lastly, fanatics have insulted him for those very parts that deserve the thanks of the human race.

In spite of its faults, this work will always be valued by men because the author has said sincerely what he thinks, whereas the majority of writers from his country, starting with the great Bossuet, have very often said what they were not thinking. Everywhere in the book he has reminded men that they are free. He presents human nature with its rights, rights lost in most parts of the world. He fights superstition, he inspires morality.

I'll admit to you how distressed I am that a book that could be so useful should be based on a chimerical principle. Virtue, he says, is the principle of republics, honour that of monarchies. You can be sure that republics have never been created by virtue. Public interest opposed rule by a single man; the property ethos, the ambition of each individual, acted as a curb on the urge to loot. The pride and arrogance of each citizen keeps close watch on the pride and arrogance of his neighbour. Nobody wished to be the slave of someone else's capricious whims. This is what establishes a republic, and this is what keeps it going. It's ridiculous to imagine that a Grison needs more virtue than a Spaniard!

That honour should be the principle of monarchies alone is an equally chimerical idea; he makes this very clear himself unconsciously. 'The nature of honour', he says in chapter 7, Book III, 'is to ask for marks of preference and distinction. Things being what they are, it is thus located in monarchical government.'

Certainly, things being what they are, people would ask for praetorships, consulships, acclamations, triumphal arches: those are marks of preference and distinction well worth the titles of rank often bought in monarchies at a fixed price. There is another principle behind his book that's just as misleading: this is the division of governments into republics, monarchies and despotisms.

Our authors have been pleased (I don't know why) to call the sovereigns of Asia and Africa *despots*. In days gone by, it was understood that by despot was meant a minor European prince, a vassal of the Turk, a disposable vassal, a kind of crowned slave governing other slaves. Originally this word *despot* had meant with the Greeks, *master of the house, father*. Today we make free with this title for the Emperor of Morocco, the Great Turk, the Pope, the Emperor of China. At the start of the second book (ch. 1), Montesquieu defines despotic government thus: 'A single man, without laws or rules, who carries everyone along by willpower and impulse.'

Now it's quite wrong to think that such a government exists and, it seems to me, quite wrong to think that it could exist. The Koran and the authorised commentaries are the laws of the Muslims. All monarchs of this religion swear on the Koran to observe these laws.

The old officer corps and the lawyers have immense privileges, and when the sultans wished to break those privileges they were all strangled, or at least solemnly deposed.

I've never been to China, but I've seen more than twenty people who have made the journey, and I think that I've read all the authors who have spoken about that country. I know, with far more certainty than Rollin knew ancient history, I know from the unanimous reports from our missionaries of various sects, that China is governed by laws, and not by a single arbitrary will. I know that in Peking there are six supreme courts with jurisdiction over forty-four other courts. I know that when these six supreme courts address remonstrations to the Emperor it has the force of law. I know that at the far outposts of the Empire a street porter or a charcoal-burner are not executed without the trial proceedings having been sent to the supreme court at Peking, which reports them to the Emperor. Is that an arbitrary and tyrannical government? The Emperor is more revered there than the Pope is in Rome; but to be respected, must one reign without the curb of the law? One proof that the laws reign in China is that the country is more heavily populated than the whole of Europe. We've transported to China our holy religion, and it's been a failure. We might well have taken its laws in exchange, but perhaps we don't know how to trade like that.

It's an absolute certainty that the Bishop of Rome is more despotic than the Emperor of China, for he is infallible and the Chinese Emperor is not. However, that bishop is still subject to the law.

Despotism is just the abuse of monarchy, a corruption of a fine system of government. I could more easily accept highwaymen in political office than I can tyrants as kings.

A

You say nothing to me about the venality of judgeships, this fine trade in the law that only the French in the whole wide world know about. Those people must be the biggest traders in the universe since they sell and buy even the right to judge men. Devil take it! If I had the honour to have been born in Picardy or in Champagne, and to be the son of a tax-farmer or royal victualler, I could, with the help of twelve or fifteen thousand *écus*, become absolute master of the lives and fortunes of my fellow citizens! I would be called *monsieur* in accordance with the protocol used by my colleagues, and I would call litigants by their plain surnames, whether they be Châtillons or Montmorencys and, to get my money's worth, I would be a Guardian of Kings! It's an excellent deal. In addition, I would have the pleasure of having every book that displeased me burnt by someone whom Jean-Jacques Rousseau wishes to make the Dauphin's stepfather. It's a great right.

B

True, Montesquieu does have the weakness to say that the venality of offices *is good in monarchical states*. What do you expect? He was a high court president complete with mortar. I've never seen a mortar, but I imagine that it's a superb adornment. It's very difficult for the most philosophical mind not to pay tribute to pride. If a spice merchant talked about legislation, he would want everyone to buy cinnamon and nutmeg.

A

All that doesn't stop the *Spirit of the laws* from having some excellent bits in it. I like thinking people who make me think. How would you rank this book?

B

With works of genius that make you yearn for perfection. It appears to me to be a building with poor foundations, and an irregular structure, in which there are a lot of fine, well-polished, gilded apartments.

A

I'd happily spend a few hours in these apartments, but I can't stay a moment in the ones belonging to Grotius: they are too well set up, with furniture that is a little too old-fashioned. But how do you find the house that Hobbes built in England?

B

It's a bit too much like a prison, for he accommodates hardly anyone apart from criminals and slaves. He says that each man is born enemy to every other man, that the basis of society is the union of all against all. He claims that authority alone constitutes the law, that *truth*[3] has nothing to do with it. He makes no distinction between kingship and tyranny. With him force is everything. There is of course some truth in a few of these ideas; but his errors have outraged me so much that I've no wish to be either a citizen in his city when I read his *De cive*, nor eaten by his great beast Leviathan.

C

Gentlemen, you seem to me to be very discontented with the books that you've read, but to have gained something from them.

A

Yes, we take what we like from Aristotle down to Locke, and don't give a damn for the rest.

---

[3] 'The word *truth* is used here rather inappropriately by Hobbes; he should have said *justice*' (Voltaire's note).

C

I'd very much like to know what the results of your reading and your reflections are.

A

Nothing very much.

B

No matter. Let's try to sum up simply and straightforwardly this 'nothing very much' that we do know, without any foolish deference to intellectual tyrants or to the views of the tyrannised man in the street; in short, with all the good faith of reason.

Second conversation.
On the soul.

B

Let's begin. Before being certain of what is just, honest, and decent in [the world of] human souls, it's a good thing to know where they come from, and where they are going; you need to have a deep knowledge of the people you are dealing with.

C

That's right, although it hardly matters. Whatever the origin and destiny of the soul, the essential thing is that it should be just. But I always like discussing a subject in which Cicero took so much pleasure. What do you think, Mr A? Is the soul immortal?

A

But the question is a little blunt, Mr C. It seems to me that in order to discover by oneself whether the soul is immortal, you must be certain first of all that it exists; and my only knowledge of that is through faith which cuts through all difficulties. Lucretius said eighteen hundred years ago:

> Ignoratur enim quae sit natura animai.[1]

We don't know what the nature of the soul is. He could have said: We

[1] 'For none knows what is the nature of the soul', Lucretius, *De rerum natura* (Of the nature of things), I, line 113.

don't know whether it exists or not. I've read two or three hundred dissertations on this vast subject; they've never taught me anything. Here I am answering you in the same way that Saint Augustine answered Saint Jerome. Augustine said quite frankly that he knew nothing about the soul. Cicero, who was a better philosopher than Augustine, had often said the same thing before him, and much more elegantly. Our young graduates doubtless know more about it, but I know nothing about it, and at the age of eighty I feel that I'm no further forward than on the day I was born.

C

You're talking nonsense. Aren't you certain that animals have life, that plants have [powers of] growth, that the air has fluidity, that the winds have their currents? Have you any doubt that you have an old soul in control of your old body?

A

It's precisely because I know nothing of any of the things that you postulate that when I listen only to the weak voice of my reason, I've absolutely no knowledge of whether or not I have a soul. I can see perfectly well that the air is not still, but I see no real entity in the air called *wind current*. A rose grows, but there is no little secret individual entity in the rose that is *growth*. Philosophically speaking, that would be as absurd as saying that fragrance is in the rose. Yet this absurdity has been advanced for centuries. The whole of the ancient world's ignorant science of physics said: fragrance leaves the flowers and goes up my nose; colours leave objects and reach my eyes. Smell, taste, vision and hearing were given a kind of separate existence. People went as far as to say that life was something that created the living animal. The misfortune of the whole ancient world was thus to change words into real entities. It was claimed that an idea was an entity. Ideas, archetypes existing I know not where, had to be consulted. Plato gave full reign to this jargon, called *philosophy*. Aristotle reduced the fantasy to a method: hence all those entities, quiddities, haecceitas, and all the other barbarisms of the schools.

A few wise men perceived that all these imaginary entities are just words invented to bring relief to our understanding; that the animal's life is nothing more than the animal living; that its ideas are the animal thinking; that a plant's powers of growth are just the plant growing; that the movement of a ball is nothing more than the ball changing position; in short, that every metaphysical entity is just one of our ideas. Two thousand years had to pass for wise men to be right.

C

But if they are right, if all these metaphysical entities are just words, is your soul, which is presumably a metaphysical entity, nothing therefore? Have we really no soul?

A

I don't say that; I say that [without having recourse to anything] outside myself I know nothing about it. I just think that God has given us five senses and a brain, and it could well be the case that we are in God, as Aratus and Saint Paul say, and that we see things as part of God, as Malebranche says.

C

In that case, therefore, I would have thoughts without having a soul: that would be very odd.

A

Not all that odd. Don't you agree that animals have feelings?

B

Of course, not to accept that would be a denial of common sense.

A

Do you think that there's a strange little entity inside them called *sensitivity, memory, appetite*, or to which you give the vague, inexplicable term *soul*?

B

Of course not. None of us believe any of that. Animals have feelings because that is of their nature, because that same nature has given them all the organs of feeling, because the Author, the principle behind all nature, has determined it so for ever.

A

So! This eternal principle has arranged things in such a way that should I have a well-made head, should my cerebellum not be too moist or too dry, I will have thoughts, and I thank him from the bottom of my heart for them.

C

But how do you have thoughts in your head?

A

Again, I know nothing about that. One philosopher has been persecuted for having said forty years ago,[2] at a time when in his country people dared not think: 'The problem is not just to know whether matter can think, but to know how a being, of whatever kind, can have thought.' I agree with that philosopher, and I'll tell you, in the face of persecuting fools, that I know absolutely nothing of the first principles of things.

B

You know very little, and neither do we.

A

Agreed.

[2] The reference is to the *Philosophical letters* (Letter 13).

B

Why therefore are we discussing things? How will we know what is just or unjust if we don't even know what a soul is?

A

There's a big difference: we know nothing of the principle of thought, but we know very well where our interest lies. It's apparent to us that it's in our interest to be just towards other people, and that others should be just towards us so that we can all be on this pile of mud doing as little harm to each other as possible for the time allotted to us by the Being of Beings to grow, feel and think.

Third conversation.
On whether man was born wicked and the child of the Devil

B

You're an Englishman, Mr A. Give us your frank opinion on justice and injustice, government, religion, war, peace, laws, etc., etc., etc., etc.

A

With pleasure. What I find to be most just is *freedom* and *property*. I'm very happy to make an annual contribution of a million pounds sterling to my king for his household, provided that I enjoy my wealth and possessions in my own. I want everyone to have his *prerogative*. I only know laws that protect me, and I find our system of government to be the best on earth because each man knows what he has, what he owes, and what he can do. Everything is subject to the law, starting with royalty and religion.

C

Do you not admit the principle of divine right in society?

A

Everything goes back to divine right, if you want, because God made men, and because nothing happens without his divine will and without the interaction of divine laws, put into eternal effect. The

Archbishop of Canterbury, for example, is archbishop no more by divine right than I am a member of Parliament by right of birth. When it pleases God to come down to earth to give a priest a living with twelve thousand guineas income, then I'll say that this living comes from divine right, but until then I'll believe that his living is very human.

B

So everything is by agreement with men; it's pure Hobbes.

A

As far as that is concerned, Hobbes is just echoing the views of all sensible people. Everything is either a matter of contractual agreement or force.

C

So there's no natural law?

A

Certainly there is: self-interest and reason.

B

So in fact was man born in a state of war, since our self-interest almost always conflicts with the self-interest of our neighbours, and since our reason is used to support the self-interest driving us?

A

If man's natural state was war, all men would slaughter each other. It's a long time since we were in that state (thank God). What happened to those men born from Cadmus' dragon-teeth would have happened to us: they fought and not one survived. Man born to kill his neighbour, and to be killed by him, would necessarily fulfil his destiny, just as vultures fulfil theirs by eating pigeons, and beech-martens fulfil theirs by sucking the blood from my chickens. We have seen people who have never waged war: they say that Brahmans didn't; they say that several tribes in the American islands didn't, whom Christians exterminated, not being able to convert them. Primitives we call *Quakers* are starting to set an important country up in Pennsylvania, and they all abhor war. The Lapps, the Samoyeds, have never killed anyone as front-line soldiers. War is thus not part of the nature of the human species.

B

Yet the desire to hurt, the pleasure of exterminating one's neighbour for minor reasons of self-interest, the most horrible wickedness and the blackest perfidy must be the distinctive characteristic of our species, at least since the time of original sin, for our nice theologians assure us that from that moment on the Devil took our whole race over. Now the Devil is our master, as you know, and a very wicked master. So all men are like him.

A

I grant you that the Devil has taken possession of theologians, but not of me, I assure you. If the human species was directly governed by the Devil, as people say it is, clearly every husband would beat his wife senseless, every son would kill his father, every mother would eat her child, and the first thing a child would do, as soon as it had teeth, would be to bite its mother, always supposing that its mother had not spitted it first. Now, as none of that happens, people are demonstrably pulling our legs when they tell us that we are in the power of the Devil. That is the most foolish blasphemy ever spoken.

C

When I look at it closely, I confess that the human race is not quite as bad as certain people proclaim loudly in the hope of governing it. They are like those surgeons who assume all the ladies of the court have been struck down by that shameful disease that produces a lot of money for those who treat it. Diseases exist, of course; but the whole world is not in the hands of the Faculty of Medicine. There are major crimes, but they are rare. For more than two hundred years, no pope has resembled Pope Alexander VI; no European king has imitated Christian II of Denmark or Louis XI of France. Only one archbishop of Paris has been seen going to the *parlement* with a dagger in his pocket. The Saint Bartholomew massacre is quite horrific, whatever *abbé* Caveyrac says about it. But when you see the whole of Paris preoccupied with Rameau's music, or with *Zaïra*, or the *Opéra-Comique*, or with art exhibitions, or with Ramponeau, or Nicolet's monkey, you forget that half the nation cut the throats of the other half over theological arguments on what will be soon two hundred years ago to the day. The revolting executions of the Jane Greys, the Mary Stewarts and the Charles Is do not recur every day in your country.

These epidemics of horror are like those great plagues that sometimes ravage the earth; after which people plough, sow, harvest, drink, dance, make love on the ashes of the dead which are trampled under foot; and as a man who has spent his whole life feeling, arguing and joking once said, 'If everything isn't good, everything is at least tolerable.'

Take a province like the Touraine, for example, where a major crime hasn't been committed for a hundred and fifty years. Venice has seen four centuries flow by without the slightest revolt taking place within its walls, without a single rowdy gathering. There are a thousand villages in Europe where not one murder has been committed since the practice of cutting throats for religion fell out of fashion. Farm-workers don't have time to shirk; their wives and daughters help them; they sow, weave, knead dough, put the bread in ovens (not like Archbishop La Casa).[1] All these good people are too busy to think of doing wrong. After what is for them pleasant work, because they find it necessary, they have a light meal, for which their appetite provides the best sauce, and yield to the need for sleep so that they can start again the next day. My only fear for them is on feast-days, which are devoted so absurdly to singing psalms in harsh discordant voices in a Latin that they don't understand, and to drinking themselves senseless in a tavern, which they understand only too well. Again, if everything isn't good, everything is at least tolerable.

---

[1] 'Look at the *Capotili* by monsignor La Casa, Archbishop of Benevento: you will see how he used to put bread in the oven' (Voltaire's note).

B

What madness allowed people to imagine that there existed a goblin with gaping mouth, four lion-claws and a serpent's tail; that he is accompanied by a thousand million imps made like him, all of them having descended from heaven, all of them locked away in an underground fiery furnace; that Jesus Christ went down into that furnace to chain up all these beasts; that ever since they have come out of their dungeon every day; that they tempt us; that they enter into our bodies and our souls; that they're our absolute sovereigns, and that they inspire us with all their devilish perverseness. What can be the source of such an extravagant view, of such an absurd tale?

A

The ignorance of doctors.

B

I didn't expect that.

A

But you ought to expect it. You know well enough that before Hippocrates, and since his time even, doctors have understood nothing about diseases. Where did grand-mal epilepsy come from, for example? From malevolent gods, evil spirits. It was also called the *holy sickness*. It was the same with scrofula. These illnesses were the effects of a miracle; a miracle was needed to cure them; people made pilgrimages, had themselves touched by priests. This superstition spread around the world; it's still fashionable with the rabble. On a trip to Paris I saw epileptics in Ladychapel and Saint Maurus scream and writhe about from Maundy Thursday night until Good Friday. And our ex-King James II, as a holy person, imagined that he was able to cure scrofula sent by the Evil One. In the past all unknown disease was thus a case of possession by an evil spirit. The melancholy Orestes was supposed to be possessed by Megaera, and he was sent off to steal a statue in order to be cured. The Greeks, who were a very new nation, got this superstition from the Egyptians. The priests and priestesses of Isis went all over the place telling fortunes, and for money they rescued fools under the sway of Typhon. They performed their exorcisms with tambourines and castanets. The wretched Jewish nation, freshly established in its rocks between Phoenicia, Egypt and Syria, adopted all the superstitions of its neighbours and, in the depths of its brute ignorance, added new superstitions to them. When this little horde was enslaved in Babylon, it learned there the names of the Devil, of Satan, Asmodeus, Mammon, Beelzebub, all of them servants of Ariman, the principle of evil. And it was at that time that the Jews attributed diseases and sudden deaths to devils. Their holy books, written since then, when they had the Chaldean alphabet, occasionally speak of devils.

You see that when the angel Raphael descended from the Empyrean specifically to make Gabel the Jew pay a sum of money to Tobias the Jew, he took little Tobias to Raguel, whose daughter had already married seven husbands who had been strangled by the devil Asmodeus. Devil doctrine found great favour with the Jews. They admired an enormous number of devils in a hell about which the laws of the Pentateuch had said not a single word: almost all of their sick people were possessed by the devil. Instead of doctors they had exorcists who, by virtue of their office, got rid of evil spirits with a root called barathrum, prayers and contortions.

Wicked people were considered to be possessed more than the sick were. Debauchees [and] perverts are always called children of Belial in Jewish scripture.

Christians, who for a hundred years were just half-Jews, took up demonic possession, and boasted of driving off the Devil. The mad Tertullian carried this insanity to the point of saying that by making the sign of the cross every Christian forced Juno, Minerva, Ceres, Diana to confess that they are devils. Legend has it that a donkey drove off the devils of Senlis by tracing a cross in the sand with its hoof on Saint Rieule's command.

Gradually, it was generally established that all men are born possessed by the Devil and damned: without doubt a strange idea, an abominable idea, a horrible insult to the Divinity to imagine that the Divinity continually creates sensitive, rational beings just to be tortured forever by other beings, who are themselves eternally engulfed in torment. If the executioner in Carlisle, who in one day tore the hearts from eighteen supporters of Prince Charles-Edward, had been given the responsibility of founding a dogma, this is the one that he would have chosen. Moreover, it would have been necessary for him to have been drunk on brandy, for unless he had both the soul of an executioner and that of a theologian, he would never have been able to invent in cold blood a system by which so many thousands of infants still at the breast are delivered up to eternal executioners.

B

I fear that the Devil will reproach you for being a bad son who rejects his father. Your outlandish statements will seem to good Roman Catholics to prove that you are possessed by the Devil, and that you don't want to acknowledge it. But I'm curious to know how this idea of an infinitely good being creating millions of people every day in order to damn them could have entered people's minds.

A

By a misleading ambiguity, just as papal power is based on a play of words: 'Thou art Peter, and upon this rock I shall build my church.'[2]

Here is the ambiguity that damns all infants. God forbids Eve and her husband from eating the fruit of the Tree of Knowledge that he had planted in his garden. He says to them: 'On the day that you eat from it, you will die from death.'[3] They eat it and don't die from it at all. On the contrary, Adam lived another nine hundred and thirty years. We must therefore understand by that a different kind of death: the death of the soul, damnation. But it's not said that Adam is damned: therefore it will be his children who are. And how does that come about? Because God condemned the serpent, who had seduced Eve, to walk on its belly (for previously, as you will readily understand, it walked on its legs); and Adam's race is condemned to be bitten on the heel by the serpent. Now the serpent is obviously the Devil, and the heel he bites is our soul. 'Man shall crush the heads of serpents as much as he is able.'[4] Clearly, we must understand by that the Messiah, who triumphed over the Devil.

[2] The pun on *Pierre/pierre* is lost in translation. See Matthew, XVI.18.
[3] Genesis, II.17.
[4] Genesis, III.15.

But how did he crush the head of the old serpent by delivering up to him all unbaptised infants? There's the mystery. And how is it that children are damned because their first father and mother had eaten of the fruit in their garden? There's another mystery.

C

I'll stop you there. Isn't it because of Cain that we are damned, and not because of Adam? For we look as though we descend from Cain, if I'm not mistaken, given that Abel died unmarried; and it seems to make more sense to me to be damned for fratricide than for an apple.

A

It can't be because of Cain, for it's stated that God protected him and gave him a sign in case he should be beaten or killed. It's even stated that he founded a town [at a time] when he was still almost alone on the earth with his father, his mother, his sister, who became his wife, and a son named Enoch. I've even seen one of the most boring books, entitled *The science of government*, by some seneschal from Forcalquier named Réal, in which the law is derived from the town built by our father Cain.

But, however that may be, it's beyond doubt that the Jews had never heard of original sin, nor of the eternal damnation of infants who died without being circumcised. The Sadducees, who didn't believe in the immortality of the soul, the Pharisees, who believed in metempsychosis, could not accept eternal damnation, however much inclined the fanatics are to believe conflicting accounts.

Jesus was circumcised when he was eight days old and baptised as an adult, in accordance with the custom of a few Jews who looked upon baptism as the cleansing of the soul's stains. This was an old custom of the peoples of the Indus and the Ganges who had been convinced by the Brahmans that water washes sins like it washes clothes. In short, Jesus, circumcised and baptised, doesn't speak of original sin in any of the Gospels. No apostle says that unbaptised infants will be burnt eternally because of Adam's apple. None of the early fathers of the Church proposed this cruel fantasy, and what's more, you realise that Adam, Eve, Abel and Cain have only ever been known to the little Jewish nation.

B

So who was the first to say that clearly?

A

Augustine the African, a respectable man, by the way, but one who twists the meaning of a few of Saint Paul's texts in order to infer from them, in his letters to Evodius and Jerome, that God hurls children who die very young straight down into hell from their mother's breast. Read especially the second book of the review of his works, chapter 45: 'The Catholic faith teaches that all men are born sinful, and that even children are surely damned if they die without having been reborn in Jesus.'

It's true that nature, sickening the heart of this great talker, forces him to flinch at the barbarous sentence. However, he says it, and the man who changed his view so often does not retract. The Church asserts the authority of this terrible system in order to make its baptisms more necessary. Today, the reformed churches detest the system. The majority of theologians no longer dare accept it; however, they continue to acknowledge that our children belong to hell. So true is this that the priest, while baptising these small creatures, asks them whether they renounce the Devil, and the godfather, who answers for them, is kind enough to say yes.

C

I'm happy with everything that you've said. I think that man's nature is not completely diabolical. But why do people say that man is always inclined towards evil?

A

He's inclined towards his well-being, which is only evil when it oppresses his fellow men. God has given him pride, which is useful to him; benevolence, which is useful to his neighbour; anger, which is dangerous; compassion, which disarms it; affection for several of his companions; dislike for others. A lot of needs, a lot of ingenuity, instinct, reason and passions, that's man. When you're one of the gods, try to make a man based on a better model.

Fourth conversation.
On natural law, and on curiosity

B

We are quite convinced that man is not an entirely detestable being; but let's come to the point: what do you call just and unjust?

A

What appears to be so to the whole world.

C

The world is made up of a lot of people. They say that in Sparta people approve of pilfering, for which you are sentenced to the mines in Athens.

A

That's a misuse of words. Pilfering cannot be committed in Sparta when everything is held in common. What you call *theft* was the punishment for *greed*.

B

It was forbidden to marry your sister in Rome. Among the Egyptians, the Athenians, and even with the Jews you were allowed to marry your half-sister on your father's side, for in spite of *Leviticus* young

Tamar said to her brother Amnon: 'Brother, don't be silly, just ask my father for my hand; he won't say no to you.'[1]

A

All that is just the law of convention, arbitrary customs, fashions that fade away. What is essential stays for ever. Show me a country where robbing me of the fruits of my labour is an honest thing to do, where it is honourable to break one's promise, to tell harmful lies, to slander, to murder, to poison, to be ungrateful to your benefactor, to strike your father and mother when they feed you.

B

This is what I read in a proclamation that was quite well-known in its time. I've translated this bit which seemed odd: 'The first person who, having enclosed a piece of land, ventured to say *This is mine*, and found people simple-minded enough to believe him, was the true founder of civil society. What crimes, what wars, what murders, what misery and horror might have been spared the human race if, tearing up the stakes and filling in the ditches, someone had said to his fellow men: 'Take care not to listen to this imposter; you are lost if you forget that the fruits of the earth are for everyone, and that the earth belongs to no-one.'[2]

C

It must have been some highwayman, some clever wit, who wrote that piece of impertinence.

A

I just suspect that it was a very lazy beggar, because instead of spoiling the land of a wise and industrious neighbour, all he had to do was to imitate him; and if the father of [every] family had followed this example, you would soon have a very pretty village. The author of this passage seems to me to be a very unsociable animal.

[1] Kings, II.13.
[2] Jean-Jacques Rousseau, *Discourse on the origin of inequality* (Part 2), p.66.

B

So you think that by attacking and robbing the fellow who fenced off his garden and chicken run with a quickset hedge, he has failed to meet the first obligations of natural law?

A

Yes, definitely. There is such a thing as natural law, and it doesn't consist in doing harm to others, or in taking pleasure in their misfortune.

C

Still, there are people who say that nothing is more natural than doing harm. Lots of children enjoy plucking feathers from sparrows, and there's hardly a man born who doesn't take secret pleasure in wandering along the shore enjoying the sight of a ship battered by the wind, gaping open, and being swallowed up gradually by the waves, while the passengers raise their hands to the heavens and plunge into the watery depths with their wives holding their children in their arms. Lucretius tells us the reason why:

> ... Quibus ipse malis careas quia cernere suave est.[3]
> *You look with pleasure on evils that do not affect you.*

A

Lucretius doesn't know what he's saying; and he is quite prone to doing this himself, in spite of his fine descriptions. People flock to such a sight out of curiosity. Curiosity is a feeling natural to man, but there isn't a single one of those spectators who wouldn't make every effort, if he could, to save those drowning people.

When small boys and girls pluck feathers from their sparrows, it's purely out of curiosity, just as when they take their petticoats and dolls to bits. It's this passion alone that brings so many people out to public executions. 'The strange urge to see the wretched', the author of a tragedy once said.[4]

---

[3] Lucretius, *De rerum natura* (Of the nature of things), II, line 4.
[4] Voltaire in *Tancred*, act III, scene 3.

I remember being in Paris when Damiens was made to suffer one of the most refined and atrocious deaths you can imagine. All the windows looking out over the square were rented out at a high price to ladies. Certainly none of them were consoled by the thought that his breasts wouldn't really be torn by red-hot pincers, that molten lead and boiling resin wouldn't really be poured into his wounds, and that four horses wouldn't really tear apart his dislocated, bleeding limbs. One of the executioners made a sounder assessment than Lucretius, for when one of the members of the Paris Academy[5] wanted to get into the enclosure to take a closer look, and was held back by the guards, he said: 'Let the gentleman enter, he's an amateur', that's to say, he's just curious, he hasn't come here out of wickedness; it's not to do some soul-searching, to savour the pleasure of not being quartered; it's simply out of curiosity, like going to observe a physics experiment.

B

Alright. I understand that man only likes and does evil for his own advantage; but so many people are inclined to seek their advantage in the misfortune of others. Vengeance is such a violent passion; there are such dreadful examples of it; ambition, even more deadly, has flooded the earth with so much blood that when I call to mind the horror of all this again, I'm tempted to retract and accept that man is very much like the Devil. No matter that I have in my heart a notion of what's just and what's unjust; an Attila, to whom Saint Leo pays court; a Phocas, whom Saint Gregory flatters with the most contemptible cowardice; an Alexander VI, stained with so much incest, so many murders, so many poisonings, with whom the weak Louis XII, known as the *good*, makes the closest and most unworthy alliance; a Cromwell, whose protection was sought by Cardinal Mazarin, and for whom he drove out of France the descendants of Charles I, Louis XIV's first cousins, etc., etc., etc. A hundred similar examples upset my ideas, and I no longer have my bearings.

A

So! Do storms stop us from enjoying the lovely sunshine today? Does the earthquake that destroyed half the city of Lisbon stop you from

[5] La Condamine.

making a very comfortable trip from Madrid to Rome on firm ground? If Attila was a brigand, if Cardinal Mazarin was a rogue, are there no princes and ministers who are honest people? And doesn't the idea of justice always survive? It's on this that all laws are founded. The Greeks called them *daughters of heaven*; that simply means daughters of nature.

C

No matter, I'm also ready to retract; for I see that laws are only made because men are wicked. If horses were always docile, you would never put a bridle on them. But, without wasting our time probing the nature of man and comparing so-called savages with so-called civilised people, let's have a look at which bridle suits our mouths best.

A

I warn you that I can't bear anyone to bridle me without consulting me first, that I wish to bridle myself, and cast my vote in order to know at least who is going to ride on my back.

C

We come more or less from the same stable.

Fifth conversation.
On the ways of losing and keeping one's freedom, and on theocracy

B

Mr A, you seem to me to be a very wise Englishman. How do you imagine all those systems of government, whose names we can hardly remember, were founded: monarchical, despotic, tyrannical, oligarchical, aristocratic, democratic, diabolical and other combinations of these precedents?

C

Yes, everybody has his own version, because we have no true historical account.

A

Since you want to, I'll fritter my time away talking to you, and you can fritter yours away listening to me.

I imagine that first of all two small neighbouring tribes, each consisting of about a hundred families, are separated by a stream, each cultivating a reasonably good piece of land, for if they settled in that particular spot, it's because the land is fertile.

As each individual has received equally from nature two arms, two legs and a head, I find it inconceivable that the inhabitants of this little canton were not at first all equal. And, as these tribes are separated by a stream, I find it equally inconceivable that they were not enemies, for there would have been necessarily some difference between them in the way they pronounced the same words. The inhabitants south of the stream would certainly have made fun of those living to the north, and that cannot be excused. There would have been great rivalry between the two villages; some girl or woman would have been abducted. The young men would have fought frequently with their fists, with sticks and stones. All things being equal up to that point, the man considered to be the strongest and cleverest from the northern village says to his comrades: 'If you will follow me and do as I tell you, I'll make you masters of the southern village.' He spoke so confidently that he got their vote. He made them take up better weapons than the opposing village had. 'So far you have only fought in daylight,' he said, 'you must attack your enemies while they are asleep.' This idea seemed like a great [stroke of] genius to the mob from the north. They attacked the southern mob during the night, killed a few sleeping inhabitants, maimed several (as the noble Ulysses and Rhesus did), abducted the girls and the rest of the livestock. After all this, the victorious town-sized village quarrels inevitably over the sharing of the spoils. Naturally, they refer the issue to the leader whom they chose for this heroic expedition. So there he is, set up as commander and judge. The device of taking by surprise, looting and killing his neighbours has stamped terror on the south, and respect on the north.

The new leader is considered a great man throughout the land; people get used to obeying him, and he gets even more used to giving orders. I think that could well be the origin of monarchy.

C

It's true that the great art of taking by surprise, killing and looting is a most ancient form of heroism. I can find no military strategy in Frontin comparable to that of the children of Jacob, who in fact came from the north and surprised, killed and looted the Shechemites, who lived in the south. It's a rare example of sane politics and sublime bravery. For as the King of Shechem's son was hopelessly in love with Dina, the daughter of Jacob the patriarch, who was already nubile, being at least six years old, and as the two lovers had slept together, the children of Jacob proposed to the King of Shechem, to his son the prince, and to all the Shechemites, that they should get themselves circumcised so that they could all form a single nation.

And as soon as the Shechemites, having cut off their foreskins, had gone to bed, two patriarchs, Simeon and Levi, acting on their own, took all the Shechemites by surprise,[1] killed them, and the ten other patriarchs plundered them. However, that does not fit in with your theory, because it was the ones who were taken by surprise, killed and looted who had a king, and the murderers and thieves who did not yet have one.

A

It would appear that the Shechemites had taken some similarly splendid action before, and that eventually their leader had become a monarch. I can understand that there were thieves who had leaders, and other thieves who didn't. The desert Arabs, for example, were nearly always thieving republicans, but the Persians [and] the Medes, were thieving monarchists. Without arguing with you further about Shechem's foreskins and thieving Arabs, I have it [firmly] in my mind that a war of aggression created the first kings, and that a defensive war created the first republics. A robber-baron like Dejoces (if he existed), or Cosrou, otherwise known as Cyrus, or Romulus, the murderer of his brother, or Clovis, another murderer, Genseric [and] Attila all made themselves kings. Nations who live in caves, on islands, in marshes, in mountain gorges, on cliffs, keep their freedom like the Swiss, the Grisons, the Venetians, the Genoans. You once saw the Tyrians, the Carthaginians and the Rhodians keep theirs as long as no-one had access to them by sea. The Greeks were free for a long time in a country bristling with mountains; within their seven hills the Romans took back their freedom as soon as they could, and then took it away from several other nations by taking them by surprise, killing them and looting them, as has already been said. And in the end the earth belonged everywhere to the strongest and the cleverest.

As men's minds became more sophisticated, systems of government were treated like [pieces of] fabric, with variations in grounding, design and colour. Thus the Spanish monarchy is as different from the English as the climate. The Polish bears no resemblance to the English. The Venetian republic is the opposite to the Dutch.

[1] Genesis, XXXIV.25.

C

All that is plainly true; but among all those types of government, has there ever really been a theocracy?

A

That is proved by the fact that theocracies are still to be found everywhere, and that from Japan to Rome you can be shown laws emanating from God himself.

B

But these laws are all different, they all conflict. Human reason might very well not understand how God came down to earth to decree what was right and what was wrong, to order the Egyptians and the Jews never to eat pork, having once cut off their foreskins, and to leave us with our foreskins and fresh pork. He surely could not have forbidden eels and hares in Palestine while allowing people to eat hares in England and ordering papists to eat eels on fast days. I confess that I tremble to examine things too closely; I fear of finding some contradictions in them.

A

So what? Don't doctors recommend completely different cures for the same illness? One recommends a cold bath, the other a hot bath; one bleeds you, another one purges you, a third one kills you; a newcomer poisons your son and becomes your grandson's soothsayer.[2]

C

That's strange. Apart from Moses and other genuinely inspired people, I would really like to have seen the first impudent fellow to make God speak.

---

[2] The reference is to Gérard Van Swieten who was a doctor at the imperial court in Vienna, and an enemy of enlightenment.

A

I think that he was someone who combined fanaticism with deceit. Fraud alone would not be enough; that bewitches, but fanaticism subjugates. Probably, as one of my friends says, this profession starts with dreams. A man with an inflamed imagination sees his mother and father die in a dream. Both are old and sick, and they die. The dream comes true, and there he is, convinced that God has spoken to him in a dream. In addition to being a brazen fellow and a rogue (two very common things), he starts making predictions in the name of God. In a war he sees that his countrymen have an advantage of six to one; he predicts victory for them, provided he gets a handsome cut.

It's a good trade; my little charlatan trains pupils with the same self-interest that he has. Their authority increases with their numbers. God reveals to them that the best slices of mutton and beef, the plumpest chickens, the best vintages, belong to them.

The priests eat roast beef, and the people stare.[3]

The King of the country first makes a deal with them in order to be better obeyed by the people; but soon the monarchy is duped as a consequence of the deal: the charlatans use the power over the riff-raff that the King has delegated to them to enslave the King himself. The monarch kicks against this, the priest strips him of his authority in the name of God. Samuel dethrones Saul, Gregory VII dethrones Emperor Henry IV, depriving him of a Christian burial. This diabolo-theocratic system lasts until reasonably well-educated princes come along with enough intelligence and courage to cut the Samuels and the Gregorys down to size. That, it seems to me, is the story of the human race.

B

No need to have read much to judge that things must have happened like that. You only have to look at the half-witted population of a

---

[3] Voltaire is quoting in English, probably from memory. The source might be Theodosius Forrest's *The roast beef of Old England*, a well-known cantata inspired by Hogarth's picture of *The Gate of Calais, or the roast beef of Old England* (1748). Cf. Henry Fielding *The Grub Street opera*, Act 3, scene 3.

provincial village where there are a couple of monasteries, some educated magistrates and a sensible [garrison] commander. The people are always ready to flock around the Franciscans and the Capuchins. The commander wants to keep the crowd under control. The magistrate, who is angry with the commander, issues a warrant that deals rather gently with the monks' insolence and the people's credulity. The Bishop is even more angry with the magistrate for having meddled in divine business, and the monks stay powerful until a revolution abolishes them.

> Humani generis mores tibi nos se volenti
> Sufficit una domus.[4]

---

[4] Juvenal, *Satires*, XIII.159.

Sixth conversation.
On three systems of government, and a thousand ancient errors

B

Let's get to the point. I confess that I could put up quite well with a democratic government. I think that philosopher was wrong who said to a supporter of a system of government by the people: 'Let's start by trying it in your own house, you'll soon regret it.'[1] With all due respect to him, a house and a city are two very different things. My house belongs to me; my children belong to me; my servants, when I pay them, belong to me; but by what right do my fellow citizens belong to me? All those with possessions in the same territory have equal right to the maintenance of law and order in the territory. I like to see free men themselves make the laws under which they live, just like they have made their houses. I find it pleasing that my mason, my carpenter, my blacksmith, who all helped me build my house, my neighbour the farmer, and my friend the mill-owner, all rise above their trades, and understand the public interest better than the most arrogant Tchaouch in Turkey. No ploughman, no artisan in a democracy has to fear harassment and contempt. No-one is in the position of that hatter who presented his bill to a peer and duke so that he could be paid for his services: 'Have you received nothing on account, my dear fellow?' 'Sorry, my lord, I did receive a slap in the face from his lordship your Intendant.'

It's very nice not to be liable to be dragged off for life to some dungeon for not having paid a man you don't know a tax whose value and reason for existence are unknown to you.

[1] Lycurgus. See Plutarch, *The Banquet of the seven wise men.*

To be free, to have only equals, is the true, natural life of man. Anything else is shameful pretence, a black comedy in which someone plays the part of the master and someone else the part of the slave, one that of parasite, the other that of pimp. You'll agree with me that men can only have left their natural condition through cowardice and stupidity.

This much is clear: people can only have lost their liberty through being unable to defend it. There were two ways of losing it: either when fools were deceived by rogues, or when the weak were subjugated by the strong. There's talk of some defeated people being forced by some conqueror or other to lose an eye; there are nations forced to lose both eyes like old nags made to turn the millstone. I want to keep my eyes; I suppose that you would lose one in a state run by the aristocracy, and both in a monarchical state.

A

You're talking like a citizen of Northern Holland, but I forgive you.

C

Me, I only like the aristocracy. The people are not fit to govern. I could not bear my wig-maker to be a legislator; I would prefer never to wear a wig. Only those who have had a very good education are fit to lead those who haven't had any. The Venice system is the best. This aristocracy is the most ancient state in Europe. After it I would rank the system of government in Germany. Make me a noble Venetian or a count of the Empire, I tell you, I can only live joyfully in either one of those stations in life.

A

You're a rich lord, Mr C, and I strongly approve of your way of thinking. I see that you would support the Turkish system of government if you were Emperor of Constantinople. For my part, although I'm just a member of the Parliament of Great Britain, I consider my own constitution to be the best of all, and to support my case, I'll cite irrefutable evidence: that of a Frenchman who, in a poem devoted to truth and not to frivolous make-believe, speaks thus of our system:

Within Westminster's walls you can see three powers
Appear together, astonished at the knot that joins them:
The representatives of the people, the nobility, the King,
Divided by self-interest, united by the law,
All three sacred members of that invincible body.
To itself dangerous, to its enemies terrible[2]

C

To itself dangerous! So do you have great abuses in your country?

A

I expect so. Just as the Romans had, or the Athenians, and just as there always will be with men. The culmination of human perfection is to have power and happiness, and enormous abuses; this is what we have achieved. It's dangerous to eat too much, but I still want my table to be well laden.

B

Would you like us to examine in depth all the systems of government in the world, from the Chinese Emperor Hiao, and the Hebrew hordes, [down] to the latest disputes in Ragusa and Geneva?

A

Good Heavens, no! I just have to comb through foreign archives to set the record straight. Quite a few people who could not govern a maidservant or a valet have undertaken to govern the world with their pens. Would you like us to waste time reading that book by Bossuet, Bishop of Meaux, called *The politics of holy scripture*? Nice politics, those of an unhappy people who were bloodthirsty without being warlike, usurious without being commercial, brigands without being able to hold on to their spoils, almost always enslaved and almost always in revolt, sold in markets by Titus and Adrian just as the animal called unclean by the Jews is sold, and which was more useful than they were. I'll leave to the declaimer Bossuet the politics of the little kings of Judah and Samaria, who understood only murder, starting with their own David who, having followed the trade of a robber

---

[2] *Henriade*, I, lines 313–18.

in order to become king, murdered Uriah as soon as he was master. And that wise Solomon who started off by murdering his own brother Adonias at the foot of the altar. I'm tired of the education of the young being devoted by these ridiculous pedants to the study of the history of such a people.

I'm no less tired of all those books which repeat the tales of Herodotus and his ilk about the ancient monarchies of Asia and about republics that have all disappeared.

There they go, telling us yet again how a certain Dido, supposedly Pygmalion's sister (not at all African names) escaped from Phoenicia to buy as much land in Africa as a bull's hide could cover, and that, cutting it into [thin] strips she encircled an immense territory on which she founded Carthage; there they go, these story-telling historians, following so many others, with so many others following them, talking about the prophecies fulfilled by Apollo, and about Gyges' magic ring, and about Smerdis' ears, and about Darius' horse that made its master king of Persia; there they go, expanding on the laws of Charondas, telling us yet again that the little town of Sybaris put three hundred thousand men in the field against the little town of Croton, which could only put a hundred thousand men under arms. We must consign all these stories to the same place as the she-wolf of Romulus and Remus, the Trojan horse and Jonas' whale.

So let's leave the whole of ancient so-called history there, and with regard to modern history, let everyone try to learn from the mistakes of his own country and from those of his neighbours. It will be a long lesson, but let's also look at the fine institutions by which modern nations distinguish themselves: that will be an even longer lesson.

B

And what will we learn from it?

A

That the closer the laws of convention are to natural law, the more tolerable life is.

C

Let's see then.

Seventh conversation.
That modern Europe is better than ancient Europe

C

Would you be so bold as to maintain that you English are better than the Athenians and the Romans, that your cockfights and gladiatorial combats in rings made of rotten wooden planks surpass the Coliseum? Are the cobblers and clowns who play roles in your tragedies superior to the heroes of Sophocles? Do your orators makes us forget Cicero and Demosthenes? And finally has London got a better system of law and order than ancient Rome?

A

No, but London is ten thousand times better than Rome was then, and the same goes for the rest of Europe.

B

Ah! Please make an exception for Greece, which obeyed the Great Turk, and Italy which obeyed the Pope.

A

I make those exceptions as well; but just think that Paris, which is only a tenth smaller than London, was only a little barbarian city then. Amsterdam was just marshland, Madrid a desert, and from the right bank of the Rhine to the Gulf of Bothnia everything was uncivilised. The inhabitants of those regions lived, as the Tartars have always lived, in ignorance, in want, and in barbarity.

Do you place so little value on the fact that today there are philosophers on thrones in Berlin, in Sweden, in Poland, in Russia, and that the discoveries of our great Newton have become the catechism of the cream of Moscow and Saint Petersburg?

C

You'll grant me that this is not the case on the banks of the Danube and the Mançanares; the light came from the north, for as far as I am concerned, having been born below the forty-fifth parallel, you are northern people. But do all these innovations make people in those countries happier than they were when Julius Caesar landed on your island and found you all running around half-naked?

A

I firmly believe so. Good houses, good clothing, a good standard of living, with good laws and freedom are better than want, anarchy and slavery. Those who are unhappy with London just have to go off to the Orkneys; there they will live as we used to in London in Caesar's time; they'll eat oat bread, cut each other's throats for sun-dried fish and a straw hut. Those who recommend it should set us an example.

B

But at least they would live in accordance with natural law. Pure nature is unaware of parliamentary debates, or crown prerogatives, or the East India Company, or tax on land at three shillings in the pound, and a shilling on windows. You might well have corrupted nature. It hasn't been tainted in the Orkneys or in the land of the Topinambous.

A

And what if I said to you that it is the savages who have corrupted nature, and that we are following nature?

C

You surprise me. What! Consecrating an archbishop of Canterbury is following nature? Calling a transplanted German *your majesty*? Only being able to marry one wife, and paying out more than a quarter of your income every year [in tax]? Apart from other transgressions against nature that I won't mention.

A

Yet I'll prove it to you, unless I'm very much mistaken. Is it not true that instinct and judgement, two of the oldest sons of nature, teach us to seek out our well-being in everything, and to secure that of other people when it is obvious that their well-being makes for ours? Is it not true that if two old fasting cardinals met dying of hunger beneath a plum-tree, automatically they would help each other to climb the tree and pick the plums, and that two little scamps from the Black Forest or from the Chicachas would do the same?

B

So? What conclusion do you draw from that?

A

The same one drawn by the two cardinals and the two little wretches, namely that in all such circumstances we must help each other. Those who help society most, therefore, are those who follow nature closest. Those who invent the arts (which is a great gift from God), those who propose laws (which is infinitely easier) are, therefore, those who have obeyed natural law best: thus the more the arts are cultivated and the more people's property is protected, the more natural law will in fact have been observed. So when we all agree to pay tax at three shillings in the pound, when we agree to choose a German to be, with the title of king, the preserver of our freedom, the arbiter between the Lords and the Commons, the Head of the Republic, when we marry only one woman for the sake of economy and to have some peace at home, when (because we are rich) we put up with an archbishop of Canterbury having an income of twelve thousand [pounds] in cash to relieve the poor, to preach virtue, if he knows how to preach, to keep the clergy quiet, etc., etc., we are doing more than simply perfecting natural law, we are exceeding the objective. But what does the solitary, wild savage (if there are such animals on the earth, which I very much doubt) do from morning until night but pervert natural law by being useless to himself and to others?

A bee that makes neither honey nor wax, a swallow that does not make its nest, a hen that never lays eggs, would corrupt their own natural law, which for them is instinct; men who are unsociable corrupt the instinct of human nature.

C

So the man who is concealed beneath sheep's wool and silk-worm droppings, inventing gunpowder to destroy himself, and travelling two thousand miles from home to find syphilis, is natural man, and the naked Brazilian is artificial man?

A

No, but the Brazilian is an animal who has not yet reached the full potential of his species. He is a bird with only very late plumage, a caterpillar inside its chrysalis which will not change into a butterfly for a few centuries. One day he will have his Newtons and his Lockes perhaps, and then he will have completed the full course of human development, assuming that the Brazilian's physical constitution is sufficiently strong and flexible to reach that point, for everything depends on our physical constitution. But what do I care about the characteristics of a Brazilian and the feelings of a Topinambou? I'm neither one nor the other; I want to be happy in my own way in my own place. We must examine the country in which we live, and not one where we cannot live.

Eighth conversation
On physical serfdom

B

It seems to me that Europe today is like a huge bazaar. You find there everything you think is necessary to life; there are guards to watch over the security of shops, rogues winning at dice money [that is] lost by fools, layabouts asking for charity, and marionette shows, all in the same marketplace.

A

All that is by way of convention, as you can see. And these marketplace conventions are based on man's needs, on his nature, on the development of his intelligence, on the first cause that drives the mechanism of secondary causes. I'm sure that it's like that in a republic of ants. We always see them in action without being able to discern very well what they are doing. They appear to be running around all over the place. Possibly they make the same judgement about us. They are holding their market, just like we hold ours. As far as I'm concerned, I'm not totally unhappy with my little stall.

C

Among the conventions of this great world market that displease me, there are two in particular that make me angry: [the fact] that slaves are sold there, and [the fact] that there are charlatans for whose quack remedies we pay far too much. I was highly delighted by

Montesquieu in his chapter on the negroes. He's very amusing; he triumphs by making fun of our injustice.

A

In truth, we don't have the natural right to go and capture a citizen of Angola, take him off and beat him into working in our sugar plantations in Barbados in the same way that we have the natural right to take a dog we have fed hunting; but we have the right by convention [to do it]. Why is this negro sold? Or why does he let himself be sold? I bought him; he belongs to me. What wrong am I doing him? He works like a horse, I feed him badly, I dress him likewise, he is beaten when he disobeys; what's surprising about all that? Do we treat our soldiers any better? The only difference between the negro and the soldier is that the soldier costs a lot less. The going rate for a fine negro currently is at least one hundred and fifty *écus*, and a fine soldier costs barely fifty. Neither may leave the place where he is confined; both are beaten for the slightest misdemeanour. The wages are more or less the same; and the negro has the advantage over the soldier of not risking his life, and of spending it with his negress and piccaninnies.

B

What! You think that a man can sell his liberty, which is priceless?

A

Everything has its price; too bad for him if he sells me something so precious cheaply. You can say that he's a fool, but don't say that I'm a rogue.

C

It looks as though Grotius, in Book II, chapter 5,[1] strongly approves of slavery; he even finds the condition of a slave to be much more

---

[1] *De jure belli et pacis.*

advantageous than that of a journeyman, who doesn't always know where the next meal is coming from.

B

But Montesquieu looks upon slavery as a kind of sin against nature. So here we have a free Dutch citizen who wants slaves, and a Frenchman who doesn't want any. He doesn't even believe in the right to wage war.

A

And what other right can there be then in war other than that of the strongest? Suppose that I find myself in action against the Spanish in America? A Spaniard has wounded me; I am all set to kill him; he says: 'Brave Englishman, don't kill me and I'll serve you.' I accept the proposal, I please him, I feed him garlic and onions; every evening he reads *Don Quixote* to me at bedtime: what's the harm in that, if you please? If I surrender to a Spaniard under the same conditions, how can I reproach him? All there is in a deal is what you put into it, as the Emperor Justinian said.

Didn't Montesquieu himself accept that there were nations in Europe where it was quite common to sell oneself, as in the case of the Russians, for example?

B

It's true, he does say that, and he also quotes Captain John Perry in the *Present state of Russia*;[2] but he quotes in his usual way. John Perry says exactly the opposite. Here are his own words: 'The Czar ordained that no-one in future should call himself his slave, his *kholop*, but only *rab*, which means subject. The truth is that the people gained no real advantage from this, for they are still enslaved today.'

In fact, all farmers, all the inhabitants of the lands belonging to Boyars, or to priests, are slaves. If the Empress of Russia is starting to create free men, she will make her name immortal by so doing.

---

[2] Captain John Perry's *The state of Russia under the present Czar* (1716) was translated into French in 1717. See the 1771 article 'Slaves' in *QE*.

Moreover, to humanity's shame, farmers, artisans, bourgeois who are not citizens of great cities, are still slaves, feudal serfs, in Poland, Bohemia, Hungary, several German provinces, half of Franche-Comté, a quarter of Burgundy, and what is something of a contradiction is that they are slaves of priests. There are some bishops who have hardly anyone except feudal serfs in mortmain on their lands. Such is humanity, such is Christian charity. As for people enslaved in wartime, the only people you can see in the country of the religious Knights of Malta are slaves from Turkey or from the coastal regions of Africa, chained to the oars in Christian galleys.

A

By God, if bishops and prelates have slaves, I want some too.

B

It would be better for nobody to have any [at all].

C

This will follow as sure as night follows day when the *abbé* Saint-Pierre's perpetual peace[3] is signed by the Great Turk and all the powers, and when Arbitration Village has been built next to the hole that people want to dig down to the centre of the earth in order to know precisely how to conduct themselves on its surface.

[3] The *abbé* de Saint-Pierre's *Project for perpetual peace* was published in 1713.

Ninth conversation.
On the serfdom of minds

B

If you accept physical slavery, at least you wouldn't approve of slavery of the mind, would you?

A

Please let's not misunderstand each other. I don't accept physical slavery as part of the principles of society. I only say that it's better for the vanquished to be enslaved than to be killed, just in case he prefers life to liberty.

I say that the negro who sells himself is a fool, and that the negro father who sells his piccaninny is a barbarian, but that I'm a very sensible man to buy that negro and make him work on my sugar plantation. It's in my interest that he should be in good health so that he can work. I'll treat him humanely, and I'll demand no more gratitude from him than from my horse, to which I'm obliged to give oats if I want him to be of use to me. I stand in more or less the same relationship to my horse as God does to man. If God has made man to live a few minutes in the world's stable, it was clearly necessary for him to provide man with food, for it would be absurd if he had given man the gifts of hunger and a stomach, and had then forgotten to feed him.

C

And what if your slave is of no use to you?

A

I'll give him his freedom unconditionally, even if he has to go off to be a monk.

B

But what do you think about slavery of the mind?

A

What do you mean by slavery of the mind?

B

I mean that practice whereby the minds of our children are shaped just like Caribbean women knead the heads of their children; whereby their mouths are first of all taught to mumble nonsense which we ourselves ridicule; whereby they are made to believe nonsense as soon as they start believing; the practice whereby every care is thus taken to make a nation stupid, faint-hearted and barbaric; lastly, the practice whereby laws are passed stopping men from writing, talking and even thinking, a bit like that play in which Arnolphe wants the only desk in the house to be his alone, and to make an imbecile of Agnès in order to take his pleasure with her.[1]

A

If there were such laws in England, I would either hatch a fine plot to get rid of them, or flee from my island forever, after having first set fire to it.

C

But it's a good thing that everyone does not speak his mind. You should not insult by what you write, or what you say, those laws under whose protection you enjoy your wealth, your freedom, and all the comforts of life.

---

[1] Molière, *School for wives*, act III, scene 2.

A

Of course not, and reckless traitors must be punished; but because writing can be abused, must men be forbidden to do it? I would like that no more than if you were to be made dumb to stop you arguing badly. People are robbed in the streets, must they be forbidden from walking in them because of that? People say stupid and insulting things, but must speaking be forbidden? Everybody can write what they think in my country at their own risk; it's the only way to speak to one's country. If it finds that you have spoken foolishly, it boos you; if seditiously, it punishes you; if wisely and nobly, it loves you and rewards you. The freedom to speak to men through one's pen is well-established in England, as it is in Poland, in the United Provinces and most recently in Sweden, where we are imitated. It will be in Switzerland; without it Switzerland does not deserve freedom. Without the freedom to explain what one thinks, there is no freedom among men.

C

And what if you had been born in modern Rome?

A

I would have raised an altar to those ancient Romans, Cicero and Tacitus; I would have ascended the altar and, wearing Brutus' hat and with his dagger in my hand, I would have reminded the people of the natural rights that they have lost. Like Nicholas Rienzi, I would have re-established the Tribunate.

C

And you would have ended up like him.

A

Perhaps; but I can't tell you how much horror I felt at the subservience of the Romans when I was last there. I shuddered at the sight of recollects at the Capitol. Four of my fellow-countrymen chartered a boat to go off and sketch the useless ruins of Palmyra and Baalbek. I was tempted a hundred times to arm a dozen boats at my own expense to lay ruin to the lairs of the Inquisitors in those countries where man is enslaved by these monsters. My hero is Admiral Blake. He was sent by Cromwell to sign a treaty with John of Braganza, King of Portugal. This prince apologised for not signing because the Grand Inquisitor would not tolerate negotiations with heretics. 'Leave it to me', Blake told him, 'he'll come to sign the treaty on my ship.' This monk's palace was on the river Tagus, facing our fleet. The admiral let him have a red-hot broadside; the Inquisitor came to ask for pardon, and signed the treaty on his knees. In all that, the admiral did only half of what he should have done. He should have prohibited all inquisitors from tyrannising souls and burning bodies, just like the Persians, and after them the Greeks and the Romans, prohibited Africans from practising human sacrifice.

B

You always talk like a true Englishman.

A

Like a man, and like all men would speak if they dared. Shall I tell you what the human race's greatest fault is?

C

Please do; I'd like to understand my species.

A

The fault is that of being fools and cowards.

C

But all nations show courage in time of war.

A

Yes, like horses trembling at the first sound of the drum, and advancing proudly when under the discipline of a hundred drumbeats and a hundred whip strokes.

Tenth conversation.
On religion

C

Since you believe that the lot of good men is to be able to speak freely what is in their minds, do you wish to see anything printed about government and religion?

A

Whoever keeps silent on these two subjects, whoever cannot look closely at these two polarities of human life, is just a coward. If we had not known how to write, we would have been oppressed by James II and Jeffreys, his chancellor; and my Lord of Canterbury would have whipped us at the door of his cathedral. Our pen is the first weapon against tyranny, and our sword the second.

C

What! Writing against the religion of your country!

B

Ah! You're not thinking, Mr C. If the first Christians had not been free to write against the religion of the Roman Empire, they would never have established their own. They composed the Gospel of Mary, of James, of Christ's childhood, of the Hebrews, Barnabas, Luke, John, Matthew, and Mark; they wrote fifty-four of them. They composed Jesus' letters to a little king of Edessa, the letters of Pilate to Tiberius, of Paul to Seneca, of the acrostic prophecies of the Sybils, the symbol of the twelve apostles, the testament of the twelve patriarchs, the Book of Enoch, five or six apocalypses, and false apostolic successions, etc., etc. What didn't they write? Why do you want to deprive us of the freedom they had?

C

God save me from outlawing that precious freedom! But I want to see some tact in it, as in decent conversation; everyone says what he thinks, but no-one insults the whole company.

A

I'm not asking you to insult society either, but to enlighten it. If a country's religion is sacred (for every country boasts that it is), a hundred thousand volumes written against it will do it no more harm than [that done] to rock-solid walls by a hundred thousand snowballs. The gates of Hell shall not prevail against it, as you know! How can a few black letters traced on paper destroy it?

But if fanatics or rogues, or people combining the features of both, go as far as to corrupt a pure and simple religion, if Magi and Bonzes happen to add absurd ceremonies to holy laws, impertinent mysteries to the sacred morality of the Zoroastras and Confuciuses, should the human race not be grateful to those who are cleansing the temple of God of the dirt that these wretched people have piled up there?

B

You seem to be very wise. What are these precepts of Zoroastra and Confucius then?

A

Confucius did not say: 'Do not do to others what you would not wish them to do to you.'

He said: 'Do what you would want others to do to you; forget insults, and remember only favours.' He made friendship and humanity into a duty.

I'll quote only one law from Zoroastra, which contains the essence of morality, and which is for that reason the opposite to the Jesuits' famous probabilism: 'When you are unsure whether an action is good or bad, refrain from doing it.'

No moralist, no philosopher, no legislator has ever said, or ever could say, anything better than this maxim. If, afterwards, Persian or Chinese theologians supplemented the worship of a God and the doctrine of virtue with weird fantasies, apparitions, visions, predictions, miracles, possessions, scapulas, if they wanted people to eat certain foods in honour of Zoroastra and Confucius, if they claimed knowledge of all the family secrets of these two great men, if they argued for three hundred years over whether Confucius was created or born, if they introduced superstitious practices which channelled the money of devoted souls into their pockets, if they built their temporal greatness on the foolishness of people with little real religion, if finally they armed fanatics to maintain their imaginings by sword and fire, it is beyond dispute that we must curb these imposters. Whoever has written in favour of natural, divine religion, and against the abhorrent abuses of the religion of sophists, is his country's benefactor.

C

These benefactors have often been ill-rewarded. They have been burned alive or poisoned, or they died upside down, and every reform has produced wars.

A

That's the fault of legislative systems. There have been no more wars of religion since governments have been wise enough to curb theology.

B

In the name of reason, I would like it to have been abolished instead of curbed. It's just too shameful to have made a science out of this madness. I fully understand the point of a parish priest who keeps a register of births and deaths, who collects alms for the poor, who comforts the sick, who brings peace to families, but what is the use of theologians? What is the advantage to society, when it has been well understood that an angel is infinite, *secundum quid*, that Scipio and Cato are damned because they were never Christians, and that there is an essential difference between *categoramatic* and *syncategoramatic*?

Don't you just admire a Thomas Aquinas who decides that 'the irascible and concupiscible parts are not part of the intellectual appetite'? He examines at length whether legal ceremonies are pre-legal. A thousand pages are devoted to these wonderful issues, and five hundred thousand men study them.

Theologians have long enquired into whether God can be a pumpkin or a beetle; whether, having received the Eucharist, you then give it back in the lavatory.

These extravaganzas have preoccupied the long-beards in countries that have produced great men. On this point one writer, a friend of reason,[1] has said several times that the main trouble with us is that we still do not know how far below the Hottentots we are in certain subjects.

We have advanced further than the Greeks and the Romans in several arts, and we are brute beasts in this area, like those animals on the Nile [made] partly of living matter and partly of mud.

Who would believe it? A madman, after having regurgitated for two years all the scholastic idiocies, receives his cap and bells at a ceremony. He struts about like a peacock; he hands down decisions; and this is the school of bedlam that leads to fame and fortune. Altars are raised to Thomas and Bonaventure, and those who invented the plough, the sister-block, the plane, and the saw are unknown.

A

Theology must be destroyed absolutely, just as judicial astrology, magic, the divining rod, the Cabbala, and the Star Chamber have been destroyed.

---

[1] Voltaire himself.

C

Let's destroy these caterpillars in our gardens as much as we can so that only nightingales remain; let's preserve what is useful and pleasing: that's what man is all about; but as for everything that's disgusting and poisonous, I agree to its extermination.

A

A good, honest religion, as I live and die! clearly established by act of Parliament, clearly dependent on the sovereign, that's what we need, and let's put up with all the others. We are happy only from the moment we are free and tolerant.

C

The other day I was reading a French poem on *Grace*, a didactic poem that's a bit tedious on account of its monotony. Speaking of England, from which God's grace has been withheld (in spite of the fact that your monarch calls himself king by grace of God, like any other), this author expresses himself thus in rather flat verse:

> England, this island seed-bed of Christians,
> Where once so much light shone,
> Today, by taking in so many religions,
> Is nothing more than a sad gathering of mad visions . . . .
> Yes, Lord, we are the most precious of your peoples,
> It is on us that you shine your brightest rays.
> Truth ever pure, o eternal doctrine!
> France is today your faithful kingdom.[2]

A

There's an original for you, with his seed-bed and bright rays! A Frenchman always thinks that he sets the pace for other nations; you would think it's all about a minuet or a new fashion. He pities us for being free! In what way, if you please, is France the faithful kingdom of *eternal doctrine*? Was it when an absurd bull, concocted in Paris in

---

[2] Louis Racine, *Poem on grace* (1720), IV, lines 129–46.

a college of Jesuits, and sealed in Rome in a college of cardinals, divided the whole of France, and made more prisoners and exiles than there were soldiers? O faithful kingdom!

Let the Anglican Church respond, if it wishes, to these rhymsters of the Gallican Church; I for one am certain that none of us will miss *those bygone times when so much light shone*. Was that when the popes sent their legates to us to give away our livings to Italians, and impose tithes on us to pay for their prostitutes? Was it when our three kingdoms swarmed with monks and miracles? This tedious poet is a very bad citizen. He would have done better to wish for enough bright rays to enable his own country to see what it would gain by imitating us. These rays make clear that Gallicans should not send twenty thousand pounds sterling to Rome every year, and that Anglicans, who once paid Peter's pence, were immersed at the time in the most stupid barbarity.

B

Well said. Religion is not at all about transferring money to Rome. That truth is recognised not only by those who have broken that yoke, but also by those who are still burdened with it.

A

Religion must clearly be purged; the whole of Europe is crying out for it. This great work was started almost two hundred and fifty years ago; but men are only enlightened gradually. Who would have believed then that people would analyse the sun's rays, produce electricity with lightning, discover gravity, that law which governs the universe? It is time for men who are so enlightened to stop being slaves of the blind. I laugh every time I see an academy of science forced to defer to the decision of a congregation of the Holy Office.

Theology has only served to subvert minds, and sometimes states. It alone creates atheists, for the vast majority of minor theologians, who are sensible enough to see the silly side of this fantastical discipline, don't know enough about it to replace it with a sane philosophy. Theology, they say, is the *science of God*, according to the meaning of the word. Now the rascals who have desecrated this science have given people some absurd ideas about God, and from that people have concluded that the Divinity is a fantasy because theology is fantastical. That's exactly the same as saying that you must never take quinine for a fever, or diet when the blood is too rich, or be bled when you have a seizure, because there are bad doctors. That amounts to denying the movement of the planets because there are astrologers, or denying the clear effects of [chemical processes] because charlatan chemists have claimed to make gold. People in the street, even more ignorant than these minor theologians, are saying: 'Here are bachelors and masters of arts who do not believe in God; why should we?'

Friends, a false science creates unbelievers; a true science makes man bow down before the Divinity; it makes just and wise what theology makes iniquitous and insane.

That's more or less what I've just read in that recent little book,[3] and I've declared my faith in it.

B

That's really the faith of all decent people.

---

[3] *Letters to His Highness monsignor the Prince of* *** (see Moland, XXVI.488).

Eleventh conversation.
On the code of war

B

We have dealt with subjects that concern us all very closely; and people are quite mad to prefer hunting or playing piquet to educating themselves on such important issues. Our initial plan was to go more deeply into the code of war and peace; we haven't yet talked about this.

A

What do you mean by the code of war?

B

You put me on the spot there; but de Groot or Grotius has written a fat treatise on it, in which he quotes more than two hundred Greek or Latin authors, and even Jewish ones.

A

Do you think Prince Eugene and the Duke of Marlborough had studied it when they drove off the French miles away from home? I know a little about the code of peace; it's the code of keeping your word, and of allowing all men to enjoy the laws of nature; but as for the code of war, I don't know what it is. The code of murder seems to me to be a strange concept. I expect that we'll soon have a jurisprudence for highwaymen.

C

How then can we reconcile such an ancient and universal abomination as war with notions of what is just and unjust, with this compassion for our fellow men that we claim is born within us, with τὸ καλὸν,[1] beauty and honesty?

B

Not so fast. This crime that consists of committing so many crimes when called to the colours is not as universal as you say. We have already noted that Brahmans and the primitives called *Quakers* have never been guilty of this abomination. Nations beyond the Ganges spill blood very rarely; and I haven't read that the Republic of San Marino has ever waged war, although it has almost as much land as Romulus. The peoples of the Indus and the Hydaspes were very surprised to see the first armed thieves coming to take possession of their beautiful country. Several American nations had never heard of this horrible sin before the Spaniards came, Gospel in hand, to attack them.

Nowhere is it said that the Chamani had ever gone to war against anyone when a horde of Jews suddenly appeared, reduced the towns to ashes, slaughtered the women over the dead bodies of their husbands, and massacred the children on their mothers' bellies. How shall we explain this mad frenzy in [the context of] our principles?

A

In the same way that wicked people rationalise the plague, the two poxes and madness: these are illnesses linked to our physical make-up. People are not always struck down by madness or plague. For rabid madness to be communicated in three months to four or five hundred thousand men it often only takes one rabid minister of state to bite another.

C

But, when one has these illnesses, there are a few cures. Do you know any for war?

[1] 'the beautiful, the noble'. The notions of nobility and beauty are inseparable in Greek. Stoic usage would prefer 'honourable' to 'noble'.

A

I know of only two, which tragedy has seized upon: fear and pity. Fear often forces us to make peace; and pity, which nature has ingrained in us as an antidote to flesh-eating heroism, stops us from treating the vanquished too severely. It is in our interest even to deal mercifully with them so that they will serve their new masters without too much loathing. I'm perfectly well aware that there have been ruthless men who have made subjugated nations feel the full weight of their chains pretty harshly. To that I can only respond with a line from a tragedy called *Spartacus*, written by one Frenchman who thinks deeply:

The law of the universe is: *Woe to the vanquished.*[2]

I've tamed a horse; If I'm wise, I feed it well, I pat it, and I mount it; if I am a frenzied maniac, I slit its throat.

C

That's not much consolation, for after all nearly all of us have been subjugated. You English were by the Romans, the Saxons and the Danes, and then by a bastard from Normandy. The cradle of our religion is in Turkish hands. A handful of Francs conquered Gaul. In turn, the Tyrians, the Carthaginians, the Romans, the Goths, the Arabs subjugated Spain. In short, pretty well the whole world, from China to Cadiz, has belonged to the strongest. I know of no conqueror who came with his sword in one hand and a book of laws in the other; laws were made after the conquest, that is, after the looting; and they made those laws precisely to maintain their tyranny. What would you say if some Norman bastard were to take possession of your England so that he could come and impose his laws on you?

A

I wouldn't say anything; I would try to kill him as soon as he landed in my country. If he were to kill me, I would have no ready response; if he were to subjugate me, I would have only two options: to kill myself or to serve him well.

[2] Bernard-Joseph Saurin, *Spartacus*, act IV, scene 3.

B

There are some sad alternatives for you. What! No code of war? No law of nations?

A

Sorry, but there's nothing else apart from being always on one's guard. All kings, all ministers think the same way as we do, and that's why today in Europe twelve hundred thousand mercenaries parade in peacetime.

Should a prince dismiss his troops, let his fortifications crumble, spend his time reading Grotius, in two or three years you will see whether or not he has lost his kingdom.

C

That would be a great injustice.

A

I agree.

B

And is there no remedy for that?

A

None, apart from preparing yourself to be as unjust as your neighbours. Then ambition is contained by ambition. Then equally matched dogs bare their teeth, and only tear at each other when they have prey to quarrel over.

C

But what about the Romans, those great legislators, the Romans?

A

I tell you, they made laws like the Algerians who subjugate their slaves by regulation, but when they fought to reduce nations to slavery, then the sword was their law. Look at great Caesar, husband to so many wives, and wife to so many husbands. He crucified two thousand citizens from the Vannes area so that the rest would learn to be more pliant. Then, when the whole nation is well tamed, come the laws and the fine regulations. Circuses, ampitheatres are built, aqueducts are put up, public baths are constructed, and the subjugated peoples dance in their chains.

B

Yet people say that in war some laws are observed: for example, people have a truce for a few days to bury the dead; it's stipulated that fighting will not take place in certain areas, a besieged town is allowed to surrender; they are allowed to buy their church bells back; pregnant women are not disembowelled when a surrendered town is occupied; you salute a wounded officer whom you have captured, and if he dies you give him a burial.

A

Don't you see that in those cases the laws of peace, the laws of nature, primeval laws, are being applied on a reciprocal basis. War has not dictated them; they make themselves heard in spite of war; and without that three quarters of the globe would just be a desert littered with bones.

If two eager litigants, on the point of being ruined by their attorneys, reach an agreement that leaves each of them with a little bread, would you call that agreement a *law of the bar*? If a horde of theologians, on their way to a ceremonial burning of a few rationalists they call *heretics*, learn that the next day it will be the turn of the heresy party to burn them, and if they reprieve them so that they might be reprieved, would you say that that was a theological law? You'll agree that they have listened to nature and self-interest, in spite of theology. It's the same thing with war. The evil that war does not do is prevented by need and self-interest. War, I tell you, is a horrific disease which infects one nation after the other, but which nature cures in the long run.

C

What! You don't accept the notion of a just war?

A

I've never known one of that sort; to me it seems an impossible contradiction.

B

What! When Pope Alexander VI and his infamous son Borgia looted Romania, disembowelled and poisoned the whole of that country's nobility, while offering them indulgences, was it not permitted to arm oneself against those monsters?

A

Don't you see that it was those monsters who were waging war? Those defending themselves were keeping it going. In this world there are certainly only offensive wars; a defensive war is nothing other than resistance to armed thieves.

C

You're making fun of us. Two princes are quarrelling over an inheritance; their rights are a matter of legal dispute, their arguments are equally plausible; war must necessarily decide the issue: so this war is a just one on both sides.

A

You're the one making fun. It's physically impossible for one of them not be wrong, and it is absurd and barbaric for whole nations to perish because one of these two princes has argued badly. Let them fight each other in judicial combat if they want, but allowing a whole people to be sacrificed to their interests, that's what is horrible. For example, Archduke Charles quarrels with the Duke of Anjou over the throne of Spain, and before a judgement on the case can be reached it has cost more than four hundred thousand men their lives. I ask you if that is justice.

B

No, I agree. Some other basis of agreement had to be found.

C

It was found; the matter had to be referred back to the nation over which it was wished to rule. The Spanish nation said: We want the Duke of Anjou; his grandfather, the King, has named him in his will as his successor; we have subscribed to that; we have recognised him as our king; we have begged him to leave France and come and govern us. Whoever wishes to oppose a law based on the wishes of the living and the dead is clearly unjust.

B

Alright. But what if the nation is divided?

A

Then, as I told you, the nation and those participating in the quarrel are sick with a rabid madness. Its horrible symptoms last for twelve years, until the madmen, exhausted and unable to do more, are forced to reach agreement. Chance happenings, a mixture of good and bad results, plots, weariness, put out this fire that other chance happenings, other plots, greed, jealousy, expectations had lit. War is like Mount Vesuvius; its eruptions swallow up towns, and its conflagrations then stop. There are times when wild animals come down from the mountains, eat some of your produce, and then return to their lairs.

C

What a disaster man's condition is!

A

That of partridges is worse: foxes, birds of prey eat them; hunters kill them; cooks roast them, and yet they are still here. Nature preserves species, and is not much concerned with individuals.

B

You're a hard man, and morality doesn't fit in with these maxims.

A

It's not I who am hard, it's destiny. Your moralists do well to keep on shouting: 'Wretched mortals, be just and beneficent; cultivate the earth, and do not spill blood on it. Princes, do not lay waste to the inherited land of others in case you are killed in your own territory. Stay at home, poor little would-be barons, patch up your hovels; make the return on your assets double what it used to be; fence in your field with quickset hedges; plant mulberry trees; let your sisters make you silken stockings; improve your vineyards; and if neighbouring peoples want to come and drink your wine against your wishes, defend yourself with courage, but don't sell your blood to princes who don't know you, who will never give you a passing glance, and who treat you like the hunting dogs that they set on the wild boar, and then leave to die in a kennel.'

Perhaps these statements will impress three or four clear minds, while a hundred thousand others will not so much as hear them, and will try hard to become lieutenants in the Hussars.

As for the other professional moralists, called *preachers*, they have never dared so much as to preach against war. They rail against sensual appetites, after drinking their chocolate. Love is anathema to them, and on leaving their pulpits, where they have been sounding off, gesticulating and sweating, they have their brows wiped by their devout followers. They shout themselves hoarse proving mysteries about which they haven't got the slightest clue; but they take great care not to denounce war which brings together all the most cowardly perfidiousness in proclamations, all that is most base in the cowardly racket of arms-dealing, all the horrors of banditry, pillage, rape, robbery, homicide, devastation and destruction. On the contrary, these good priests bless ceremonially the banners of murder; and their colleagues sing Jewish songs for money when the earth has been soaked in blood.

B

In fact, I don't remember ever having read in the works of the wordy, argumentative Bourdaloue, the first to give sermons the semblance of reason, I repeat, ever having read a single page against war. The elegant, mild Massillon did express some wish for peace, while he was blessing the Catinat regiment's flags, it's true; but he authorised ambition: 'This wish', he said, 'to see your services rewarded, if it is modest . . . if it does not lead you down paths of iniquity to achieve your ends . . . contains nothing that could be offensive to Christian morality.' Finally, he asks God to send the Destroying Angel on ahead of the Catinat regiment. 'Please God, make victory and death precede it always; spread among its enemies spirits of terror and confusion.' I don't know whether victory can precede a regiment, or whether God can spread spirits of confusion around; but I do know that the Austrian preachers said the same thing to the Emperor's cuirassiers, and that the Destroying Angel didn't know which regiment to listen to.

A

Jewish preachers went even further. It's edifying to see the humane prayers which fill their psalms. They're all about girding on your holy sword, disembowelling women, and smashing against walls children still at their mothers' breasts. The Destroying Angel was not happy in his campaigns, and became the Angel Destroyed; and the Jews, for all the good their psalms did them, were always defeated and enslaved.

Whichever way you turn, you will see that priests have always preached carnage, from Aaron, who, it is claimed, was the pontiff of a horde of Arabs, to the preacher Jurieu, prophet of Amsterdam. The tradesmen of that town, who were as sensible as the poor fellow was mad, let him go on talking, and went on selling their cloves and cinnamon.

C

Well! Let's not go to war, and let's not get ourselves killed on the off-chance for the sake of money. Let's be happy defending ourselves well against those thieves called *conquerors*.

Twelfth conversation.
On the code of perfidy

B

And what shall we say about the code of perfidy?

A

By George! What did you say? I've never heard of that code. In which catechism did you read about that Christian duty?

B

I find it everywhere. The first thing that Moses did, with his holy people, was by an act of perfidy to borrow valuables from the Egyptians in order to go off into the desert, he said, to make sacrifices.[1] This act of perfidy was, it is true, only accompanied by robbery. Those that are associated with murder are much more admirable. The perfidies of Ehod, of Judith, are very well-known. Those of the patriarch Jacob towards his father-in-law and his brother were just [like] master Gonin's [magic] tricks,[2] since he murdered neither his brother nor his father-in-law. But three cheers for David's perfidy. David, after having assembled for himself four hundred rogues steeped in debt and debauchery, and having entered into an alliance with a certain petty king called Achish, went and slaughtered the men, women and children of the villages under the protection of this

---

[1] Exodus, XI.2.
[2] The allusion is to Mercury in the *Cymbalum mundi* (*Dialogue II*).

petty king, and made him think that he had only slaughtered the men, women and boys belonging to little King Saul! Three cheers especially for his perfidy towards old Uriah also. Hurrah for the perfidy of the wise Solomon who, inspired by God, had his brother Adonias killed, after having sworn to protect his life.

Then we have some very celebrated acts of perfidy by Clovis, first Christian king of the Francs, which could well serve as the perfect example of morality. I respect especially his conduct towards the murderers of a certain Regnomer, King of Le Mans (always supposing there was ever a kingdom of Le Mans). He struck a deal with these brave assassins to kill the King from behind, and paid them in false coinage; but as they grumbled about not having received their due, he had them murdered to get his base coins back.

Almost all of our history is filled with similar acts of perfidy, committed by princes who all built churches and founded monasteries.

Now the examples provided by these brave people ought certainly to serve as a lesson for the human race: for from whom should they seek such a lesson other than from the Lord's anointed?

A

It matters very little to me that Clovis and his ilk were anointed, but I confess to wishing that the whole of civil and ecclesiastical history could be thrown on the fire for the moral improvement of the human race. I can see hardly anything else in it other than the annals of crime, and whether these monsters were anointed or not, the only thing [you get] from studying their history is the example of wickedness.

I remember having once read the *History of the great western schism.*[3] I could see a dozen popes all equally perfidious, all equally deserving to be hanged at Tyburn. And since the papacy has survived in the middle of such a long, vast torrent overflowing with all possible crime, and since the records of these horrors have mended the ways of no-one, I conclude that history has no good purpose.

C

Yes, I agree that a novel is more valuable; there at least you are free to invent examples of virtue; but Homer never dreamed up a single

---

[3] By Louis Maimbourg. Published in 1678.

virtuous, honest action in the whole of that monotonous novel, the *Iliad*. I would much prefer *Telemachus*[4] if the whole thing did not consist of digressions and declamations. But since you raise the matter, here's a bit of *Telemachus* about treachery on which I would like to have your views.

In one of the digressions in this novel, in Book XX, Adrastus, King of the Daunians, rapes the wife of someone called Dioscorus. This Dioscorus seeks refuge with the Greek princes, and listening only to the voice of vengeance, he offers to kill their enemy, the rapist, for them. Telemachus, inspired by Minerva, persuades them not to listen to Dioscorus and to send him back to King Adrastus, bound hand and foot. What do you think of this decision of the virtuous Telemachus?

A

It's horrible. Apparently it was not Minerva but Tisiphone who inspired him. What! Send the poor man back so that he can be given an agonising death, and so that Adrastus can be completely like David who enjoys a wife while having her husband killed! The greasy author of *Telemachus* didn't think. That's not the action of a noble heart, but of a wicked and treacherous man. I wouldn't have accepted Dioscorus' proposal, but I wouldn't have delivered this wretch up to his enemy. Dioscorus was quite vindictive, as far as I can see, but Telemachus was perfidious.

B

And do you accept that there can be perfidy in treaties?

C

I assure you, it's very common. I would be hard-pressed if I had to decide who were the greatest rogues in negotiations, the Romans or the Carthaginians, Louis XI, the most Christian, or Ferdinand the Catholic, etc., etc., etc., etc. But I wonder if it isn't permissible to be a rogue in the interests of the state.

---

[4] By Fénelon. Published in 1695.

A

It seems to me that there are roguish tricks that are so clever that everybody pardons them; there are others so crude that they are universally condemned. As far as we English are concerned, we have never caught anybody. Only the weak deceive. If you want some good examples of perfidy, take the Italians in the fifteenth and sixteenth centuries.

A good politician is one who plays well and wins in the end. A bad politician is one who can only cheat at cards, and who is found out sooner or later.

C

Very good; and what if he is not found out, or if he is not found out until after he has won all our money [off us] and made himself too powerful for us to force him give it back.

A

I think that turn of events is rare and that history provides us with more famous knaves who were punished than famous knaves who were happy.

B

I've just one question to ask you. Do you think it a good thing for a nation to poison a public enemy in accordance with this maxim: *Solus republicae suprema lex esto*?

A

Good Heavens! That's a question you should ask casuists. If anyone made that proposal in the House of Commons I would vote (God forgive me!) for him to be poisoned himself, in spite of my horror of drugs. I would very much like to know why what is a heinous crime in the case of one individual is blameless in the case of three hundred senators, or even three hundred thousand. Is it the number of guilty people that changes crime into virtue?

C

I'm happy with your reply. You're a good man.

Thirteenth conversation.
On basic laws

B

I'm always hearing about basic laws; but are there any?

A

Yes, there's the law of justice; and never was such a basic thing more often shattered.

C

Not long ago, I read in one of those very rare bad books, much sought after by the curious, how naturalists collect pieces of fossilised animal or vegetable matter, thinking that in so doing they will discover the secret of nature. This book is by a Paris lawyer named Louis Dorléans who pleaded the case against Henry IV before the League,[1] and who lost, fortunately. Here are the views of this legal expert on the basic laws of the Kingdom of France: 'The basic law of the Hebrews was that lepers could not rule. Henry IV is a heretic; he is thus leprous; thus he cannot be King of France by the basic law of the Church. The law requires that a King of France should be Christian as well as male. Whoever does not accept the Catholic, apostolic and Roman faith is not a Christian and cannot believe in God. He

---

[1] An association founded in 1576 under Henry, third Duke of Guise, to defend the Catholic Church against the Calvinists. The League was eventually defeated by Henry IV in 1589–90, and was brought to an end with Henry's conversion to Rome in 1594.

can no more be King of France than the biggest scoundrel in the world, etc.'[2]

It's perfectly true that in Rome any man who doesn't believe in the Pope doesn't believe in God. But that's not completely true for the rest of the world: some tiny reservation has to be made, and it seems to me that, taking everything into consideration, *master* Louis Dorléans, lawyer to the Paris *parlement*, did not reason quite as well as Cicero and Demosthenes.

B

It would give me pleasure to see what would happen to the basic law of the Holy Roman Empire if one day the electors took it into their heads to choose a Protestant Caesar in the proud town of Frankfurt-am-Main.

A

The same thing would happen as happened with the basic law establishing the number of electors at seven because there are seven heavens and seven branches to a chandelier in a Jewish temple.

Isn't it the case that a basic law of France is that the Crown's lands are inalienable? And yet isn't it almost entirely alienable? You'll acknowledge that all of these basic laws are built on shifting sands. The laws called *basic laws* are, like all others, just laws based on convention, on ancient customs, ancient prejudices which change with the times. Ask today's Romans if they have kept the basic laws of the old Roman Republic. It was a good thing for the territory of the kings of England, France [and] Spain to remain the property of the Crown when kings lived off the produce of their land, like you and me. But what of today, when they live on taxes and duties, whether they have territory or not. When Francis I broke his word to his conqueror, Charles V, when he seriously violated the oath to surrender Burgundy to him, he had his lawyers make the case that the Burgundians were inalienable, but if Charles V had put the con-

---

[2] *Response of true French catholics to the notice to English catholics for the exclusion of the King of Navarre from the crown of France* (1588), p. 224.

trary case to him at the head of a great army, the Burgundians would have been very alienable.

Franche-Comté, whose basic law was to be free under the protection of the House of Austria, depends in a close and essential way on the French Crown. The Swiss have depended essentially on the Empire, but depend essentially today on freedom.

This freedom is the basic law of all nations; it's the only law against which nothing can be ordained, because it's the law of nature. The Romans can say to the Pope: Our basic law was first of all to have a king who reigned over a few miles of territory; then it was to elect two consuls, then two tribunes; then our basic law was to be devoured by an emperor, then devoured by northerners, then to be in a state of anarchy, then to starve under the government of a priest. At last we are returning to the true basic law, which is to be free. Go away, and hand out your indulgences *in articula mortis* somewhere else, and leave the Capitol which was not built for you.

B

Amen!

C

We really must hope that this will happen one day. It will be a fine sight for our grandchildren.

A

If only the grandfathers could have the joy of it too. Of all revolutions, this is the easiest one to accomplish; yet nobody is thinking about it.

B

That's because, as you say, the main characteristics of man are foolishness and cowardice. The Roman rats still don't know enough to bell the cat.

C

Do we not recognise any other basic law?

A

Freedom covers all of them. Let the farmer not be harassed by some petty tyrant; let it not be possible to imprison a citizen without bringing him to trial promptly before his natural judges, who then decide between him and his persecutor; let a man's meadow and vineyard not be taken from him on the pretext of the public interest without generous compensation; let priests teach morality and not corrupt it; let them set nations an example instead of wishing to dominate them while they grow fat on the people's produce; let the law rule, not capricious impulse.

C

The human race is ready to put its name to all that.

Fourteenth conversation.
That every state must be independent

B

After having talked about the code of killing and poisoning in wartime, let's have a little look at what we'll do in peacetime.

First of all, how will states, whether republican or monarchical, be governed?

A

They will govern themselves, obviously, without depending for anything on any foreign power, unless these states are made up of idiots and cowards.

C

Thus it was very shameful for England to be under the suzerainty of a legate *a latere*, a legate *of the side*. Do you remember a certain comedian named Pandulf who made your King John kneel before him to receive from him the troth and homage of a liegeman, in the name of the Bishop of Rome, Innocent III, God's deputy, servant of God's servants, on the day before Holy Thursday, on 15 May 1213?

A

Yes, yes, we remember him so that we can treat this insolent servant as he deserves [to be treated].

B

For goodness sake, Mr C! Let's not give ourselves too many airs. There's not a single kingdom in Europe that the Bishop of Rome has not given away by virtue of his humble and holy power. God's deputy Stephanus took the Kingdom of France from Chilpericus to give it to his head servant, Pipinus, as your own Eginhard says, if the writings of this Eginhard have not been faked by monks, as so many other writings have, and as I suspect is the case here.

God's deputy Silvester gave Hungary to Duke Etienne in the year 1001 to please his wife Giselle, who had a lot of visions.

In 1247 God's deputy Innocent IV gave the Kingdom of Norway to a bastard named Haquin whom this same pope, exercising his full rights, declared legitimate, in return for fifteen thousand silver marks. And as those fifteen thousand silver marks were not to be had in Norway, it was necessary to borrow in order to pay.

For two whole centuries were the kings of Castile, Aragon and Portugal not required to pay an annual tribute of two pounds in gold to God's deputy? We know how many emperors have been deposed, forced to ask for pardon, or murdered or poisoned by virtue of a papal bull. I tell you, not only has the servant of God's servants given away, without exception, all the kingdoms in communion with Rome, but he has kept for himself the best and most useful land; there's no kingdom on which he has not levied tithes and tributes of all kinds.

He's still today suzerain of the Kingdom of Naples; liege-homage has been paid to him for seven hundred years. That descendant of so many sovereigns, the King of Naples, still pays him a tribute. Today the King of Naples is the only vassal-king; and whose vassal is he? For God's sake!

A

I advise him not to be for very long.

C

I'm always dumbfounded when I see the traces of ancient superstition still surviving. By what strange twist of fate did almost every prince for so many centuries run like this straight into the yoke presented to them?

B

There's a very natural explanation. Kings and barons could neither read nor write; the court of Rome could; that alone gave it a huge advantage, some trace of which it still retains.

C

And how could free princes and barons surrender in such a cowardly way to a few tricksters?

A

I can see quite clearly why. The roughnecks knew how to fight, and the tricksters knew how to rule; but when the barons learned how to read and write, when the leprosy of ignorance abated among magistrates and leading citizens, people looked the idol, before which they had licked dirt, straight in the face; instead of homage, half of Europe paid the servant of servants back with atrocity for atrocity. The other half, while still kissing his feet, tied his hands. At least, that's what I read in a history book which, although it's a contemporary work, is true and objective.[1] I'm sure that if tomorrow the King of Naples and Sicily wished to renounce this unique prerogative that he has of being the Pope's liegeman, of being the servant of the servant of God's servants, of giving him every year a little horse with two thousand gold *écus* round its neck, he would be applauded by the whole of Europe.

B

He has the right to do it, for it wasn't the Pope who gave him the kingdom of Naples. If Norman murderers, to dress up what they had usurped, and to be independent from the emperors to whom they paid homage, made themselves into oblates of the Holy Church, the King of the two Sicilies, a direct descendant of Hugh Capet and not of the Normans, is in no way obliged to be an oblate. He just needs the will.

---

[1] Voltaire is referring to his own *Age of Louis XIV*. See chapter 2.

Just one word from the King of France and the Pope would have no more credibility than [he has] in Russia. No more annates would be paid to Rome; permission would no longer be purchased there to marry your cousin or your niece. Take my word for it, those tribunals in France called *parlements* would register that edict without protest.

People don't know their strength. Fifty years ago whoever proposed getting rid of the Jesuits in so many Catholic states would have been considered one of the biggest dreamers around. That colossus had a foot in Rome and another in Paraguay; it embraced a thousand provinces and held its head high. Yet it passed away, and lo! it was not.[2]

You just need to puff on all the other monks, they will disappear from the surface of the earth.

A

It isn't our concern whether or not France has fewer monks and more men, but I do dislike the monk's cowl so much that I would prefer seeing variety shows in France rather than religious processions. In short, as a citizen, I don't like citizens who cease to be citizens, subjects who subject themselves to a foreigner, patriots with no more *homeland*. I want each state to be completely independent.

You said that men were blind for a long time, then deaf, and that they are starting to enjoy [seeing] with both eyes. Who do they have to thank for that? Five or six eye surgeons who came on the scene at various times.

B

Yes; but the terrible thing is that there are some blind men who want to fight the very surgeons eager to cure them.

A

Oh well! Let's give light only to those who ask us to remove their cataracts.

---

[2] Psalms, XXXVI.36.

Fifteenth conversation.
On the best legislation

C

Which of all the states is the one which seems to you to have the best laws, the legal system that accords best with the general good, and with the good of individuals?

A

My own country, without any doubt. The proof is that with all the differences between us we always speak highly of *our happy constitution*, and that in almost all other kingdoms people want a different one. Our criminal system is equitable and in no way barbarous: we have abolished torture, against which the voice of nature is raised in vain in so many other countries; this terrible means of making a weak, innocent man die and of saving a strong guilty one came to an end with our infamous Lord Chancellor Jeffries, who was happy to make use of this hellish practice in the reign of James II.

Every accused person is judged by his peers; he is only found guilty when they are unanimous; the law alone condemns him for the proven crime, and not the arbitrary sentences of judges. The death penalty is a straightforward death, and not a death accompanied by refined tortures. To stretch a man out on a Saint Andrew's cross, break his arms and thighs, and then to put him in that state on a carriage wheel, seems to us to be a barbarity too offensive to human nature. If, for crimes of high treason, you then tear out the heart of the culprit after he is dead, that is an old cannibal practice, an instrument of terror which horrifies the spectator, without hurting the person executed. We don't add torment to death; counsel is not refused the defendant, as is the case elsewhere; a witness who has testified without due consideration is not made to lie by being threatened with punishment if he retracts; witnesses are not heard in secret – that would make informers of them; the procedures are public: secret trials have only been the invention of tyrannies.

We don't have the idiotic barbarity of punishing indecent behaviour with the same penalty used for punishing parricide. That form of cruelty, as stupid as it is abominable, is unworthy of us.

In civil life, the only judge is the law; interpreting it is not permissible: that would amount to abandoning the fate of citizens to caprice, to favouritism and to hatred.

If the law cannot make provision for a particular case that comes up, then you appeal to the court of equity, before the Chancellor and his advisors; and if the case raises important issues, a new law is drafted in Parliament for the future, that is to say, with all the estates of the nation assembled.

Litigants never solicit their judges; that would amount to saying: I wish to seduce you. A judge who receives a visit from a litigant would be dishonoured; they don't seek that ridiculous honour that flatters bourgeois vanity. Thus they have not bought the right to judge: magistrates' positions are not sold in our country like the produce of a smallholding. If members of Parliament sell their votes now and again to the Court, they are like those beauties who sell their favours, and don't tell. In our country the law ordains that nothing but land and the produce of the land will be sold; whereas in France the law itself fixes the price of counsellor appointments to the King's Bench that is called *parlement*, and appointments to the presidencies of High Courts called *presidencies with mortar*. Almost all official positions and honours are sold in France, as herbs [are sold] at market. The Chancellor of France is often drawn from the ranks of counsellors of state; but in order to be a counsellor of state, you have to have bought an appointment as master of the rolls. A regiment is not a reward for service; it's the reward that comes from a sum of money that a young man's parents have deposited so that he can go and keep an open house for three months of the year in some town in the provinces.

You see clearly how happy we are to have laws that protect us from such abuses. At home there is nothing arbitrary except for the pardons that the King might wish to grant. Blessings emanate from him; the law does the rest.

If authority trespasses illegally on the freedom of the least important of citizens, then the law avenges him; the minister has to pay an immediate fine to the citizen, and he pays it.

Add to all these advantages the right of every man among us to speak to the entire nation through his pen. The admirable art of printing is as free as talking in our island. How can you not like such a system of law?

It's true that we always have two parties, but they keep the nation on guard, rather than dividing it. These two parties keep watch on each other, and compete for the honour of being the guardians of public freedom. We do have our quarrels, but we always bless this happy constitution that brings them about.

C

Your system of government is a fine creation, but it's fragile.

A

We give it some hard blows sometimes, but we don't break it.

B

Preserve this precious monument built with intelligence and courage: it has cost you too much for you to allow it to be destroyed. Man was born free: the best form of government is the one that preserves this gift of nature for each mortal as far as possible.

But look here, sort things out with your colonies, and don't let a mother and her daughters come to blows.

Sixteenth conversation.
On abuses

C

People say that the world is ruled only by abuses; is that true?

B

I think that in the civilised nations half is abuse and half tolerable practice, half unhappiness and half good fortune, just as at sea you find over the year a fairly equal distribution of storms and fine weather. That's what caused the two barrels of Jupiter and the Manichean sect to be dreamed up.

A

Why of course! If Jupiter had two barrels, the barrel of evil was a Heidelberg cask;[1] the barrel of good was barely a quarter-cask. There are so many abuses in this world that when I was in Paris in 1751 appeals against abuses were made six times a week throughout the year to the King's Bench they call the *parlement*.

B

Yes, but to whom shall we appeal against the abuses that reign supreme in the way the world is run?

[1] A cask holding the equivalent of a hundred barrels.

Isn't it an enormous abuse that all animals kill each other with savage eagerness to feed themselves, and that men kill each other with much greater ferocity without the thought of eating each other even occurring to them?

C

Oh! Excuse me. We did once make war in order to eat each other; but in the long run all good institutions degenerate.

B

I read in one book[2] that on average we have only twenty-two years to live; that of those twenty-two years, if you take out the time lost in sleep and the time lost awake, hardly fifteen years are left; that of these fifteen years you must exclude childhood, which is just a transition from nothingness to a state of being; and that if you take away the body's sufferings and the torments of what is called the soul, that leaves only three years free for the happiest among us, and barely six months for the rest. Isn't that an intolerable abuse?

A

Eh? What the devil are you getting at? Will you command nature to be organised in a different way?

B

I would wish it so, at least.

A

That's a sure way of shortening your life even more.

C

Let's leave aside the blunders made by nature: children are often conceived in the womb only to die there and kill their mothers; the

[2] *LHQE*

176

source of life poisoned by a venom passed on from hole to hole-plugger, from America to Europe; smallpox which decimates the human race; plague, still surviving in Africa; the poisons covering the earth that are so easily self-generating, while wheat can only be grown with incredible difficulty. Let's just talk about the abuses that we've introduced ourselves.

B

That would be a long list in a society so perfect as ours, for leaving aside the art of regularly murdering the human race through war, which we've already discussed, we have the art of snatching the food and clothing away from those who sow the corn and process the wool; the art of amassing a whole nation's treasure in the money coffers of five or six hundred people; the art of killing in public with full cere-mony, on the authority of half a sheet of paper, people who displease, like the wife of a Field-Marshal d'Ancre, a Field-Marshal Marillac, a Duke of Somerset, a Mary Stuart; the practice of preparing a man for death through torture in order to find out who his associates are, when he couldn't possibly have had any; the burnings at the stake, the sharpened daggers, the scaffolds erected to settle obscure, incom-prehensible arguments; half the nation continually engaged in the loyal harassment of the other half. I could speak for longer than Esdras, if I wanted to put all our abuses on the record.

A

That's all true; but you must agree that most of these horrible abuses have been abolished in England, and are beginning to be mitigated in other countries.

B

Agreed; but why are men better and a little less unhappy than they were in the time of Alexander VI, the Saint Bartholomew Day mas-sacre, and Cromwell?

C

That's because people are starting to think, to become enlightened and to write well.

A

I agree; superstition raises storms, and rational thinking abates them.

Seventeenth conversation.
On curious matters

B

By the way, Mr A, do think the world is very old?

A

Mr B, I imagine it's eternal.

B

That can be supported by means of hypothesis. All the ancient philosophers believed that matter was eternal. Now there's only one small step from raw matter to organised matter.

C

Hypotheses are very amusing. They're of no importance. They're dreams that the Bible dispels, for we must always come back to the Bible.

A

Certainly, and in this year of grace 1760 all three of us believe sincerely, don't we, that from the creation of the world, that was made out of nothing, to the Great Flood, made with water created specially for the purpose, 1656 years passed according to the *Vulgate*, 2309

according to the Samaritan text, and 2262 according to that miraculous translation that we call the Septuagint version. But I've always
been surprised that Adam and Eve, our father and mother, Abel,
Cain and Seth, were unknown to everyone else in the world except
for the little horde of Jews, who kept the matter secret until the Jews
of Alexandria, in the reign of Ptolemy I and Ptolemy II, took it upon
themselves to translate their absurdities into very bad Greek, which
were totally unknown to the rest of the world until then.

It's funny that our family's title-deeds should have been deposited
only with one branch of our house and, what's more, with the most
despised [branch], while the Chinese, the Indians, the Persians, the
Egyptians, the Greeks and the Romans had never heard of either
Adam or Eve.

B

There's worse to come: Sanchoniathon, who unquestionably lived
before the time in which we locate Moses, and who created his own
version of Genesis, as did so many others, speaks neither of Adam
nor Eve. He gives us quite different parents.

C

On what do you base your judgement that Sanchoniathon lived before
the time of Moses, Mr B?

B

It's just that if he had lived in the time of Moses, or after him, he
would have mentioned him. He was writing in Tyre, which flourished
long before the Jewish horde had acquired a bit of land near Phoenicia. The Phoenician language was the country's mother tongue; the
Phoenicians had been cultivating the arts for some time. Jewish books
acknowledge this in several places. It's said explicitly that Caleb took
possession of the city of letters, called Kirjath-sepher, that is, *City of
Books*, later called Debir. Sanchoniathon would have certainly spoken
of Moses, had he been his contemporary or younger brother. It's not
natural for him to have omitted from his history the fantabulous
adventures of Moshe or Moses, such as the ten plagues of Egypt,

and the waters of the Red Sea suspended in mid-air to the right and to the left in order to let three million fleeing thieves through without getting their feet wet, and those same waters then falling down again on millions of other men pursuing the thieves. Those are not obscure little everyday banalities that a serious historian would pass over in silence. Sanchoniathon does not mention the miraculous feats of *Gargantua*. Thus he knew nothing about them; thus he lived before Moses, as did Job, who doesn't speak of him. Eusibius, his abridger, would not have failed to have availed himself of such brilliant evidence.

A

That reasoning is irrefutable. In earlier times no nation spoke of the Jews, nor did any speak like the Jews; none had a cosmogony that had the slightest relation to that of the Jews. These wretched Jews came on the scene so recently that they didn't even have in their language a name to signify God. They were forced to borrow the name Adonai from the Sidonians, and the name Jehovah or Iao from the Syrians. Their obstinacy, their new superstitions, their time-honoured usury, are the only things that belong to them, properly speaking. And it seems highly likely that these rascals, to whom the words *geometry* and *astronomy* were totally unknown, only finally learned to read and write when they became slaves in Babylon. It has already been proved that it was there that they learned the names of the angels, and even the name Israel, as that Jewish turncoat Flavius Josephus himself acknowledges.

C

What! Do all ancient peoples have origins going back further than those of the Jews, and origins [that are] completely different?

A

Beyond any doubt. Look at the *Shasta* and the *Veidam* of the Indians, the *Five Kings* of the Chinese, the *Zen* of the early Persians, the *Theaetetus* or *Mercury Trismegistus* of the Egyptians. To them Adam was as unknown as the ancestors of so many of the marquises and barons who swarm over Europe.

C

No Adam! That's really sad. All our almanachs are calculated from Adam's time.

A

I don't care how they are calculated; the *pretty Christmas-boxes* are not my archives.

B

So are we to assume that Mr A is pre-Adamite?

A

I'm pre-Saturnian, pre-Osirite, pre-Abrahamite, pre-Pandorite.

C

And what do you base your fine hypothesis of an eternal world on?

A

To explain it to you, you must listen patiently to a few little preliminaries:

I don't know whether we've argued well or badly so far; but I do know that we've argued, and that all three of us are intelligent beings. Now, intelligent beings can't have been created by a brutish, blind insensitive being. There's certainly some difference between Newton's ideas and donkey droppings. Newton's intelligence came therefore from another intelligence.

When we see a wonderful machine, we say there's a good machine-designer, and that this machine-designer has an excellent brain. The world is certainly an excellent machine, so somewhere or other there's an excellent intelligence behind it. This is an old argument, but none the worse for that.

All living bodies consist of levers and pulleys that work in accordance with the laws of mechanics, fluids that are continually circulated by the laws of hydrostatics; and when one thinks that all these beings have feelings that are entirely separate from their physical make-up, one is astonished.

The movement of the planets, that of our little earth around the sun, everything works by virtue of the laws of higher mathematics. How is it that Plato, who didn't know a single one of these laws, Plato the dreamer, who said that the land rested on an equilateral triangle and water on a right-angled triangle, that ridiculous Plato who said that there could only be five worlds, because there are only five regular forms, how, I repeat, could the ignorant Plato, who didn't even know about spherical trigonometry, have nevertheless the sharpness of mind, the happy instinct, to call God the *Eternal Geometer*, to sense that a creative intelligence existed?

B

I once amused myself by reading Plato. We clearly owe him the whole of Christian metaphysics; all the Greek fathers were unquestionably Platonists; but what's that got to do with the eternity of the world that you were talking about?

A

Let's take it step by step, please. There's an intelligence which animates the world; Spinoza himself acknowledged it. It's impossible to argue against that truth which surrounds us, and presses [in] on us from all sides.

C

But I've known awkward people who say that there's no creative intelligence, and that movement alone has created everything we see and everything we are. They'll tell you bluntly: The arrangement of the universe was possible, since it exists; thus it's possible that movement alone arranged it. Just take four planets, Mars, Venus, Mercury and Earth; let's just think about their position first of all, putting everything else to one side, and let's see how high the probability is for movement alone to have put them in their respective positions. We have only twenty-four possibilities for this arrangement, that is to say, there are only odds of twenty-four to one that those planets could be where they are in relation to each other. Add Jupiter to those four planets: there will only be odds of a hundred and twenty to one that Jupiter, Mars, Venus, Mercury and our planet would be positioned as we see them.

Finally, add Saturn: there will only be odds of seven hundred and twenty to one for those six huge planets to be placed a set distance apart in the relative positions they maintain. It is thus demonstrated that in seven hundred and twenty throws of the dice, movement alone could line these major planets up in their order.

Then take all the secondary planets, all their combinations, all their movements, all the beings that vegetate, live, feel, think, act on all those planets, you only have to increase the odds; if you multiply that number through eternity, up to the number that our limited minds call *infinity*, you will always have a calculation that favours movement alone having created the world as we know it. Thus it's possible that through all eternity the movement of matter alone could have produced the entire universe as we know it. That's how these gentlemen argue.

A

Excuse me, C, my dear friend. This theory seems to me to be grotesque and ridiculous for two reasons: the first is because in this universe there are intelligent beings, and that you cannot prove that movement alone can produce intelligence. The second is that, as you yourself acknowledge, the odds are infinity to one that an intelligent creative cause animates the universe. When you're one against infinity, you're in a really bad way.

And again, Spinoza himself admits the possibility of this intelligence. Why do you want to go further than he did, and through foolish pride let your feeble mind plunge down an abyss into which Spinoza did not dare to fall? Do you not sense the utter madness of saying that a blind force causes the square of a planet's revolution always to be the square of the revolutions of other planets, as the cubed root of its distance is to the cubed root of the distance of the others to a common [central] point? Friends, either the planets are great geometers, or the planets have been arranged by the eternal geometer.

C

No insults, please. Spinoza didn't say on this issue that it's easier to insult than it is to reason. I agree with you that there is a creative intelligence abroad in this world; I will gladly say with Virgil:

> Mens agitat molem et magno se corpore miscet.[1]

I'm not one of those people who say that planets, men, animals, vegetation [and] thought are the effects of the throws of a dice.

A

I'm sorry for getting angry; I was feeling depressed; but I was none the less right for all that.

B

Let's get to the point without anger. How, by admitting the existence of a God, can you support the hypothesis that the world is eternal?

A

In the same way that I support by proposition that the sun's rays are as old as this planet.

C

That's a funny idea! What! Dungheaps, bachelors of theology, fleas, monkeys and ourselves, we're all emanations of the Divinity?

[1] Virgil, *Aeneid*, VI.727.

A

The divine is certainly present in a flea: it can jump fifty times its height; it did not give itself that advantage.

B

What! Fleas have existed throughout all eternity?

A

Necessarily so, since they exist today, existed yesterday, and there's no reason to think that they haven't always existed. For if they serve no useful purpose, they ought never to exist, and as soon as a species exists it's impossible to prove that it hasn't always existed. Would you wish the eternal geometer to have been in a dumb trance for the whole of eternity? It's not worth the bother of being a geometer and an architect just to spend eternity without arranging and building things. It's of his nature to create; since he has created, he necessarily exists; thus everything that is in him is a necessary part of his essence. You cannot strip a being of its essence, because then it would cease to exist. God is active, therefore he has always been active; thus the world emanates eternally from him; thus whoever accepts the existence of a God must accept the notion of an eternal world. Light rays have been coming from the sun through all eternity, and all the patterns of the universe have been coming from the Great Pattern-Maker throughout all eternity. Man, the snake, the spider, the oyster [and] the snail have always existed, because they were possible.

B

What! You believe that the Demi-Ourgos, the power of creation, the Great Being, has created everything that there was to create?

A

I imagine that's how it was. Otherwise, he would not have been a being who was necessarily creative. You would turn him into an ineffective or lazy workman who had worked only on a small part of his creation.

C

What! Is it likely that other worlds are impossible?

A

That could well be the case. Otherwise we would have an eternal, necessary cause, active by nature, which, being capable of creating them, would not have created them; now such a cause without an effect seems as absurd to me as an effect without a cause.

C

But many people say, however, that this eternal cause has chosen this world from all other possible worlds.

A

They don't seem to be possible, if they don't exist. Those gentlemen might just as well have said that God made a choice from all impossible worlds. The eternal craftsman would have arranged these possible worlds in space. There's enough room to spare there. Why, for example, did the universal, eternal, necessary mind that presides over this world reject the notion of a world without poisonous vegetation, without the pox, without scurvy, without the plague, and without the Inquisition? It's quite possible that such a world exists; it must seem better than ours to the great Demi-Ourgos; however, we have got the worse one. To say that this perfect world is possible, and that he didn't give it to us, is to say unquestionably that he is neither rational, nor benevolent nor powerful; now that's what you just can't say; so if he hasn't given us this perfect world, it would appear that it wasn't possible to create it.

B

And who told you that this world doesn't exist? It's probably on one of the planets circling Sirius, or Canis minor or in the eye of Taurus, the Bull.

A

In that case, we agree; the supreme intelligence has done all that it was possible for him to do; and I stick to my idea that things that don't exist cannot exist.

C

So the theory is then that space is full of planets that all enter into perfect existence one after the other; and that we have necessarily [drawn] one of the poorest prizes. That's a wonderful concept, but not a very consoling one.

B

So in the end you think that everything that exists emanates necessarily from this eternal creative power, from the universal mind, in a word, from the Great Being?

A

It looks like it to me.

B

But in that case, was the Great Being free?

A

Freedom, as I've told you a hundred times in other conversations, is power. He had power, and he acted. I cannot conceive of any other sort of freedom. Freedom in neutral isolation is a word with no meaning, you know.

B

In all conscience, are you really sure of your system?

A

Me! I'm sure of nothing! I believe that there's an intelligent being, a creative force, a God. On everything else I'm feeling my way in the darkness. I give my support to an idea one day, and have doubts about it the next; and every day I could be making a mistake. All philosophers of good faith I have seen have confessed to me, after a few glasses of wine, that the Great Being hasn't provided them with a scrap of evidence stronger than mine.

Do you think that Epicurus always had a very clear view of his variation theory of atoms, that Descartes was fully persuaded by his theory of striated matter? Believe me, Leibnitz laughed at his monads and his theory of pre-established harmony. Telliamed[2] laughed at his theory of mountains made by the sea. The author who wrote about organic molecules is wise and honourable enough to laugh about it. Two augurs laugh like mad when they meet, as you know.[3] There's only the Irish Jesuit Needham who doesn't laugh at all at his eels.

B

It's true that when it comes to systems you must always reserve the right to laugh tomorrow at the ideas you had the night before.

C

I'm very pleased to have found an old English philosopher who can laugh after getting angry, and who believes sincerely in God. That's very edifying.

A

Yes, by Heaven! I believe in God, and I've a firmer belief in him than the Universities of Oxford and Cambridge, and all the priests in my country, for all those people have closed ranks somewhat in wanting people to have adored God only for about the last six thousand years, and I want them to have adored him throughout eternity.

[2] De Maillet spelt backwards.
[3] Cicero, *De natura deorum* (Of the nature of the gods), I, line 26.

I know of no master without servants, no king without subjects, no father without children, no cause without effect.

C

Alright, we agree. But look, put your hand on your heart: do you believe in a God of Vengeance and Retribution, who hands out prizes and penalties to creatures who have emanated from him, and who necessarily are in his hands like clay in the hands of a potter?

Don't you find it quite absurd for Jupiter to have kicked Vulcan out of Heaven and down on to Earth because Vulcan had a bad limp. I know of nothing more unjust. Now the eternal Supreme Intelligence must be just; eternal love must cherish its children, spare them kicks, and not throw them out of the house for having itself caused them to be born with bad legs.

A

I'm familiar with everything that's been said on this abstruse question, and I'm not much concerned by it. I want my attorney, my tailor, my servants, even my wife, to believe in God, and I fancy that as a result I shall suffer from less theft and less cuckoldry.

C

You're making fun of people. I know of twenty devout ladies who have given their husbands heirs that don't belong to them.

A

And I've known just one whom the fear of God restrained, and that's enough for me. Come on! Are you of the opinion that your twenty sluts would have been more faithful had they been atheists? In short, all civilised nations have accepted gods of vengeance and retribution, and I'm a citizen of the world.

B

Well done; but wouldn't it have been preferable for the creative intelligence to have had nothing to punish? And, what's more, when and by what means will it punish?

A

I haven't any idea, myself; but again, you mustn't shake loose a concept that is so useful to the human race. I'll concede you all the rest. I'll concede you my eternal world theory even, if you insist, although I'm very keen on that system. After all, what does it matter to us whether the world is eternal, or whether it dates from the day before yesterday? Let's live peacefully in it, let's adore God, let's be just and let's do good: that's the essential thing, that's the conclusion to every argument. Let intolerant barbarians be detested by the human race, and let everyone think what he wants!

C

Amen. Let's raise our glasses, rejoice and bless the Great Being.

Other writings

Republican ideas.
By a member of a public body

I

Pure despotism is the punishment for men's bad behaviour. If a community is governed by a single person or by several, that is clearly because it has not had either the courage or the skill to govern itself.

II

A society of men governed arbitrarily resembles perfectly a herd of cattle yoked in the service of a master. He feeds them only so that they are in a condition to serve him; he only tends them when they are ill so that in [good] health they will be useful to him; he fattens them up so that he can obtain nourishment from what their bodies produce; he uses the skins of some to harness others to the plough.

III

Thus a nation is subjugated either by a skillful fellow-countryman, who has profited from its stupidity or divisiveness, or by a thief, known as a conqueror who, with other thieves, has taken possession of its territory, killed those who resisted, and made slaves of the cowards he allows to live.

IV

This thief, who deserves to be broken on the wheel, sometimes has altars built to himself. The enslaved nation has seen in the thief's children a race of gods; they have viewed any questioning of their authority as blasphemy, and the slightest attempt to gain freedom as sacrilege.

V

The most absurd of all despotisms, the most humiliating for human nature, the most contradictory and lethal, is that of priests; and of all the priestly empires, that of the priests of the Christian religion is without a doubt the most criminal. It is an affront to our Gospels, for Jesus said in twenty places: 'But many that are first shall be last; my kingdom is not of this world; the son of man came not to be served, but to serve etc.'[1]

VI

When our bishop, made to serve and not to be served, made to give relief to the poor and not to devour all they have, made to teach the catechism and not to rule, dared in times of anarchy to give himself the title of prince over a town for which he was just the pastor, he was obviously guilty of rebellion and tyranny.

VII

In this way, the bishops of Rome, who were the first to set this fatal example, made their rule and simultaneously their sect into something ugly throughout half of Europe; in this way several bishops in Germany sometimes became the oppressors of peoples to which they should have been a father.

VIII

Why is it in man's nature to be more horrified by those who have subjugated us by trickery than by those who have enslaved us by force of arms? It is because at least tyrants who have subdued men have shown some courage, and those who have deceived them have shown only despicable cowardice. The valour of conquerors is hated,

---

[1] Mark, x.31; John, xviii.36; Matthew, xx.28.

but respected; people hate imposture, and despise it. Hatred added to contempt makes all kinds of yokes shake.

IX

When we have destroyed in our city some papist superstitions like the worship of corpses, the tax on sins, the affront to God of remitting for money the penalties by which God deters crime, and so many other inventions that stupefy human nature; when, by throwing off the yoke of these monstrous errors we have sent the papist bishop who dared to call himself our sovereign packing,[2] all we have done is to re-establish the rights of reason and freedom of which we have been deprived.

X

We have taken up municipal government again such as it was more or less under the Romans, and it has been given lustre and solidity by that freedom bought with our blood. We have never known that odious and humiliating distinction between nobles and commoners, which meant originally lords and slaves. Having all been born equal, we have remained so; we have given honours, that is to say burdens of public duty, to those who seem to us the most suitable to hold them.

XI

We have set these priests up so that they are no more than what they should be: teachers of morality to our children. These teachers must be paid and accorded respect, but they must not have any claim to law-making, inquisitorial functions or to honours; in no case must they place themselves on the same footing as magistrates. An ecclesiastical assembly that presumed to make a citizen kneel before it[3] would play either the role of a pedant correcting children, or a tyrant punishing slaves.

---

[2] The reference is to the expulsion from Geneva of Pierre de La Baume in 1534.
[3] Robert Covelle.

XII

It is an insult to reason and to the law to say these words: *civil and ecclesiastical government.* You must say *civil government and ecclesiastical regulations*; and none of these *regulations* must be made by anything other than the civil authorities.

XIII

Civil government is the will of all, carried out by a single person or by several persons, in accordance with laws that have been made by all.

XIV

The laws pertaining to the constitution of governments are all made to counter ambition; everywhere people have given thought to erecting dams to hold back the torrents that would engulf the world. Thus, in republics, the primary laws regulate the rights of each public body; thus kings, when they are crowned, swear to protect the rights of their subjects. In Europe there is only the King of Denmark who is above the law, by virtue of the law itself. The meeting of the estates-general in 1660 declared him to be the absolute sovereign arbiter. It seems that they foresaw that Denmark would have wise and just kings for more than a century. Perhaps in later centuries it will be necessary to change that law.

XV

Some theologians have claimed that popes possessed, through divine right, the same power over the whole world that Danish monarchs have over a small piece of territory; but then they are theologians ... ; the world has booed them loudly, and the Capitol muttered darkly at the sight of Hildebrand the monk speaking as a ruler in that sanctum of the laws where the Catos, Scipios and Ciceros used to speak as citizens.

XVI

Everywhere the laws concerning distributive justice, jurisprudence to put it properly, have been inadequate, equivocal, uncertain, because the men who were heads of state have always been more concerned about their private interest than about the public interest. In the twelve great courts of France there are a dozen different judicial systems. What is true in Aragon becomes false in Castillon; what is just on the banks of the Danube is unjust on the banks of the Elba. Roman laws themselves, to which today all courts lay claim, have sometimes been contradictory.

XVII

When a law is obscure, everyone has to interpret it, because everyone has passed it; unless they have appointed *a few* [men] with the express purpose of interpreting laws.

XVIII

When times have palpably changed, there are laws that have to be changed. Thus, when Triptolemus brought the plough into use in Athens, it was necessary to abolish the corn regulations. In those times, when academies were made up only of priests, and when they alone knew the jargon of science, it was acceptable for them alone to appoint professors: it was the corn regulations all over again; but today, now that the laity are enlightened, the civil authorities must resume their right to appoint to all chairs.

XIX

The law permitting the imprisonment of a citizen without preliminary investigation and without judicial formalities would be tolerable in times of disturbance and war; in peacetime it would be iniquitous and tyrannical.

XX

A sumptuary law, that is good in a poor republic bereft of the arts, becomes absurd when the city has become busy and opulent. It means depriving artists of the legitimate profits to be made from the rich; it means depriving those who have made their fortunes of the natural right to enjoy them; it means stifling all industry; it means frustrating the rich and the poor [alike].

XXI

The clothing of the rich man must be regulated no more than the rags of the poor man. Both, who are equally citizens, must be equally free. Everyone dresses himself, feeds himself, and houses himself as best he can. If you forbid the rich man to eat grouse, you are robbing the poor man who would be keeping his family on the cost of the fowl that he sells to the rich man. If you do not want the rich man to make his house more ornate, you ruin a hundred artists. The citizen who humiliates the poor man by his ostentatious wealth enriches the poor man much more than he humiliates him by means of that very same wealth. Poverty must work for opulence in order one day to be its equal.

XXII

A Roman law which had said to Lucullus: Spend nothing, would in effect have said to Lucullus: Become even richer so that your grandson can buy the republic.

XXIII

The sumptuary laws can only please the idle, haughty, jealous pauper who wants neither to work nor to allow those who do work to enjoy the benefits of it.

XXIV

If a republic has been created during a time of religious war, if during these troubles it has removed sects that are hostile to its own from its territory, it has behaved wisely, because it saw itself at the time as a country surrounded by those stricken with plague, and feared that someone might bring the plague in. But when those dizzy times have passed, when tolerance has become the dominant dogma of all respectable people in Europe, is it not a ridiculous barbarity to ask a man who has just settled in our country and brought his wealth to it: 'What religion do you belong to?' Gold and silver, industry and talents do not belong to any religion.

XXV

In a republic worthy of the name, the freedom to publish one's thoughts is the natural right of the citizen. He can use his pen as he uses his voice; he must no more be forbidden to write than to speak, and crimes committed with the pen should be punished in the same way as crimes committed by word of mouth. Such is the law of England, a monarchical country, but one where men are freer than elsewhere because they are more enlightened.

XXVI

Of all republics it would seem that the smallest must be the happiest when its freedom is assured by its location, and when it is in the interests of its neighbours to preserve it. The mechanism is apparently simpler and more regular in a small machine than in a large one whose springs are more complicated, and where a more violent friction interferes with its running. But as pride enters everybody's mind; as the craze to lord it over one's equals is the dominating passion of the human mind; as, when seeing each other at closer quarters, people can hate each other more, it sometimes happens that a small state is more troubled than a large one.

XXVII

What is the cure for this evil? Reason, which makes itself heard in the end, when the passions are weary of shouting. Then the two sides back off a little for fear of something worse; but time is needed.

XXVIII

In a small republic it seems that the people must be listened to more than in a large one because it is easier to make a thousand people assembled together listen to reason than forty thousand. Thus it would have been very dangerous to wish to rule Venice, which had waged war for so long against the Ottoman Empire, like Saint Martin, who had only ever been able to conquer a mill, that it was forced to surrender.

XXIX

It seems very strange that the author of the *Social contract* should take it upon himself to say that the whole English nation should have a seat in Parliament, and that it stops being free when its right consists of having itself represented in Parliament by deputies. Would he like three million citizens to come and vote at Westminster? Are the peasants of Sweden represented in any other way except by deputies?

XXX

It is said in this same *Social contract* that 'monarchy is suitable only for very rich nations; aristocracy for states of modest wealth and size; democracy for small, poor states'.

But in the fourteenth and fifteenth centuries, and at the start of the sixteenth, the Venetians were the only rich nation; they still have a lot of wealth; however, Venice has never been, and never will be, a monarchy. The Roman Republic was very rich from the time of Scipio down to Caesar. Lucca is small and not very rich; opulent and clever Athens was a democratic state.

We have very rich citizens, and we make up our government out of a mixture of democracy and aristocracy. Thus we must beware of all of these general rules which only owe their existence to writers' pens.

XXXI

The same writer, speaking of different systems of government, expresses himself thus: 'One person finds it admirable to be feared by one's neighbours; another prefers to be unknown to them. One person is happy when money circulates; another demands that the people should have bread.'

The whole of this article seems to be puerile and contradictory. How can one be unknown to one's neighbours? How are you safe if your neighbours do not know that there is danger in attacking you? And how can this very same state which could make itself feared be unknown? And how can the people have bread without money circulating? The contradiction is obvious.

XXXII

'At that moment when the people are legally assembled in a sovereign body, the whole jurisdiction of the government ceases, executive power is suspended' etc. This proposition from the *Social contract* would be pernicious, if it were not so obviously false and absurd. When Parliament assembles in England, no jurisdiction is suspended; and in the smallest state, if, while the assembly is sitting, a murder or a robbery is committed, the criminal is, and must be, handed over to law officers. Otherwise, an assembly of the people would be a solemn invitation to commit crimes.

XXXIII

'In a state that is truly free, the citizens do everything with their hands, and nothing with money.' This thesis from the *Social contract* is just foolish. A bridge is to be built, a road is to be paved; will it be necessary for magistrates, businessmen and priests to pave the road and build the bridge? For sure, the author would not want to cross a bridge built by their hands. This is an idea worthy of a teacher who, with a young gentleman to bring up, teaches him the trade of carpentry. But not every man should be a manual worker.

XXXIV

'The trustees of executive power are not the people's masters, but their officials . . . ; it can appoint them and remove them from office when it pleases; for them it is a question not of contract, but of obedience.'

It is true that magistrates are not the masters of the people: the law is master; but the rest is absolutely wrong; it is wrong in all states, and it is wrong in your own. When we are convened, we have the right to reject or approve the magistrates and laws that are proposed to us; we do not have the right to remove state officials from office *when we please*; that right would be part of the code of anarchy. The King of France himself, when he has commissioned a magistrate, cannot remove him from office other than by putting him on trial. The King of England cannot take away a meadow that he has given to someone. The Emperor cannot dismiss a prince whom he has created *when he pleases*. Magistrates, whose commission can be revoked, can only be removed from office after their period of service [has ended]. It is no more permissible to demote a magistrate at whim than to imprison a citizen as the fancy takes you.

XXXV

'It is a mistake to consider the government of Venice to be a true aristocracy. It may be true that the people have no part in government there, but there the aristocracy itself is the people. A crowd of poor barnabites never got [anywhere] near any magistracy.'

All that is revolting error. That is the first time that anyone has said that the government of Venice was not entirely aristocratic. In truth, it is a foolish statement, but it would be severely punished in the Venetian state. It is wrong to say that the senators, whom the author dares to call contemptuously barnabites, have never been magistrates. I could cite more than fifty who have held the most important positions.

What he then says is no more true, namely that: 'our peasants represent the mainland subjects of the Venetian Republic'. Among these mainland subjects there are in Verona, in Vicenza, in Brescia, and in many other towns, titled lords of the most ancient nobility, several of whom have commanded armies.

So much ignorance, coupled with so much presumptuousness, is an affront to every educated man. When this presumptuous ignorance treats noble Venetians so outrageously, one asks who is the potentate who has forgotten himself like this? When you finally learn who the author of these follies is, you just laugh.

XXXVI

'Those who succeed in monarchies are more often than not merely petty muddlers, petty rogues, or petty plotters, whose petty talents, which make for promotion to high office in court life, only serve to reveal to the public their ineptitude once they have achieved office.'

This indecent heap of cynical antitheses is in no way appropriate in a book on government, which ought to be written with wisdom and dignity. When a man, whoever he might be, thinks enough of himself to give lessons on public administration, he must give the appearance of good sense and impartiality, like the laws themselves which he is invoking.

We recognise with some distress that in republics as well as monarchies, plotting succeeds where official appointments are concerned. There were people like Verres, Milo, Clodius and Lepidus in Rome; but we are compelled to accept that no modern republic can pride itself on having produced ministers like Oxenstiern, Sully, Colbert and the great men chosen by Elizabeth of England. Let us not insult either monarchies or republics.

XXXVII

'Czar Peter did not have true genius, genius that creates and makes something of nothing. A few of the things that he did were fine; most were misplaced ... His subjects or neighbours, the Tartars, will become his masters and ours; this revolution seems to me to be a certainty.'

It seems certain to him that wretched hordes of Tartars, who have sunk to their lowest point, will subjugate in the near future an empire defended by two hundred thousand soldiers who are among the best troops in Europe. Has the fortune-teller's column in the *Old Moore's almanach* ever made predictions like that? The Court at Saint Petersburg will consider us great astrologers if it learns that one of our apprentice clockmakers has set the hour at which the Russian Empire is to be destroyed.

XXXVIII

If you trouble yourself to read carefully this book on the *Social contract*, there will not be a single page on which you will not find mistakes or contradictions. For example, in the chapter on civil religion: 'Two peoples, always alien and hostile to each other, could never recognise the same god; two armies fighting a battle could never obey the same commander. Thus from national divisions results polytheism, and from that religious and civil intolerance, which is of course the same thing.'

So many words, so many errors: The Greeks, the Romans, the peoples of Greater Greece recognised the same gods while waging war on each other; they all adored the gods *majorum gentium*, Jupiter, Juno, Mars, Minerva, Mercury, etc. Christians, when they wage war on each other, worship the same god. The polytheism of the Greeks and the Romans did not result from their wars at all: they were all polytheists before they had anything between them to settle; lastly, in their countries there was never civil or religious intolerance.

XXXIX

'A society of true Christians would no longer be a society of men', etc. Such an assertion is very strange. Does the author mean that it would be a society of animals or a society of angels? Bayle has treated in some depth the question of whether the Christians of the early Church could have been philosophers, politicians and warriors. This issue is a little futile. People want to go one better than Bayle; they repeat what he said; and for fear of being just plagiarists, they use foolhardy terms which basically mean nothing. For whatever beliefs nations have, they will always wage war.

This book has been burned in our country. The process of burning it has perhaps been as odious as that of composing it. There are things that a wise administration will ignore. If this book was dangerous, it had to be refuted. Burning a book containing reasoned arguments is to say: We have not got enough sense to answer it. The books that should be burned are slanderous books whose authors should be punished severely, because slander is a crime. A bad argument is only a crime when it is clearly seditious.

XL

A court must have fixed laws for the criminal code as for the civil code. Nothing must be arbitrary, and even less so when it is a matter of honour and life than when the issue is simply about money.

XLI

A criminal code is absolutely necessary for citizens and for magistrates. Citizens will then never have anything to complain about with regard to sentences, and magistrates will have nothing to fear from incurring hatred, because sentences will not be the result of their will, but of the law. One power is needed to pass judgement by that law alone, and another to grant mercy.

XLII

With regard to finance, it is a commonplace that it is up to the citizens to rule on what they think they should contribute to the expenses of the State; it is a commonplace that this contribution should be managed efficiently by those who administer it, and bestowed in noble style on grand occasions. On this point there is no cause to reproach our republic at all.

XLIII

There has never been a perfect government, because men have passions; and if they did not have passions, there would be no need for government. The most tolerable of all systems is undoubtedly the republican one, because that is the one which brings men closer to a state of natural equality. Every father must be master in his own house, and not in his neighbour's. As a society is made up of several houses and of several pieces of land attached to them, it is a contradiction for one man to be the master of all those houses and all those pieces of land; and it is in nature for each master to have a vote for the good of society.

XLIV

Should those without land or house in that society be able to vote? They have no more right to that than a clerk paid by merchants has in the running of their business; but they can be honorary members, either for having given service, or for having paid for their membership.

XLV

That country, governed on a common basis, should be richer and more populated than if it were governed by a master; for each person, in a true republic, secure in his property, his possessions and his person, works confidently for himself, and by improving his own condition improves that of the public as a whole. Under one master the contrary can happen. Sometimes a man can be taken completely by surprise to hear that neither his person nor his property belong to him.

XLVI

A Protestant republic should be a twelfth richer, more industrious, more populated than a papist one, assuming that they have an equal amount of equally good territory, by reason of the fact that there are thirty feast days in a papist country, consisting of thirty days of idleness and debauchery; and thirty days are a twelfth of the year. If in this papist country there is a twelfth of the priests, of the apprentice-priests, of the monks and of the nuns, as in Cologne, it is obvious that a protestant country of similar size must have a population that is a twelfth as big again.

XLVII

The accounts of the Treasury in the Low Countries, located at present in Lille, record that Philip II did not get eighty thousand *écus* from the seven United Provinces; and according to a revenue return from the single province of Holland, made out in 1700, his income amounted to twenty-two million, two hundred and forty-one thousand, three hundred and thirty-nine florins, which in French currency come to forty-six million, seven hundred and six thousand, eight hundred and eleven *livres* and eighteen *sous*. That was more or less what the King of Spain possessed at the beginning of the century.

XLVIII

Let people compare what we were in our bishop's time with what we are today. We used to sleep in hovels, we used to eat off wooden platters in our kitchens; our bishop was the only one to have silver plate, and went about his diocese, which he called his states, with forty horses. Today we have citizens with three times his income, and in the city and in the country we have far finer houses than the one he called his palace, and which we have made into prisons.

XLIX

Half of the land in Switzerland is made up of cliffs and precipices, and the other half is not very fertile; but when free hands, controlled at last by enlightened minds, cultivated that land, it flourished. The land of the Pope, on the contrary, from Orvieto to Tarracina, with roads stretching for more than a hundred and twenty miles, is uncultivated, uninhabited and [has been made] unhealthy through famine. You can travel for a whole day there without coming across any people or any animals. There are more priests than farmers; there people hardly eat any bread other than unleavened bread. This is the land that in the time of the ancient Romans was covered with opulent towns, splendid houses, harvests, gardens, ampitheatres. Let us add to this contrast that fact that six Swiss regiments could take possession of the whole of the Pope's estates in two weeks. Had anyone predicted all this to Caesar, when he passed through and fought nearly four hundred thousand Swiss on the way, it would have really surprised him.

L

It is perhaps useful for a republic to have two parties, because one can keep an eye on the other, and because men need to be watched over. It is not perhaps as shameful as one thinks for a republic to need mediators. In truth, that proves that there is obstinacy on both sides, but it also proves that on both sides there is plenty of spirit, plenty of enlightenment, a great wisdom in the interpretation of laws in different ways. That is when arbiters are needed to illuminate disputed laws, to change them if need be, and to avert fresh changes as much as possible. It has been said a thousand times that authority always wants to grow, and the people always want to complain; that it is necessary neither to concede all of their representations nor to reject them all; that there must be a curb on authority and on freedom; that the scales must be kept balanced. But where is the fulcrum? Who will determine it? This will be a masterpiece of reason and impartiality.

LI

Examples are deceptive; the inferences drawn are often badly applied; the quotations to support these inferences are often wrong. 'The nature of honour', said Montesquieu, 'is to ask for signs of preference, marks of distinction. Honour is thus, by its very nature, located in monarchical government.' The author forgets that in the Roman Republic people asked for consular office, triumphal arches, ovations, crowns, statues. There is no republic so small that people do not look for honours.

LII

That superb man with his ingenious and profound thoughts shining with a light that dazzled him, was not able to subordinate his genius to the order and method that is necessary. The fire of his great genius stops objects from being clear and distinct; and when he quotes, he almost always mistakes his imagination for his memory.

[The rest of this section, together with sections LIII-LVII have been omitted. The missing text is identical to that printed in the First Conversation of ABC, see p. 91, l.25 – p. 93, l.27.]

LVIII

It seems to me that it is an even greater abuse to cite the laws of Bantam, Bago, Cochin and Borneo to prove to us truths that have no need of such examples. The illustrious author of the *Spirit of the laws* often falls into this affectation. He tells us that in Bantam 'the king takes the whole of a father's estate, house, wife and children'. He says that this is to be found in a collection of travel tales. But the whole thing is impossible, for within two generations the King would have taken possession of every house and every wife. A traveller often says things that should never be repeated by a man writing as a legislator.

[Section LIX has been omitted. The missing text is identical to that printed in the First Conversation of ABC, see p. 95, l.1–6.]

LX

In a work dealing with the law neither off-the-cuff conjecture, nor examples taken from unknown peoples, nor witticisms, nor irrelevant digressions are necessary. What does it matter to our laws, our administration, 'that the only navigable river in Persia is the Cyrus'? No doubt the author should not have left out the Tigris, the Euphrates, the Araxes, the Phasis, and the Oxus. But what is the point of displaying such erroneous geographical information when he ought only to tell us about what is important to us?

[Sections LXI-LXII have been omitted. The missing text is identical to that printed in the First Conversation of ABC, see p. 95, l.6 – p. 96, l.20.]

LXIII

Will it be through books which destroy superstition, and which make virtue attractive, that we will succeed in making men better? Yes; if young people read these books carefully, they will be protected from all kinds of fanaticism. They will feel that peace is the fruit of tolerance, and the true aim of every society.

LXIV

Tolerance is as necessary in politics as it is in religion. Pride alone is intolerant. It is pride that gives men's minds a feeling of revulsion when it makes us want to force them to think as we do; this is the secret source of all divisiveness.

LXV

Politeness, caution, forbearance consolidate that sense of union between friends and within families. They will have the same effect in a small state, which is a big family.

Thoughts on public administration[1]

I

I was quite right to suggest twenty years ago that we must not ask what the nature of a people's government and its interests is, but what its interests and its government are in a given year. Machiavelli claimed that the strength of the kings of France lay in their *parlements*. If he was alive today, he would say: The strength of the kings of France lies in an army of two hundred thousand men.[2]

Pufendorf, and those who write like he does on the interests of princes, are making defective almanachs for the current year, and almanachs that are absolutely worthless for the year after.

II

Those who wrote fifty years ago that the House of Prussia was destined always to be attached to the House of Austria would be somewhat disconcerted today.[3]

Whoever would have said at the Peace of Nijmegen that one day Spain, Mexico, Peru, Naples, Sicily and Parma would belong to the House of France?

III

Who would have said in the last century that the Russians would shake the Ottoman Empire, and would send an army of forty thou-

---

[1] The title in the first edition was *Thoughts on government*.
[2] The above paragraph was printed only in the 1752 and 1754 editions.
[3] The above paragraph was printed only in the 1752 and 1754 editions.

sand men against France? Three centuries ago, they were subjugated by the Tartars; and if ever the Empire of Constantinople should fall, it will be by their hands. The disciplined Russians will conquer the undisciplined janissaries, who despise them.[4]

When Charles XII was ruling Sweden as a despot, did anyone foresee that his successors would have no more authority than the Polish kings?

IV

When some Czars in Russia shocked nature with so many terrible tortures, which they carried out themselves in days gone by, could anyone foresee the advent of an empress who would vow never to condemn anyone to death, and who would faithfully keep to that oath?[5]

A century ago the kings of Denmark were doges; now they are absolute rulers.

V

Once upon a time, the Russians themselves were sold like negroes; now they think so highly of themselves that they do not accept foreign soldiers into their armies, and they look upon it as a point of honour never to desert. But they need more foreign officers because the country has not yet acquired as much skill as it has courage, and it still knows only how to obey.

VI

Animals accustomed to the yoke present themselves for yoking of their own accord. I do not know who the compiler of the *Letters from Queen Christine* was[6] who outraged the human race by justifying the murder of Monaldeschi, assassinated at Fontainebleau on the orders of a Swedish lady, on the pretext that this Swedish lady had been a queen. The only assassins in the whole world to claim that it was

---

[4] The above paragraph was printed only in the 1752 and 1754 editions.
[5] The above paragraph was printed only in the 1752 and 1754 editions.
[6] Johann Arckenholtz, *Memoirs concerning Christine, Queen of Sweden* (1751–60), II, p. 9.

permissible for this princess to commit at Fontainebleau what would
have been a crime in Stockholm were the ones employed by her.

VII[7]

The government under which a certain number of men would be
allowed to say: 'It's up to those who work to pay; we owe nothing
because we're idle', would be worthy of the Hottentots.

VIII

That government which would allow citizens to say: 'The state has
given us everything; we owe it only our demands', would outrage
God and man.

IX

In becoming perfect, reason destroys the seed of religious wars. It is
the spirit of philosophy that has banished this plague from the world.

X

If Luther and Calvin were to come back, they would make no more
of an impact than the Scotists and the Thomists. Why? Because
they would be born in a time when men are starting to become
enlightened.

XI

It is only in times of barbarism that you see witches, possessed people,
excommunicated kings, subjects absolved from their oaths of loyalty
by doctors of theology.

XII

There is a certain convent, useless to the world in every respect,
which enjoys an income of two hundred thousand *livres*. Reason

---

[7] Paragraphs vii–xix were added in 1756, but suppressed in Kehl.

indicates that if one were to give those two hundred thousand *livres* to a hundred officers, and if one were to marry them off, a hundred good citizens would be rewarded, a hundred girls provided for, and [there would be] at least four hundred more people in the State after ten years instead of fifty idle people. Reason indicates that if these fifty idle people were to be returned to the State, they would cultivate the soil and populate the land, and that there would be more plough-men and more soldiers. This is what everyone, from the princes of the blood down to vine-growers, want. In the past, only superstition was opposed to it; but reason, subject to faith, must crush superstition.

XIII

With a single word, the Prince can stop people from taking religious vows before the age of twenty-five. And if someone says to the sover-eign: 'What will become of these girls of quality, whose interests we normally sacrifice to those of our eldest sons?' the prince will reply: 'They will become what they become in Sweden, Denmark, Prussia, England and Holland; they will make good citizens; they were born to reproduce, and not to recite Latin verse that they do not under-stand. A women feeding two children, and who can spin, gives greater service to the State than any convent can ever give.'

XIV

The Prince and the State are very fortunate to have a lot of philo-sophers to instill all these maxims into men's heads.

XV

Philosophers, who have no private interests to serve, can only speak for reason and the public good.

XVI

Philosophers love religion, and they do princes a favour by destroying superstition, which is always the enemy of princes.

XVII

It is superstition that had Henry III, Henry IV, William of Orange, and so many others assassinated. It is superstition that has made rivers of blood flow since the time of Constantine.

XVIII

Superstition is the most horrible enemy of the human race. When it controls the Prince, it stops him from seeking the good of his people; when it controls the people, it causes them to rise against their prince.

XIX

There is not a single instance in the world of philosophers ever having opposed the Prince's laws. There is not a single century in which superstition and hysteria have not caused horrifying disturbances.

XX

Freedom consists in being dependent only on the law. On that basis, today every man is free in Sweden, England, Holland, Switzerland, Geneva and Hamburg. People are even free in Venice and in Genoa, although what does not form part of the sovereign body is not respected there. People are free in some of the imperial cities of Germany.[8] But there are still provinces and huge Christian kingdoms where most of the people are slaves.

XXI

A time will come in these countries when some prince, more skillful than the others, will make those who cultivate the land understand that it is not altogether to their advantage for a man with a horse, or several horses, that is to say a nobleman, to have the right to kill a peasant by imposing a ten-*écu* tax on his ditch. It is true that ten *écus* is a lot of money for a man born in a certain part of the world, but as the centuries pass they will work out that it is very little for a dead

---

[8] This sentence was printed only in the 1752 and 1754 editions.

man. Then it might come about that the commons will play a part in government, and the English and Swedish style of government will be established in Turkey or thereabouts.

XXII

A citizen of Amsterdam is a man; a citizen living a few degrees of longitude away is an animal in service.

XXIII

All men were born equal, but a citizen of Morocco does not suspect the existence of that truth.

XXIV

This equality does not mean the abolition of all subordination; we are all equal as men, but not [equal] as members of society. All natural rights belong equally to a sultan and to a bostandji; both should have the same power over their own persons, their families, their possessions. Men are thus equal in essential things, although on stage they play different roles.

XXV

People always ask which system of government is preferable. If you put this question to a minister or to his secretary, they will no doubt be for a system of absolute power; if you put it to a baron, he will want the baronage to share in legislative power. The bishops will say the same thing; the citizen, as might be expected, will want to be consulted, and the farmer will not wish to be forgotten. The best form of government seems to be the one where all ranks of society are equally protected by the law.

Everything that has been written for and against [the best form of government] can be reduced to this: in a mixed state, what is to be feared is confusion; in monarchical states it is the abuse of power.[9]

---

[9] The above paragraph was printed only in the 1752 and 1754 editions.

XXVI

A republican is always more attached to his country than a subject [is], by reason of the fact that one prefers what belongs to oneself to what belongs to one's master.

XXVII

What is love of country? An amalgam of self-love and prejudice, in which the good of society becomes the greatest of virtues. It is important for the vague term, *the public*, to make a deep impression.

XXVIII

When the lord in his castle or the city-dweller make accusations against the absolute power of the authorities, and express sorrow for the crushed peasant, do not believe them. People hardly ever express sorrow about evils they do not themselves feel. Citizens and gentlemen hate even more rarely the person of the sovereign, except in times of civil war. What people hate is absolute power four or five times removed; a clerk's ante-room, or the ante-room of an intendant's secretary, is the thing that makes people mutter under their breath. It is because people have been slapped in the face by some insolent valet in a palace that they grumble about the ravaged countryside.

XXIX

The English reproach the French for cheerfully serving their masters. Here is the finest thing that has been written in England on that subject:

> A nation here I pity and admire,
> Whom noblest sentiments of glory fire;
> Yet taught by custom's force, and bigot fear,
> To serve with pride, and boast the yoke they bear;
> Whose nobles born to cringe and to command,
> In courts a mean, in camps a gen'rous band
> From priests and stock-jobbers content receive
> Those laws their dreaded arms to Europe give:

Whose people vain in want, in bondage blest;
Tho' plunder'd, gay; industrious tho' oppress'd;
With happy follies rise above their fate;
The jest and envy of a wiser state.[10]

You could convey the sense of these lines thus:

Tel est l'esprit français; je l'admire et le plains.
Dans son abaissement quel excès de courage!
La tête sous le joug, les lauriers dans les mains,
Il chérit à la fois la gloire et l'esclavage.
Ses exploits et sa honte ont rempli l'univers:
Vainqueur dans les combats, enchaîné par ses maîtres,
Pillé par des traitants, aveuglé par des prêtres;
Dans la disette il chante: il danse avec ses fers.
Fier dans la servitude, heureux dans sa folie,
De l'Anglais libre et sage il est encore l'envie.

Here is the answer to all those declamations of which English poetry, pamphlets and sermons are full. It is quite natural to love a house that has reigned for almost eight hundred years. A number of foreigners, and even some English, have come to settle in France just to lead happy lives there.

XXX

A king who is not contradicted can hardly be wicked.

XXXI

A few Englishmen from the provinces, who have travelled no further than London, imagine that the King of France, in his spare time, sends for a president, and for amusement gives his property to a flunkey.

XXXII

There is hardly a country in the world where the fortunes of individuals are more secure than in France. Count Maurice of Nassau,

---

[10] Conyers Middleton.

when leaving The Hague to take command of the Dutch infantry, asked me if the income that he received from the Paris Town Hall would be confiscated. 'You will be paid', I told him, 'on the same day as Count Maurice of Saxony, the commander of the French army.' And that was literally true.

XXXIII

During his reign, Louis XI caused about four thousand citizens to pass through the hands of the executioner: it is because he was not an absolute ruler, but wanted to be. From the time of the Duke of Lauzun adventure, Louis XIV punished nobody in his court severely; that is because he was an absolute ruler. Under Charles II more than fifty important heads were chopped off in London.

XXXIV

In the time of Louis XIII not a year passed without turbulence. Louis the Just was cruel. He had started at the age of sixteen by having his prime minister assassinated. He allowed Cardinal Richelieu, who was more cruel than he was, to shed blood all over the scaffolds.

In the same circumstances, Cardinal Mazarin did not have anybody killed. As he was a foreigner, he would not have been able to maintain himself in power through cruelty. He was deceitful, not wicked. If Richelieu had not had factions to fight, he would have raised the Kingdom to a pinnacle of splendour, because his cruelty, which had to do with the haughtiness of his nature, with nothing to exercise itself on, would have given full sway to the nobility of his genius.

XXXV

In a book full of deep ideas and clever witticisms,[11] despotism has been included among the natural forms of government. The author, who is a very amusing fellow, wanted to have a joke.

There is no state that is naturally despotic. There is no country where the people have said to one man: 'Sire, we give to your Gracious Majesty the power to take our wives, our children, our posses-

---

[11] Montesquieu, *Spirit of the laws*, II.I.

sions and our lives, and to have us impaled in accordance with your own good pleasure and wonderful whim.'

The Great Lord swears on the Koran to observe the law. He cannot have anyone killed without a warrant from the Divan and a fatwa from the Mufti. He is so undespotic that he can neither alter the currency rate nor demote the janissaries. It is wrong to say that he is the master of his subjects' property. He gives away land called *timariots* just as, long ago, they used to give away fiefdoms.

XXXVI

Despotism is the abuse of kingship, just as anarchy is the abuse of republican government. A prince who, without judicial procedure and without justice, imprisons a citizen or causes him to die, is a highwayman they call *Your Majesty*.

XXXVII

A modern author[12] has said that there is more virtue in republics and more honour in monarchies.

Honour is the desire to be honoured; to have honour is to do nothing that makes you unworthy of being honoured. You would not say that a solitary man has honour. This is reserved for that degree of respect that everyone wishes to be accorded in society. It is a good thing to agree on terminology, otherwise people will no longer understand one another.

Now, in the time of the Roman Republic this desire to be honoured by statues, laurel crowns and triumphal arches made the Romans into conquerors of much of the world. Honour was dependent on a ceremony or on a sprig of laurel or parsley.

Once there was no more republic, there was no more honour of that sort.

Will republican government survive in Sweden? Yes, yes – until another Gustavus Adolphus is born.[13]

---

[12] Montesquieu, *Spirit of the laws*, III.3–6.
[13] The above paragraph was printed only in the 1752 and 1754 editions.

XXXVIII

A republic is not founded on virtue at all; it is founded on the ambition of each citizen, which keeps in check the ambition of all the others; on pride which curbs pride; on the wish to dominate which does not allow anyone else to dominate. From all that laws are formed which preserve equality as much as possible. It is a society in which the guests, having an equal appetite, eat at the same table, until a powerful, greedy man comes on the scene who helps himself to everything, leaving them the crumbs.

XXXIX

Small machines are not a success on a large scale because friction makes them go wrong. It is the same thing with states: China cannot be ruled in the same way as the Republic of Lucca.

XL

Calvinism and Lutheranism are in danger in Germany. That country is full of great bishoprics, abbacies with sovereign powers, canonries, all of them good for conversions. A Protestant prince turns himself into a Catholic in order to become a bishop or a king in a particular country, just like a princess does in order to marry.

The Lutheran religion will survive there longer because it is in nobody's interest to change it.[14]

XLI

If the Roman religion becomes top-dog again, it will be by means of the bait of fat livings and through monks. Monks are the troops who fight without let up; protestants have no troops.

XLII

It has been claimed[15] that religions are made for climates; but Christianity has reigned for a long time in Asia. It started in Palestine, and

[14] The above paragraph was printed only in the 1752 and 1754 editions.
[15] Voltaire had originally written: 'In a book so appropriately called *Wit on the laws*, it is claimed that . . . ', but he changed the text in 1756 after Montesquieu's death.

it came to Norway. The Englishman who said that religions were born in Asia and found their graves in England made a better guess.

XLIII

It must be admitted that there are ceremonies and mysteries that can only take place in certain climates. People bathe in the Ganges at [the time of] the new moon. If they had to bathe in the Vistula in January, that religious law would not be in force for very long, etc.

XLIV

It has been claimed[16] that the Muslim law forbidding the drinking of wine is the law of the climate of Arabia, because there wine would thicken the blood, and water is more refreshing. I could just as well wish for an eleventh commandment to have been made in Spain and Italy regarding iced drinks. Mohammed did not forbid wine because Arabs like water. It is said in the *Sunna* that he forbade it because he witnessed the excesses which drunkenness can make people commit.

XLV

No religious laws are the result of the nature of a climate.

Eating lamb cooked with lettuce leaves standing up, and throwing the leftovers into the fire; not eating hare because it is said that it does not have a cloven foot, and that it eats grass; putting an animal's blood into your left ear:[17] these ceremonies are hardly related to a country's temperature.

XLVI

If Leo X had given the sale of indulgences to Augustin friars, who controlled the supply of this merchandise, there would have been no Protestants. If Ann Boleyn had not been pretty, England would be Catholic. What determined that Spain did not become completely

---

[16] Montesquieu, *Spirit of the laws*, XIV.10.
[17] Leviticus, VIII.23, XI.6; Deuteronomy, XIV.7.

Aryan, and subsequently completely Muslim? What determined that Carthage did not destroy Rome?

XLVII

To deduce all the events that have happened in the world from one single event is a good problem [to have] to solve, but it is for the master of the universe to solve it.

The rights of men
and the usurpations of others.
Translated from the Italian

1. Should a priest of Christ have sovereign powers?

To understand the rights of the human race, there is no need for quotations. The time has gone when people like Grotius and Pufendorf used to look for what is your right and what is mine in Aristotle and Saint Jerome, and lavished contradictions and tedium on the question of what was just and what was unjust. We have to get down to facts.

Does one territory depend upon another? Is there some physical law that makes the Euphrates flow at China's pleasure or at that of India? Is there some metaphysical concept that makes a Spice Island submit to a piece of marshland formed by the Rhine and the Meuse? It would appear not. Is there a moral law? Just as unlikely.

How does it come about that Gibraltar, in the Mediterranean, belonged in days gone by to the Moors, and now belongs to the English, who live on islands in the Atlantic, the northernmost point of which is at about 60 degrees latitude? The reason is that they took Gibraltar. Why do they keep it? Because nobody has been able to take it off them, and subsequently it was agreed that it should remain theirs: force and agreements make empires.

By what right did Charlemagne, born in the barbarous land of the Austrasians, do his father-in-law, Didier the Lombard, out of what belonged to him, after having robbed his own nephews of their heritage? By the same right the Lombards had exercised when they came from the shores of the Baltic to sack the Roman Empire, and by the same right the Romans had to lay waste to one country after the other. In armed robbery, the strongest wins; in territorial acquisition by negotiation, the winner is the most skillful.

To rule one's brothers (what brothers! what false brothers!) by right, what does one need? The free consent of peoples.

Charlemagne came to Rome, in about the year 800, after preparing and agreeing everything with the bishop, giving his army its marching orders, and carrying his treasure-chest containing the presents intended for that priest. The Roman people named Charlemagne as their master out of gratitude for delivering them from the oppressive rule of the Lombards.

Well done the Senate and the people for saying to Charles: 'Thank you for the good you have done us; we no longer wish to obey stupid, wicked emperors who do not defend us, who do not understand our language, who give us our orders in Greek through eunuchs from Constantinople, and who take our money. Rule us better by protecting all our rights, and we will obey you.'

That is undoubtedly a fine right, and a most legitimate one.

But those poor people certainly could not do what they wanted with the Empire; they did not have an empire at their disposal; they only had themselves at their disposal. What province of the Empire could they have given away? Spain? That belonged to the Arabs. Gaul and Germany? Pépin, Charlemagne's father, had usurped them from his master. The land on this side of Italy? Charles had stolen it from his father-in-law. The Greek emperors owned the rest. Thus the people conferred only a name: that name has become sacred. Countries from the Euphrates to the Atlantic had become used to looking upon the brigandry of the Holy Roman Empire as a natural right; and the court of Constantinople always looked on the dismemberment of that holy empire as a clear violation of the people's rights, until the Turks came and taught them another set of laws.

But to say, with the mercenary lawyers of the Roman pontifical court (who laugh about it themselves) that Bishop Leo III gave the Western Empire to Charlemagne, is as ridiculous as saying that the Patriarch of Constantinople gave the Eastern Empire to Mohammed II.

On the other hand, to repeat after so many others that Pépin the Usurper and Charlemagne the Ravager gave the exarchate of Ravenna to the Roman bishops is to advance an obvious falsehood. Charlemagne was not so honest. He kept the exarchate for himself, as he did Rome. In his will, he named Rome and Ravenna as his principal cities. It is an established fact that he entrusted the government of Ravenna and Pentapolis to another Leo, the Archbishop of Ravenna, whose letter we still have stating explicitly: *Haec civitates a Carolo ipso cum universa Pentapoli mihi fuerunt concessae.*

However that may be, here it is simply a question of demonstrating how monstrous it is that, in line with the principles of our religion, as well as of our politics and our reason, a priest should give away the Empire, and that he should have sovereign territories within the Empire.

Either Christianity should be renounced completely, or observed. Neither a Jesuit, with all his distinctions, nor the Devil can find a middle way.

A religion is founded in Galilee based entirely on poverty, on equality, on a hatred of riches and of the rich, a religion in which it is said that it is harder for a rich man to enter the Kingdom of Heaven than it is for a camel to pass through the eye of a needle; where it is said that the bad rich man is condemned solely for being rich; where Anananias and Sapphira are punished with sudden death for holding on to land that was their livelihood; where the disciples are commanded never to make provision for the future; where Christ, the Son of God, God himself, pronounces those terrible oracles against ambition and greed: 'I have not come to be served, but to serve. There will never be first or last among you. That whoever wishes to raise himself up shall be cast down. That those among you who want to be the first shall be the last.'[1]

The lives of the first disciples conformed to those precepts; Saint Paul worked with his hands; Saint Peter earned a living. What connection is there between that institution and Rome's domain, and that of Sabina, Umbria, Emilia, Ferrara, Ravenna, Pentapolis, Bologna, Comaccio, Benevento, Avignon? It cannot be seen that the Bible has given those lands to the Pope, unless the Bible is like the Theatine regulation that said that the Theatines should be dressed in white, and someone had put in the margin: *that is to say, black.*

This grandeur of popes and their pretentions, [that are] a thousand times bigger, conform no more to politics and reason than they do to God's word, as they have caused upheaval and bloodshed in Europe for the last seven hundred years.

All over the world, politics and reason demand that each person should enjoy what they own, and that every state should be independ-

---

[1] Matthew, XIV.24; Luke, XVI.21–4; Acts, V.

ent. Let us see how these two natural laws, against which there can be no prescription, have been observed.

2. On Naples

The gentlemen from Normandy, who were the main tools of conquest over Naples and Sicily, performed the finest act of chivalry that has ever been heard of. Just forty to fifty men liberated Salerno when it had been taken by an army of Saracens. It took just seven other Norman gentlemen, all brothers, to drive those same Saracens right out of the country, and to seize it from the Greek Emperor, who had repaid them with ingratitude. It is quite natural that nations, whose valour these heroes had re-awakened, should get used to obeying them out of admiration and gratefulness.

There we have the first rights to the crown of the Two Sicilies. The bishops of Rome could no more give these states away as fiefdoms than they could the Kingdom of Bhutan or Kashmir. They could not even have authorised their investiture if they had been asked to; for in the age of feudal anarchy, when a lord wished to hold his freehold possessions in fief to have protection, he could only apply to his sovereign lord. Now the Pope was certainly not the sovereign lord of Naples, Apulia or Calabria.

Much has been written about this alleged vasselage, but people have never gone back to the source. I dare say that it is as much the fault of all the legal experts as [it is] of the theologians. For good or bad, everyone draws from an established principle the inferences that are most favourable to his own side; but is this principle a true one? Is this initial fact on which they are based irrefutable? That is what they take great care not to examine. They are like our old writers of romances who all assumed that Francus had brought Hector's helmet to France. The helmet was doubtless impenetrable, but had Hector in fact worn it? The Virgin's milk is also very respectable, but do those sacristies that boast of possessing half a pint of it really have any?

Giannone is the only one to have shed some light on the origin of the supreme domination assumed by popes over the Kingdom of Naples. By doing that he has rendered eternal service to the kings of that country and, as a reward, he was handed over by Emperor Charles VI, the then King of Naples, to the Jesuits to be persecuted;

betrayed after that by the most despicable perfidy, and sacrificed to the court of Rome, he ended his life in captivity. His example will not discourage us. We are writing in a free country; we were born free, and we fear neither the ingratitude of sovereigns, nor the plots of Jesuits, nor the vengeance of popes. The truth is before us, and all other considerations are irrelevant.

In those centuries of robbery, private wars, crime, ignorance and superstition, it was the custom for a weak lord, in order to be protected from the rapaciousness of his neighbours, to place his lands under the protection of the Church, and to buy this protection with some money, without which nobody ever succeeded. His lands were then deemed sacred; whoever might wish to take possession of them was excommunicated.

The men of those times, as wicked as they were stupid, were not afraid of the greatest crimes, but they dreaded excommunication, which made them abominable to other people, who were more wicked than they were, and a lot more stupid.

Robert Guiscard and Richard, the conquerors of Apulia and Calabria, were first excommunicated by Pope Leo IX. They had declared themselves vassals of the Emperor, but Emperor Henry III, who was displeased with these feudatory conquerors, had urged Leo IX to issue the excommunication at the head of an army of Germans. The Normans, who did not fear these thunderbolts as much as the princes of Italy did, beat the Germans and took the Pope prisoner; but, to stop emperors and popes henceforth from causing upsets in their possessions, they offered their conquests to the Church under the name of *oblata*. This is how England came to pay Peter's pence; this is how the first kings of Spain and Portugal, when regaining their estates from the Saracens, came to promise the Church of Rome two pounds of gold every year. Neither England, nor Spain, nor Portugal ever regarded the Pope as their sovereign lord.

Duke Robert, oblate of the Church, was no vassal of the Pope either; he could not be because the popes were not sovereign in Rome. That city was then ruled by its senate; the Bishop only had influence. The Pope in Rome was exactly what the Elector is in Cologne. There is a huge difference between being a saint's oblate and a bishop's vassal.

In his *Acts*, Baronius reports on the supposed homage given by Robert, the Duke of Apulia and Calabria, to Nicholas II, but this item is wrong; the document has never been seen, and it has never been [held] in any archive. Robert called himself *Duke by the grace of God and Saint Peter*, but Saint Peter had certainly not given him anything, and was not the King of Rome. If you wanted to go further back, you would prove irrefutably that not only was Saint Peter never Bishop of Rome, at a time when it is established beyond doubt that no priest had any particular seat, and when the rules of the nascent Church were not yet formed, but that Saint Peter had no more been to Rome than he had to Peking. Saint Paul states specifically that his mission was to preach 'the gospel of the uncircumcised, and that Saint Paul's was to preach that of the circumcised'; that is to say, Saint Peter, who was born in Galilee, was to preach only to the Jews, and that Paul, who was born in Tarsus in Karamania, was to preach only to foreigners.

The fable that tells us that Peter came to Rome in the reign of Nero, and stayed there for twenty-five years, is one of the most absurd that has ever been invented, as Nero reigned for only thirteen years. The assumption that people have presumed to make that a letter from Saint Peter, sent from Babylon, had been written in Rome, and by that Rome stands for Babylon, is such an outrageous theory that you cannot talk about it without laughing. I ask every sensible reader what kind of a right it is that is founded on such clearly confirmed deceptions.

At any rate, whether Robert gave himself to Saint Peter, or to the twelve apostles, or to the twelve patriarchs, or to the nine choirs of angels, does not give the Pope any right over a kingdom. It is just an intolerable abuse, contrary to all the old feudal laws, contrary to the Christian religion, to the independence of sovereigns, to common sense and to natural law.

This abuse has an antiquity of seven hundred years, I agree; but even if it had an antiquity of seven hundred thousand, it would still have to be abolished. I admit that there have been thirty investitures of the Kingdom of Naples granted by popes, but there have been far more bulls placing princes under the jurisdiction of the Church, and proclaiming that no sovereign under any circumstances can judge clerics or monks, nor take a farthing from them for the upkeep of his estates. There have been more bulls saying, on behalf of God, that emperors cannot be created without the consent of the Pope. All of these bulls have met with the contempt that they deserve; why

should people give any more respect to the supposed suzerainty of
the Kingdom of Naples? If antiquity consecrated errors, and made
them safe from attack, we would all still be required to go to Rome
to plead our case over [questions of] marriage, wills or tithes; we
would still have to pay taxes imposed by legates; we would still have
to take to arms every time the Pope announced a crusade; we would
still be buying indulgences from Rome, we would still be saving the
souls of the dead for money; we would still believe in witches, in
magic, in the power of relics over devils. Every priest would still be
able to cast out devils from the bodies of heretics. Every prince who
had a quarrel with the Pope would still lose his sovereignty. All that
is as old, or older, than the supposed vasselage of a kingdom which,
by its nature, should be independent.

Certainly, if the popes gave that kingdom away, they can take it
back [again]. In days gone by, they did in fact strip away the rights
of those with legitimate possessions. It is a continual cause of civil
wars. That papal right is thus in fact contrary to the Christian religion,
to sane politics, and to reason. *Quod erat demonstrandum.*

3. On the monarchy of Sicily

What is called the *privilege*, the prerogative of the monarchy of Sicily,
is a right that is linked essentially to all the Christian powers, to the
Republic of Genoa, to those of Lucca and Ragusa, in the same way
as it is to France and Spain. It consists of three main points which
were granted by Pope Urban II to Roger, King of Sicily:

The first was to receive no legate *a latere* with the functions of
pope without the consent of the sovereign.

The second was to do in his own land what this foreign ambassador
used to presume to do.

The third was to send any bishops or priests that he wanted to the
councils in Rome.

This was really the least that one could do for a man who had
freed Sicily from the yoke of the Arabs, and made it Christian. This
so-called privilege was nothing more than natural right, just as the
freedoms of the Gallican Church are simply what all churches used
to practise formerly.

These privileges were only granted by Urban II, and confirmed
and extended by some of the popes who succeeded him, in order

to turn Sicily into an apostolic fiefdom, as they had done in Naples; but the kings did not allow themselves to fall into that trap. It was quite enough for them to have forgotten their dignity to the point of being a mainland vassal. They were never [vassals] on the island.

If you want to know one of the reasons why these kings preserved their right not to receive legates, when all the other sovereigns in Europe were weak enough to accept them, you will find it in the words of John, Bishop of Salisbury: 'Legati apostolici . . . ita debacchantur in provinciis, ac Satan ad Ecclesiam flagellandam a facie Domini. Provinciarum diripiunt spolia, ac si thesaurus Craosi studeant comparare.' *They plunder the country, just like Satan flogging the Church out of the Lord's sight. They take away the spoils from the provinces as if they wanted to amass the treasure of Croesus.*

The popes soon repented of having ceded a natural right to the kings of Sicily: they wanted to retract it. In the end, Baronius maintained that this privilege was a surreptitious one, and that it had only been sold to the kings of Sicily by an anti-pope, and they had no difficulty in treating all the kings who succeeded Roger as tyrants.

After centuries of argument, and with the kings always holding on to what they possessed, the court in Rome thought that it had finally found the opportunity to subjugate Sicily when the Duke of Savoy, Victor-Amadeus, became King of that island by virtue of the treaties of Utrecht.

It is good to know what pretext the modern Roman court used to overthrow that kingdom, so dear to the ancient Romans. One day in 1711, the Bishop of Lipari sold a dozen litres of peas to a corn-merchant. The corn-merchant sold these peas in the market, and paid the three *sous* in tax levied by the government on peas. The Bishop claimed that this was a sacrilege, that these peas belonged to him by divine right, and that nothing should be paid on them to a profane court. Obviously he was wrong. The peas might have been sacred when they belonged to him, but they were no longer so once they had been sold. The Bishop maintained that their nature was ineradicable. He made so much fuss, and had so much support from his canons, that the corn-merchant had his three *sous* back.

The government thought that the matter was over, but the Bishop of Lapari had already left for Rome, after having excommunicated the government of the island and the aldermen. The monarchical court absolved them *cum reincidentia*, that is to say, suspended the sentence of censure in accordance with their right to do so.

The congregation called in Rome *the congregation of immunity* immediately sent a circular letter to all the Sicilian bishops stating that the outrage committed by the monarchical court was even more sacriligious than the one which required payment of three *sous* for the peas that came originally from a bishop's vegetable garden. A Bishop of Catania published this declaration. The viceroy, together with the monarchical court, set it aside as [being] a challenge to royal authority. The Bishop of Catania excommunicated a Baron Figuerazzi and two other officers of the court.

The indignant Viceroy issued an order through two gentlemen to the Bishop of Catania to leave the kingdom. The Bishop excommunicated the two gentlemen, interdicted his diocese, and left for Rome. Part of his possessions were seized. The Bishop of Agrigentum did his best to incur a similar order; he was given one. He did much better than the Bishop of Catania: he excommunicated the Viceroy, the court and the whole monarchy.

These trivia, which you cannot read about today without shrugging your shoulders, became a very serious issue. This Bishop of Agrigentum had three vicars who excommunicated even more people than he did. They were imprisoned. All the faithful prayed for them; Sicily was set on fire.

When the new king, Victor-Amadeus, to whom Philip V had just ceded the island, took possession of it on 10 October 1713, he had scarcely arrived when Pope Clement XI sent three briefs to the Archbishop of Palerma ordering the excommunication of the whole kingdom on pain of being excommunicated himself. Divine providence did not grant its protection to those three briefs. The boat bearing them was shipwrecked, and these briefs, which a French *parlement* would have had burned, drowned with the bearer. But Providence does not always make its presence felt through thunderbolts, it allowed other briefs to arrive, among them one which designated the monarchical court as *a certain so-called court*. In November the congregation of immunity convened all the bursars of Sicilian monasteries in Rome, and commanded them to order every monk to obey the interdiction thundered out earlier by the Bishop of Catania, and to refuse to say mass until further orders.

Good old Clement XI himself excommunicated by name the royal judge on 5 January 1714. Cardinal Paulucci commanded all the bishops (still under threat of excommunication) to make none of the payments to the State which they had agreed themselves to pay under the ancient laws of the kingdom. Cardinal La Tremouille, France's ambassador to Rome, acted as his master's mediator between the Holy Spirit and Victor-Amadeus; but negotiations did not succeed.

Finally, on 10 February 1715, the Pope thought that he could abolish the court of the Sicilian monarchy with a bull. Nothing debases fragile authority more than extreme policies that it cannot sustain. The court did not consider itself abolished at all. The Holy Father ordered all churches to be closed on the island, and that nobody should pray to God. People prayed to God in several towns in spite of the Bishop. Count Maffei, the King's envoy to the Pope, had an audience with him. Clement XI wept often, and broke just as often the promises that he had made. People said of him: 'He is like Saint Peter; he weeps and denies.' Maffei, who found him in tears because most of the churches were still open in Sicily, said to him: 'Holy Father, weep when they are closed, not when they are open.'

4. On Ferrara

If the rights of Sicily are unshakable, if the suzerainty of Naples is just an ancient chimera, the invasion of Ferrara is a new usurpation. Ferrara was a steadfast fiefdom of the Empire, like Parma and Piacenza. Pope Clement VIII stripped Caesar of Este [of it] by force of arms in 1597. The pretext for this act of tyranny was very strange for a man who proclaimed himself to be the humble Vicar of Christ. Duke Alfonso d'Este, the first of that name, the sovereign of Ferrara, of Modena, of Este, of Carpi, of Rovigo, had married an ordinary citizen of Ferrara named Laura Eustochia, with whom he had had three children prior to their marriage, solemnly recognised by him before the Church. This recognition omitted none of the formalities prescribed by law. His successor, Alfonso of Este, was recognised as Duke of Ferrara. He married Julia of Urbino, daughter of Francis, the Duke of Urbino, with whom he had this unfortunate Caesar of Este, the incontestable heir to all the family possessions, and proclaimed heir by the last duke, who had died on 27 October 1597. Pope Clement VIII, whose name was Aldobrandino, and who came from a family of Florentine traders, dared to allege that Caesar of Este's grandmother was not sufficiently noble, and that the children to whom she had given birth should be regarded as bastards. This reason is scandalous and ridiculous for a bishop; it is indefensible in all the courts of Europe; moreover, if the Duke was not legitimate, he should also lose Modena and all his other states; and if there was no flaw in his birth, he should keep Ferrara, just as he should keep Modena.

The acquisition of Ferrara was too attractive for the Pope not to take advantage of all the decretals and all the decisions of those bold theologians who assure us that the pope *can make just what is unjust.* Consequently, he first excommunicated Caesar of Este; and as excommunication necessarily deprives a man of everything he possesses, the father of all the faithful raised an army against the excommunicant in order to rob him of his heritage in the name of the Church. These troops were beaten, but the Duke of Modena and Ferrara soon saw his wealth become exhausted, and his friends become cold towards him.

The most deplorable thing about it was that the King of France, Henry IV, thought that he was obliged to take the Pope's side in order to counterbalance the influence of Philip II at the court of Rome. This was the way that good King Louis XII, for whom there is less excuse, had dishonoured himself by joining up with the monster Alexander VI and his execrable bastard, Duke Borgia. It was necessary to give way; the Pope then had Ferrara invaded by Cardinal Aldobrandino, who entered that prosperous city with a thousand horses and five thousand infantry.

Since that time, Ferrara has become a desert; its uncultivated land is covered with stagnant marshes. Under the House of Este that country had been one of the most beautiful in Italy; the people always longed for their old masters. It is true that the Duke was dismissed. He was given a nomination to a bishopric and a curacy, and he was even provided with a few pecks of salt from the shops in Cervia; but it is no less true that the House of Modena has incontestable and indefeasible rights to the Duchy of Ferrara, of which it has been stripped in such an undignified way.

5. On Castro and Ronciglione

The usurpation of Castro and Ronciglione from the House of Parma is no less unjust; but the way in which it was done was more base and despicable. In Rome there are a lot of Jews who avenge themselves on Christians as best they can by charging high interest rates on things that are pawned. The popes tried to cut them out. They set up banks called *mounts of piety*; they were pawnshops too, but with a much higher interest rate. Individuals deposit their money there, and that money is lent to those who want to borrow, and who can provide security.

Rainuce, the Duke of Parma, son of the famous Alexander Farnese who raised the siege of Rouen and the siege of Paris against Henry IV, when compelled to borrow huge sums, preferred the *mounts of piety* to the Jews. However, there was not much about the court of Rome to recommend it. The first time that he made an appearance there Sextius Quintus wanted to cut its head off in recompense for the services that his father had given to the Church.

His son, Odoardo, owed interest [as well as] the principal sum, and only extricated himself with difficulty. Barbarini or Barberini, who was then pope with the name of Urban VIII, wanted to settle the matter by marrying off his niece Barbarini, or Barbarina, to the young Duke of Parma. He had two nephews who used to be the Duke's tutors: one was Taddeo Barbarini, the prefect of Rome, and the other was Cardinal Antonio; there was in addition a brother, who was also a cardinal, but who was nobody's tutor. The Duke went to Rome to see this prefect and these cardinals, to whom he was to become the brother-in-law on condition that the interest that he owed to the *mount of piety* was reduced. Neither the deal, nor the Pope's niece, nor the behaviour of the nephews pleased him. He quarrelled with them over the big issue of modern Romans, the *puntiglio*, the science of calculating the number of steps that a cardinal and a prefect should take when escorting a duke of Parma. All the train-bearers in Rome were stirred up about this quarrel, and the Duke of Parma went off to marry a Medici.

The Barberinis or Barbarinis dreamed of vengeance. Every year the Duke sold his corn from the Duchy of Castro to the Chamber of the Apostles to redeem part of his debt, and the Chamber of the Apostles resold his corn at a very dear price to the people. The

Chamber bought it from somewhere else, and forbade corn from Castro from coming into Rome. The Duke of Parma could not sell his corn to the Romans, so he sold it elsewhere as best he could.

The Pope, who was by the way a pretty bad poet, excommunicated Odoardo, as was the custom, and incamerated the duchy of Castro. *To incamerate* is a verb peculiar to the language of the Chamber of the Apostles: each chamber has its own. It means to take, to seize, to appropriate, to reserve for ourselves what does not belong to us at all. The Duke, with the help of the Medicis and a few friends, took to arms to *disincamerate* his possessions. The Barberinis took to arms as well. It is claimed that on supplying the soldiers with blunderbusses that had been blessed, Cardinal Antonio exhorted them to always keep them clean, and to bring them back in the same state that they had been given them. We are even assured that a few blows were exchanged, and that three or four people died in this war, either from the weather or from other causes. No expenditure amounting to more than the value of the corn from Castro was allowed. The Duke fortified Castro, and irrespective of the fact that he had been excommunicated, the Barberinis were not able to take his town with their blunderbusses. All this has only a faint resemblance to the wars of the Romans of the past, and even less to the morality of Christ. It was not even a matter of *compelling them to come in*[2], but of *compelling them to leave*. This fracas went on intermittently in 1642 and 1643. In 1644 the French court secured a hollow peace. The Duke of Parma took communion, and kept Castro.

Pamphylia, Innocent X, who wrote no poetry, and who hated the two Barberini cardinals, harassed them so severely to punish them for all their harassment that they fled to France, where Cardinal Antonio became Archbishop of Reims, Grand Chaplain in charge of priests.

We will note in passing that there was a third Cardinal Barberini, who had been christened Anthony. He was the brother of Pope Urban VIII. The latter had nothing to do with either poetry or government. In his youth he had been mad enough to think that the only way of gaining Paradise was to be a lay-brother in the order of Capuchins. He assumed that rank, which is surely the lowest of all; but having subsequently become wise, it was enough for him to be a

[2] Luke, XIV.23.

237

cardinal and very rich. He lived the life of a philosopher. The epitaph that he ordered to be engraved on his tomb is odd:

> Hic jacet pulvis et cinis, postea nihil.
> *Here lies powder and ashes, and then nothing.*

That *nothing* is peculiar for a cardinal.

But let us return to the affairs of Parma. In 1646, Pamphylia wanted to give to Castro a bishop who had a very bad reputation on account of his morals, and who made all the citizens of Castro with handsome wives and pretty children quake with fear. The bishop was killed by someone who was jealous. Instead of having the guilty person found, and co-operating with the Duke in having him punished, the Pope sent in the troops and razed the city to the ground. This act of cruelty was attributed to Donna Olimpia, the Pope's sister-in-law and mistress, to whom the Duke had neglected to give presents when she was getting them from everybody else. Demolishing a city was much worse than incamerating one. The Pope erected a little pyramid on the ruins, with this inscription: *Qui fui Castro.*

This happened under Rainuce II, the son of Odoardo Farnese. A war started again which was even less bloody than the war of the Barberinis. The Duchy of Castro and Ronciglione remained confiscated, to the financial advantage of the Chamber of the Apostles, from 1646 until 1662, under the pontificate of Chigi, Alexander VII.

After this Alexander VII, over more than one issue, had defied Louis XIV, whose youthfulness he scorned, and whose greatness he did not understand, the differences between the two courts became so extreme, and the animosity so violent between the Duke of Créquy, France's ambassador to Rome, and Mario Chigi, the Pope's brother, that the Corsican guards of His Holiness fired on the carriage of the ambassador's wife, killing one of the pages at the carriage door. It is true that they were not authorised to do so by any bull, but apparently their zeal did not displease the Holy Father too much. Louis XIV made his vengeance feared. He had the papal-nuncio arrested in Paris, sent troops to Italy, and seized the county of Avignon. When the Pope, who had said at first that 'legions of angels would come to his aid', saw no angels appear, he ate humble pie, and asked for pardon. The King of France pardoned him on the condition that he surrendered Castro and Ronciglione to the Duke of Parma, and

Comaccio to the Duke of Modena, both of whom were linked to his cause, and both of whom were being oppressed.

Just as Innocent X had had a little pyramid erected in memory of the demolition of Castro, the King of France demanded the erection of a pyramid that was twice as high in Rome, in the Farnese square, where the crime of the Pope's guards had been committed. There was no mention of the page who had been killed. The Vicar of Christ at least owed a pension to that young Christian's family. The court of Rome had skilfully inserted into the treaty that Castro and Roncig-lione would only be surrendered to the Duke on payment of a sum of money almost equivalent to the sum owed by the House of Farnese to the *mount of piety*. Through this clever trick Castro and Ronciglione have always remained incamerated in spite of Louis XIV, who on occasion would explode haughtily against the court of Rome, and then make concessions to it.

It is certain that the possession of this duchy has been worth four times as much to the Chamber of the Apostles as the *mount of piety* can get from capital and interest payments. No matter, the apostles are still in possession of it. There has never been a clearer case of usurpation. Let the matter be referred to all the courts of justice from China to Corfu; is there [a single] one where the Duke would not win his case? It is just a matter of doing a sum. How much do I owe you? How much have you handled? Pay me the surplus and give me my security back. It is highly likely that when the Duke of Parma wishes to institute these proceedings, he will win his case anywhere else apart from in the Chamber of the Apostles.

6. The acquisitions of Julius II

I shall not talk here about Comaccio; that is something that concerns the Empire, and I leave that matter with the Vetzlar Chamber and the Aulic Council. But we have to see how the servants of God's servants obtained from Heaven all the territories that they possess today. From Cardinal Bembo, Guichardin and so many others, we know how Rovere, Julius II, bought his right to the papacy, and how he was elected before the conclave of cardinals had even met. He had to pay what he had promised, otherwise votes would not have been cast for him, and he risked being deposed. In order to pay some people he had to take from others. He began by raising an army, put

himself at its head, and laid siege to Perugia, which belonged to Lord
Baglioni, a weak and timid man, who did not have the courage to
defend himself. He surrendered his city in 1506. He was permitted
to leave only with his furniture, together with some *agnus-dei*. From
Perugia Julius marched to Bologna and drove out the Bentiviglios.

We know how he armed all the sovereign rulers against Venice,
and how he then allied himself with the Venetians against Louis XII.
A cruel enemy, a perfidious friend, a priest, a soldier, he embodied
all that is reprehensible about these two professions: deceit and inhumanity. This fine fellow dabbled also in excommunications. He
launched his ridiculous thunderbolt against Louis XII, King of
France and father of the nation. As one famous author tells us, he
thought that as Vicar of Christ, he could anathematise kings; and as
Vicar of the Devil, he set a price on the heads of all Frenchmen in
Italy. This is the man whose feet were kissed by princes, and whom
nations adored as if he were a god. I do not know whether or not he
had the pox, as writers have said; all I know is that his daughter,
Signora Orsini, did not have it, and that she was a highly respectable
lady. We must always be just to the gentle sex now and again.

7. On the acquisitions of Alexander VI

The world has echoed enough with stories of how much simony
the papacy was worth to this Borgia, of the extremes of frenzy and
debauchery with which his bastard children stained themselves, of
his incest with his daughter Lucretia. What a girl that Lucretia was!
We know that she slept with her brother and her father, and that she
had bishops for servants. We are pretty well informed about that
wonderful banquet in the course of which fifty naked courtesans
picked up chestnuts, adopting various postures, to amuse Her Holiness, who gave prizes to the most energetic victors of those ladies.
Italy still speaks of the poison he is supposed to have prepared for a
few cardinals, from which it is believed he died himself. Nothing of
these awful horrors remains except the memory of them; but the heirs
of those whom he and his son murdered, or strangled, or poisoned in
order to rob them of their inheritance still survive. We know the
poison that he used; it was called *la cantarella*. All the crimes of this
dreadful family are as familiar as the Bible, under whose protection
they were committed with impunity by these monsters. The question

here is only about the rights of several illustrious houses that still survive. Will the Orsinis and the Colonnas always allow the Apostolic Chamber to keep the legacies of their ancient houses?

In Venice we have the Tiepolos, who descend from the daughter of John Sforza, Lord of Pesaro, whom Caesar Borgia drove from the city in the name of his father, the Pope. There are the Manfredis, who have rightful claims on Faenza. Astor Manfredi, at the age of eighteen, surrendered Faenza to the Pope, and placed himself under the authority of the Pope's son on condition that he was allowed to enjoy the rest of his fortune. He was extremely handsome; Caesar Borgia fell hopelessly in love with him; but because he was cross-eyed, as all the portraits of him show, and because his crimes increased still further the horror that Manfredi had of him, that young man unwisely exploded with rage against the plundering ravisher; Borgia could only enjoy him by force; he then had him thrown in the Tiber along with the wife of a certain Caraccioli, whom he had kidnapped from her husband.

One can scarcely believe such atrocities. But if there is one thing established beyond doubt in history, it is the crimes of Alexander VI and his family.

The house of Montefeltro is not yet extinct. The Duchy of Urbino, which Alexander VI and his son invaded by means of the blackest and most notorious perfidy in the whole of Machiavelli, belongs to those descended from the house of Montefeltro, unless crimes constitute a prescription against their adherence to equity.

Julius Varano, Lord of Camerino, was captured by Caesar Borgia at the very moment he was signing a capitulation and, together with his two sons, he was strangled on the spot. There are still Varanos in the Romagna; Camerino belongs to them, no doubt.

Everyone who can read has seen with horror in Machiavelli how this Caesar Borgia had Vitellozzo Vitelli, Oliverotto da Fermo, *il signor* Pagolo, and Francesco Orsini, Duke of Gravina, murdered. But what Machiavelli did not say, and what modern historians teach us, is that while Borgia was having the Duke of Gravina and his friends strangled in the castle at Sinigaglia, his brother, the Pope, was having Cardinal Orsini, a relative of the Duke of Gravina, arrested, and was confiscating all the property of that illustrious house. The Pope even took possession of the furniture. He complained bitterly of not finding among these effects a large pearl with an estimated value of two thousand *ducats*, and a casket full of gold that he knew was [somewhere] in the Cardinal's house. The eighty-eight year old mother of this unfortunate priest, fearing that Alexander VI might poison her son, as was his wont, brought the pearl and the casket to him, trembling with fear; but her son had already been poisoned, and was breathing his last. It is certain that if, as they say, the pearl is still in the Pope's treasure-house, it should in all conscience be given back to the House of Urbino, together with the money that was in the casket.

Conclusion

After having reported in the most accurate way all these facts, from which a few implications can be drawn, and which can be put to some honest use, I shall draw to the attention of all those who are interested, and who might cast their eyes over these pages, that the popes do not possess an inch of land over which they have sovereign power that has not been acquired through civil upheaval or through fraud. As far as civil upheaval is concerned, you have only to read the history of the Empire and the German legal experts. As far as fraud is concerned, you have only to take a glance at the donation of Constantine and the decretals.

The donation of Countess Mathilda to the mild and modest Gregory VII is the title-deed that favours the bishops of Rome most. But in all honesty, if a woman in Paris, Vienna, Madrid or Lisbon disinherited all her relatives, and left in her will all the fiefdoms inherited from the male line of the family to her confessor, together with her rings and jewels, would that will not be broken in accordance with the explicit laws of all those states?

We will be told that the Pope is above all laws, that he can make just what is unjust: *potest de injustitia facere justitiam; papa est supra jus, contra jus, et extra jus*; that is the view of Bellarmino; that is the opinion of Roman theologians. To that we have nothing to say in response. We hold the siege of Rome in reverence; we are indebted to it for indulgences, for the ability to extract souls from purgatory; for permission to marry our sisters-in-law and our nieces one after the other, for the canonisation of Saint Ignatius; for the certainty of entering Paradise by wearing a scapular; but these benefits are not perhaps sufficient reason to hold on to other people's property.

There are some who say that if every church governed itself by the laws of the State, if a stop were to be put to the simony of paying for a benefice with annates, if a bishop, who is not normally rich before being nominated, was not obliged to ruin himself and his creditors by borrowing money to pay for bulls, the State would not be impoverished in the long run by the outflow of this money which never returns. But we shall leave the matter to be discussed by the bankers at the court of Rome.

Let us end by begging the Christian and well-intentioned reader to read the Bible again, and to see if he can find in it a single word authorising even the most minor of the tricks which we have faithfully reported. It is true that we do read there: 'we must make friends with the money of the Mammon of iniquity'.[3] Ah! *beatissimo padre*, if that is so, then let us have the money.

Padua, 24 June 1768.

[3] Luke, XVI.9.

Commentary on the book *On crimes and punishments*, by a provincial lawyer

1. The occasion for the commentary

I was immersed in reading the little book *On crimes and punishments*,[1] which is [the equivalent] in morality to what the few cures that might relieve our suffering are in medicine. I imagined fondly that this work would alleviate the barbarities that remain in the jurisprudence of so many nations. I was hoping for some reform to take place in the human race when I learned that in one province they had just hanged a pretty and shapely young eighteen-year-old girl, with some useful talents, and from a very respectable family.

She was guilty of having allowed herself to get pregnant; she was still more so for having abandoned her child. This unfortunate girl was surprised by labour pains while fleeing the family home. She gave birth alone, and without help, by a fountain. Shame, which is a violent passion in her sex, gave her enough strength to return to her father's house, and to conceal her condition there. She left her child exposed, and it was found dead the next day. The mother was discovered, sentenced to the gallows, and executed.

The first wrong done by this girl ought either to be covered up in the bosom of her family, or should deserve nothing but the protection of the law, because it is up to the seducer to make good the wrong he has done, because weakness has a right to leniency, because everything speaks in favour of a girl whose concealed pregnancy often puts her life in danger, because public knowledge of this pregnancy blights her reputation, and because the difficulty of raising her child is a further misfortune.

[1] By Beccaria.

244

The second wrong is of a more criminal nature; she abandons the fruit of her weakness and exposes it to the risk of death.

But because a child is dead, is it absolutely necessary to make the mother die too? She had not killed it; she fondly imagined that some passer-by would take pity on that innocent creature; she might well have had it in mind to go and retrieve her child, and give it the necessary succour. That feeling is so natural that one must assume it exists in a mother's heart. The law acts positively against the girl in this province I am talking about; but is this law not unjust, inhuman and pernicious? Unjust, because it has not distinguished between the person who kills her child and the person who abandons it; inhuman in as much as it causes an unfortunate girl to die a cruel death who can only be reproached for her weakness and for her readiness to conceal her misfortune; pernicious in as much as it robs society of a citizen who was destined to give subjects to the State in a province where they are complaining about depopulation.

Charity has not yet set up in this country places of shelter for the destitute, where children abandoned to the elements might be looked after. In those areas where charity fails, the law is always cruel. It would be much better to make provision for these quite commonplace misfortunes than just to punish them and nothing more. True jurisprudence lies in the prevention of crimes, and not in dealing out death to a weak sex, when it is obvious that her wrong is not accompanied by malice, and that it has caused her heartache.

Guarantee, as much as you are able, resources to whoever is tempted to do wrong, and you will have less to punish.

2. On torture

This wretched law that is so hard, which has been brought painfully home to me, has made me take a look at national criminal codes. The humane author of *On crimes and punishments* is absolutely right to complain that punishment is too often excessive in relation to the crime, and sometimes has pernicious effects for the State, for whose benefit it should be working.

Refined tortures, in which one can see how the human mind has worn itself out making death frightful, seem to be more the inventions of tyranny than of justice.

The wheel torture was introduced into Germany in times of anarchy, when those grabbing the regalia of power wished to horrify, by means of an unheard-of torture device, whoever might dare to make an attempt on their lives. In England they used to open up the stomach of a man convicted of high treason, his heart was torn out, they would slap his cheeks with it, and the heart was then thrown in the flames. But what did this crime of high treason often amount to? It meant, in the civil wars, having been loyal to an unlucky king, and of occasionally asking for the dubious rights of a victor to be justified. Eventually customs grew milder; it is true that they still tear hearts out, but always after the death of the condemned. The apparatus of death is horrific, but death is sweet, as far as it [ever] can be.

3. On the punishments for heretics

It was tyranny in particular that was the first form of government to order the death penalty for those who had a few differences in matters of dogma with the dominant church. Before the tyrant Maximinus, no Christian emperor had thought of condemning a man to be tortured just because of some controversial issues. It is true, admittedly, that it was two Spanish bishops who pushed hard for the death of the Priscillianists with Maximinus; but it is nonetheless true that this tyrant wanted to please the dominant party by spilling the blood of heretics. Barbarity and justice left him equally cold. Being jealous of Theodosius who, like him, was a Spaniard, he fondly imagined that he could take the Eastern Empire from him in the same way that he had already invaded the Western Empire. Theodosius was hated for his cruelty; but he knew how to get all the religious leaders on his side. Maximinus wished to display the same zeal, and enlist the Spanish bishops to the ranks of his bodyguards. He flattered both the old and the new religion; he was a man who was as two-faced as he was inhuman, as were all those in that period who aspired to, or succeeded to, the Empire. This vast area of the world was governed like Algeria is today. The militia made and unmade emperors; often it chose them from nations with a reputation for barbarity. So Theodosius opposed him with other barbarians from Scythia. He was the one who filled his armies with Goths, and who brought up Alaric, the conqueror of Rome. In all that horrible confusion, it was [all a matter of who] could strengthen the party supporting him the most by any means possible.

Maximinus had just murdered the Emperor Gratian, Theodosius' colleague. He had the death of Valentinian II in mind, who as a child had been proclaimed Gratian's successor in Rome. He assembled a powerful army at Trier, made up of Gauls and Germans. He was raising troops in Spain when two Spanish bishops, Idacio and Ithacus or Itacius, who at that time had a lot of influence, came to ask him for the blood of Priscillian and all his followers who said that souls emanate from God, that the Trinity does not have three hypostases and, what is more, who took sacrilege as far as fasting on Sundays. Maximinus, who was half-pagan and half-Christian, was quick to appreciate the enormity of these crimes. The holy bishops Idacio and Itacius received permission for Priscillian and his followers to be put to the question first before being put to death. They were present at this in order to ensure that everything proceeded by the book, and returned home blessing God and ranking Maximinus, defender of the faith, with the saints. But as Maximinus was defeated by Theodosius, and then murdered at the feet of his victor, he was not canonised.

It should be noted that Saint Martin, Bishop of Tours, a really good man, begged for mercy for Priscillian; but the bishops accused him of being a heretic himself, and he returned to Tours in case he was put to the question in Trier.

As for Priscillian, after having been hanged he had the consolation of being honoured by his sect as a martyr. His feast day was celebrated, and still would be if there were any Priscillianists left.

This example made the whole Church tremble, but not long after it was imitated and surpassed. The Priscillianists had been put to death by the sword, by the rope and by stoning. A young lady of good family, suspected of having fasted on Sundays, was only stoned to death in Bordeaux. These tortures seemed to be too mild. It was proved that God required heretics to be slowly roasted. The reason given arbitrarily [for this] was that God punishes them in this way in the next world, and that every prince, every lieutenant of every prince, down to the most minor magistrate, is in the image of God in this world.

It was on this principle that sorcerers, who were visibly under the control of the Devil, were burnt everywhere, and also the unorthodox who were believed to be more criminal and more dangerous than sorcerers.

We do not know exactly what the heresy was of those canons whom King Robert, son of Hugh, and Constance, his wife, had burned in their presence when they went to Orléans in 1022. How could we know? In those times there was only a very small number of clerics and monks who had the writing habit. All that is recorded is that Robert and his wife feasted their eyes on this abominable spectacle. One of the members of this sect had been Constance's confessor; that queen could not think of any better way of making up for the misfortune of having made her confession to a heretic than by seeing him swallowed up in the flames.

The habit became law, and from then on right up to the present day, that is to say, for more than seven hundred years, those who have been, or appear to have been, stained with the crime of having a wrong viewpoint have been burnt.

4. On the eradication of heresies

It seems to me that we must distinguish in a heresy between opinion and faction. From the earliest days of Christianity, opinions were divided. Christians in Alexandria did not think like Christians from Antioch on a number of points. The Achaians opposed the Asiatics. This diversity has lasted throughout the ages, and will probably last forever. Jesus Christ, who could have united all of his followers in the same sentiments, has not done so. It is to be presumed, therefore, that he did not wish to, and that his purpose was to train all his churches to be kind and charitable by allowing them to have different systems, which all came together in recognising him as their leader and master. All these sects, which the emperors had long tolerated, or which had been hidden from their view, could not persecute and ban each other since they were all equally subject to the authority of Roman magistrates. They could only argue. When the magistrates pursued them, they all claimed the same natural right; they said: Let us worship God in peace, do not rob us of the freedom that you give to the Jews. Every sect today can make the same speech to those who oppress them. They can say to the nations that gave privileges to the Jews: Treat us like you treat the children of Jacob; let us pray to God, like they do, according to our conscience; our views do no more harm to your State than Judaism does. You tolerate Christ's enemies; tolerate us therefore; we adore Christ, and only differ from you on a few theological subtleties. Do not deprive yourselves of useful subjects. It is important to you that they should work in your factories, in your navy, in the cultivation of your land, and it matters little to you that they should have a few articles of faith that are different from your own. Their arms are what you need, not their catechism.

A faction is something quite different. It always happens, and necessarily so, that a persecuted sect degenerates into a faction. Oppressed people unite and encourage each other. They have more energy to strengthen their cause than the dominant sect [has] to exterminate it. They have to crush, or be crushed. That is what happened after the persecution stirred up by Galerius Caesar in 303, during the last two years of Diocletian's empire. The Christians, having been favoured by Diocletian for eighteen whole years, had become too numerous and too rich to be exterminated; they went over to Constantius Chlorus; they fought for his son Constantine, and there was a complete revolution in the empire.

Small things and large things can be compared when the same spirit is behind them. A similar revolution occurred in Holland, in Scotland, in Switzerland. When Ferdinand and Isabella drove the Jews out of Spain, who had settled there not only before the reigning house, but before the Moors and the Goths, and even before the Carthaginians, the Jews would have had a revolution in Spain, had they been as warrior-like as they were rich, and if they had been able to reach agreement with the Arabs.

In a word, a sect has only ever changed the government when desperation provided it with weapons. Mohammed himself only succeeded because he had been driven out of Mecca, and because a price had been put on his head.

So if you want to prevent a sect from toppling a state, use tolerance. Imitate the wise policy followed today by Germany, England and Holland. With a new sect, the only position to adopt in politics is either to put to death without mercy the leaders and followers, men, women and children without exception, or to tolerate them when the sect is a large one. The first position is that of a monster, the second that of a wise man.

Chain to the State all the subjects of the State with self-interest. Let the Quaker and the Turk find it to their advantage to live under your laws. Religion comes from God to man; civil laws come from you to your people.

5. On acts of desecration

Louis IX, King of France, who is ranked among the saints for his virtues, first passed a law against blasphemers. He condemned them to a new torture: their tongues were pierced with a hot iron. It was a kind of law of retaliation: the member that had sinned suffered pain for it. But it was very difficult to decide what a blasphemy is. Expressions slip out in anger, or in joy, or in ordinary conversation which are only, properly speaking, expletives, like the *sela* or the *vah* of the Jews, the *pol* and the *aedopol* of the Latins, and the *per deos immortales*, which is used quite normally without actually taking an oath on the immortal gods.

These words, which are called *swear words, blasphemies*, are in most cases vague terms arbitrarily interpreted. The law punishing them appears to have been taken from that of the Jews which says: 'Thou shalt not take the name of God in vain.'[2] The cleverest interpreters believe that this law forbids perjury, and they are right in as much as the word *shavé*, translated as *in vain*, really means perjury. Now what relevance can perjury have to those words toned down by *cadédis, sangbleu, ventrebleu, corbleu*?

The Jews swore on God's life: *vivit Dominus*. It was an everyday expression. So it was only forbidden to lie in the name of God, who was called to bear witness.

In 1181 Philip-Augustus had condemned noblemen in his country who uttered out loud *têtebleu, ventrebleu, corbleu, sangbleu* to pay a fine, and commoners to be drowned. The first part of this decree seems puerile, the second abominable. It was a crime against nature to drown citizens for the same offence that noblemen paid for with the equivalent in those days of two or three *sous*. Also this strange law was not put into practice, like so many others, especially when the King was excommunicated and his kingdom interdicted by Pope Celestine III.

Saint Louis, in a fit of zeal, decreed without any discrimination that whoever uttered these indecent terms should have his tongue pierced or his upper lip cut off. It cost one coarse *bourgeois* his tongue, and he complained about it to Pope Innocent IV. The pontiff advised the King strongly that the punishment was too great for the crime. From then on the King refrained from using this harsh punishment.

[2] Exodus, XX.7.

It would have been a good thing for human society if popes had never had any other kind of victory over kings.

Louis XIV's statute, in the year 1666, decrees: 'That those convicted of having sworn and blasphemed on the holy name of God, on his most holy mother or on the saints, will be sentenced thus: for a first offence, to pay a fine; for a second, third and fourth offence, to have the fine doubled, tripled and quadrupled; for a fifth offence, to wear an iron collar; for a sixth offence, to be pilloried, and to have the upper lip cut off; and for a seventh offence, simply to have the tongue cut out.'

This seems to be a wise and humane law; it inflicts a cruel punishment only after six successive offences have actually occurred.

But for more serious acts of desecration, called *sacrilege*, our weighty tomes of criminal jurisprudence, whose record of decisions must not be taken for laws, speak only of theft committed in churches, and no positive law even mentions punishment by fire. These tomes do not elaborate on public impiety, either because such insanities had not been foreseen, or because it was too difficult to specify [what they were]. The punishment for this crime is thus left to the wisdom of judges. Yet justice should have nothing arbitrary about it.

In such rare cases, what must judges do? Take into consideration the age of the offender, the nature of their offence, the gravity of their wickedness, of their scandalous behaviour, of their stubbornness, the public's need to exact, or not to exact, a terrible punishment. 'Pro qualitate personae, proque rei conditione et temporis et aetitis et sexus, vel severius vel clementius stauendum.' If the law does not expressly specify death for this crime, who is the judge who feels obliged to pass this sentence? If punishment is necessary, if the law is silent, the judge should, without any difficulty, pass a milder sentence, because he is a man.

[Acts of] sacrilegious desecration are only ever committed by young rakes. Will you punish them as severely as if they had killed their brothers? Their age argues in their favour: they cannot do as they wish with their property because they are not deemed to be mentally mature enough to see the consequences of a bad deal; thus they are not mature enough to see the consequences of their impious impetuousness. Will you treat a young reprobate[3] who, in [an act of]

---

[3] De La Barre.

blindness, is supposed to have desecrated a holy statue, but without stealing it, in the same way that you treated the Brinvilliers girl, who had poisoned her father and the rest of her family? There is no explicit law against this unfortunate, and you make one up in order to expose him to the greatest torture! He deserves exemplary punishment; but does he deserve torments that horrify nature, as well as a terrible death?

Yes, he has offended God, and no doubt very seriously. Act in the same way towards him as God himself [would]. If he does penitence, God pardons him. Impose a heavy penitence on him, and pardon him.

Your illustrious Montesquieu said: 'The Divinity must be honoured, not avenged.' Think about those words carefully: they do not mean that the maintenance of public order must be abandoned. They mean, as the judicious author of *On crimes and punishments* says, that it is absurd for an insect to believe he can avenge the Supreme Being. Neither a village judge, nor a city judge is a Moses or a Joshua.

6. The leniency of the Romans in these matters

From one end of Europe to the other, the subject of conversation among respectable, educated people often turns on this enormous difference between the laws of the Romans and so many barbarous practices that have come after them, like garbage covering the ruins of a fine town.

The Roman senate certainly had as much respect for the Supreme God as we [do], and as much for the second order of immortal gods as we show towards our saints.

> Ab Jove principium ...

was the normal expression.[4] Pliny, in his panegyric of the good Trajan, starts by testifying that the Romans never failed to invoke God when beginning their business or their speeches. Cicero, Livy bear witness to that. No nation was more religious; but it was also

---

[4] Virgil, *Eclogues*, III.12. ' "Bene ac sapienter, patres conscripti, majores instituerunt, ut rerum agendarum, ita dicenti initium a precationibus capere" etc. Pliny the younger, *Panegyric of Trajan*, chapter 1' (Voltaire's note).

too great and too wise to lower itself to punish silly statements or philosophical views. It was incapable of inflicting barbaric tortures on those who had no faith in the auguries, as did Cicero, who was himself an augur, nor on those who said in the middle of senate meetings that the gods did not punish men after death.

It has been noted a hundred times or more that the senate allowed the chorus to sing on the Roman stage in the *Troad*: 'There is nothing after death, and death is nothing. Do you ask where the dead are? In the same place they were before being born.'

If ever there was a blasphemy, there it is without a doubt. And from Ennius to Ausonius blasphemies were everywhere, in spite of respect for religion. Why then did the Roman senate not suppress them? Because they had no effect whatsoever on the government of the State; because they disturbed no institution [of the State], no religious ceremony. The Romans' system of law and order was no less excellent for all that, nor were they any the less the absolute masters of the most beautiful part of the world until the time of Theodosius II.

The senate's maxim, as has been said elsewhere, was: 'DEORUM OFFENSAE DIIS CURAE: *Offences against the gods are a matter only for the gods.*' Through the wisest of institutions, senators, because they controlled religion, had nothing to fear from a college of priests forcing them to serve its vengeful purpose on the pretext of avenging Heaven. They did not say: 'Let us tear the impious limb from limb in case we are considered impious ourselves; by being cruel, let us prove to the priests that we are as religious as they [are].'

Our religion is more holy than that of the ancient Romans. Impiety with us is a greater crime than with them. God will punish it; it is man's job to punish crimes arising from public disorder caused by impiety. Now, if in an impious act no handkerchief has been stolen, if no-one has received the slightest injury, if religious rites have not been disturbed, shall we punish (to repeat once more) this impiety as if it was a parricide? Marshal d'Ancre killed a white cock under a full moon. Did Marshal d'Ancre have to be burnt for that?

> Et modus in rebus, sunt certi denique fines.
> Ne scutica dignum horribili sectere flagello.[5]

[5] Horace, *Satires*, I.1.108; I.3.119.

7. On the crime of preaching, and about Antoine

A Calvinist preacher who comes to preach secretly to his sheep in certain provinces is punished by death if he is caught,[6] and those who have given him food and shelter are sent to the galleys for life.

In other countries a Jesuit who comes to preach is hanged. Is it God whom people wish to avenge by having that preacher and that Jesuit hanged? Have people on both sides not relied on this law from the Scriptures: 'Whoever does not hear the Church, let him be treated as a pagan and a publican'?[7] But the Bible does not order people to kill the pagan and the publican.

Have people based themselves on these words from Deuteronomy: 'If there arises a prophet ... and if what he predicts comes to pass ... and he says to you: Let us follow strange gods ... and if your brother or your son, or your dear wife, or your close friend says to you: Come, let us go and serve strange gods ... kill him immediately; be the first to strike him down, and after you let all the people follow suit'? But neither that Jesuit nor that Calvinist said to you: Come let us follow strange gods.

Dubourg the counsellor, Canon Jehan Chauvin, known as Calvin, Servet the Spanish doctor, the Calabrian, Gentilis, served the same god. However, President Minard had Counsellor Dubourg hanged; and Dubourg's friends had Minard assassinated; and Jehan Calvin had Dr Servet slowly roasted, and had the consolation of making a major contribution to the beheading of the Calabrian, Gentilis; and Jehan Calvin's successors had Antoine burnt. Have all these murders been committed in the name of reason, piety and justice?

The story of Antoine is one of the strangest to be remembered and recorded in the annals of insanity. This is what I read about it in a very strange manuscript, reported in part by Jacob Spon. Antoine was born in Briey in Lorraine of Catholic parents, and studied with the Jesuits at Pont-à-Mousson. Ferry, the *preacher*, accepted him into the protestant religion at Metz. When he returned to Nancy, he was put on trial as if he was a heretic, and if a friend had not rescued him, he would have died by the rope. Having taken refuge in Sedan, he was suspected of being a papist, and people wanted to murder him.

---

[6] 'Edict of 1724, and earlier edicts' (Voltaire's note).
[7] Matthew, XVIII.17.

Seeing by what strange turn of events his life was safe neither with the Protestants nor the Catholics, he went off to Venice to become a Jew. He persuaded himself very sincerely that he was one, and maintained right until the end of his life that the Jewish religion was the only true one, and that as it had been so in the past, it must always be so. The Jews did not circumcise him for fear of having problems with the magistrate; but inside himself he was no less a Jew for that. He did not profess it openly, and when he went to Geneva as a preacher, he was even the first regent of the college there, becoming ultimately what is called a minister.

The perpetual struggle going on in his heart between Calvin's sect, to which he was obliged to preach, and the Jewish religion, which was the only one in which he believed, made him ill for a long time. He went down with melancholia and a cruel disease; upset by his pains, he cried out that he was a Jew. Some ministers came to see him, and tried to bring him back to his senses. He told them in reply that he worshipped only the god of Israel, and that it was impossible for God to have changed, that only God himself could have passed a law, engraved by his own hand, abolishing it. He spoke against Christianity; then he retracted; he wrote out a profession of faith to escape conviction, but after having written it out, the unfortunate faith of which he was persuaded did not allow him to sign it. The town council called the preachers together to ascertain what was to be done with this wretched man. A minority of priests were of the opinion that pity should be taken on him, that it was more necessary to try and cure his mental illness than punish it. The majority decided that he deserved to be burnt, and he was. The episode took place in 1632. A hundred years of reason and virtue were needed to expiate such a sentence.

8. The story of Simon Morin

The tragic end of Simon Morin is no less horrifying than that of Antoine. It was in the middle of the celebrations at a brilliant court, of love affairs and pleasures, at a time of the greatest freedom even, that this unfortunate man was burnt in Paris in 1663. He was a madman who thought he had visions, and took his madness to the point of believing himself to have been sent by God, and of being joined in Christ.

The *parlement* quite rightly sentenced him to be locked up in the madhouse. What is very strange is that in the same hospital there was another madman who said he was the Eternal Father, whose madness even became legendary. Simon Morin was so impressed by the madness of his companion that he recognised his own. He appeared to have returned to his senses for a while. He showed repentance to the magistrates and, unfortunately, for him, obtained his release.

Some time afterwards, his fits of madness recurred; he preached dogma. It was his bad fortune to have made the acquaintance of Desmarets de Saint-Sorlin, who for a few months was his friend, but who soon, through professional jealousy, became his most merciless persecutor.

This Desmarets was no less of a visionary than Morin; his first follies were, in truth, innocent: these were the tragi-comedies called *Erigone* and *Mirame*, printed with a translation of the Psalms, the novel called *Ariane*, and the poem entitled *Clovis*, printed next to the Prayer to the Virgin in verse [form]. These were dithyrambic poems enriched with invective against Homer and Virgil. From this kind of folly, he moved on to another, more serious kind. He was seen hounding Port-Royal, and after having admitted turning women into atheists, he set himself up as a prophet. He claimed that God had given him, with his own hand, the key to the treasure of the *Apocalypse*; that with that key he would reform the whole human race, and that he was going to command an army of a hundred and forty thousand men against the Jansenists.

Nothing would have been more reasonable and more just than to have put him in the same place as Simon Morin but, hard as it is to believe, he had a lot of influence over the Jesuit Annat, the King's confessor. He persuaded him that this poor Simon Morin was founding a sect almost as dangerous as Jansenism itself. Finally, having taken infamy to the point of making himself into an informer, he obtained from the lieutenant of police a warrant for the arrest of his unfortunate rival. Dare we say it? Simon Morin was sentenced to be burnt alive.

When he was being led out to his torture, a [piece of] paper was found in one of his stockings in which he asked God's pardon for all his mistakes. That should have saved him, but the sentence was confirmed, and he was executed without mercy.

Such tales make your hair stand on end. And in which country have such deplorable events not been seen? Everywhere men forget that they are brothers, and they persecute each other to death. For the consolation of the human race, we must flatter ourselves that those horrible times will not come back.

9. On warlocks

In 1749 a woman was burnt in the bishopric of Wurzburg, convicted of being a witch. It is a major phenomenon in our century. But is it possible for nations, which prided themselves on being reformed, and of trampling superstitions under foot, and which thought finally that they had perfected their powers of reason, to have still believed in sorcery, and to have burnt poor women accused of being witches, and to have done that a hundred years after the supposed reform of their reason?

In the year 1652, a peasant woman from the little territory of Geneva named Michelle Chaudron met the Devil when she was leaving town. The Devil kissed her, received homage from her, and imprinted on her upper lip and her right teat the mark that he was in the habit of applying to all those people he accepted as his favourites. This seal of the Devil is a small sign which numbs the skin, as all the legal experts in the demonography of that period confirm.

The Devil ordered Michelle Chaudron to cast a spell on two girls. She obeyed her lord punctiliously. The girls' parents made a legal accusation of Satanism against her. The girls were interrogated and confronted with the guilty woman. They testified that they felt continuous pins and needles in certain parts of their bodies, and that they were possessed. Doctors were called in, or at least people who passed for doctors at that time. They visited the girls. They examined Michelle's body for the seal of the devil which court proceedings call the *marks of Satan*. They plunged a long needle in, which in itself constituted a painful torture. Blood came out, and through her cries Michelle made it known that satanic marks do not make you numb. As the judges did not see sufficient proof that Michelle Chaudron was a witch, they put her to the question, which produced infallible evidence of the fact. That unfortunate woman, giving way to the violence of this torment, confessed as much as everyone wanted.

The doctors looked again for the mark of Satan. They found it in the form of a little black sign on one of her thighs. They plunged the needle in. The torment of being put to the question had been so awful that the poor, dying creature hardly felt the needle; she did not cry out; the crime was thus confirmed. But as customs were beginning to get milder, she was burnt only after being hanged and strangled.

All the courts of Christian Europe then echoed to the sound of similar warrants for arrest. Fires were lit everywhere for warlocks in the same way as for heretics. What people reproach the Turks most for is for not having had either warlocks or possessed people in their ranks. Being deprived of possessed people was seen as an infallible sign of a false religion.

A man with zeal for the public good,[8] for humanity, for true religion, has written in one of his publications supporting the cause of the innocent, that Christian courts have sentenced to death more than a hundred thousand so-called warlocks. If you add to these legal massacres the infinitely higher number of heretics who have been sacrificed, then this part of the world looks like a huge scaffold covered with executioners and their victims, and surrounded by judges, sbirros and spectators.

10. On the death penalty

It was said a long time ago that a hanged man is good for nothing, and that tortures invented for the good of society should be useful to that society. It is obvious that twenty robust thieves, sentenced to labour on [public works] projects for the rest of their lives, serve the State through their suffering, and that their death will only do good to the executioner, who is paid to kill people in public. In England, thieves are rarely punished by death; they are transported to the colonies. It is the same in the vast territories of Russia; no criminal was executed in the reign of the autocratic Elizabeth. Catherine II, who succeeded her, followed the same maxim. Crimes did not increase as a result of this humane policy, and it nearly always turned out that convicts transported to Siberia became respectable people there. The same thing was noted in the English colonies. This happy

---

[8] Voltaire is referring to himself.

transformation surprises us, but nothing is more natural. These convicts are forced into continuous work in order to live. They lack opportunities for vice; they marry; they multiply. Force men to work and you will make them into honest people. It is well known that great crimes are not committed in the country, except perhaps when there are too many feast days, which force a man into idleness, and lead him into debauchery.

A Roman citizen would only be condemned to die for crimes that affected the security of the State. Our masters, our first legislators, respected the blood of their fellow-countrymen. We squander the blood of ours.

For a long time people have worried away at this delicate and grievous issue: whether it is permissible for judges to punish by death when the law does not expressly stipulate the ultimate torment. This difficulty was solemnly debated before Emperor Henry VI. He made a judgement, and decided that no judge can have that right.

There are criminal acts that are either so unexpected, or so complicated, or linked to circumstances that are so bizarre, that in more than one country the law itself has been forced to leave these strange cases to the wisdom of the judges. But if in fact one case does arise in which the law might permit an accused person, for whom it has no sentence, to be put to death, there are a thousand other cases in which humanity, which is stronger than the law, should spare the lives of those whom the law itself has marked out for death.

The sword of justice is in our hands, but we must blunt it more often than we sharpen it. It is carried in its scabbard in the presence of kings to warn us that it should be rarely drawn.

We have seen judges who liked to spill blood; Jeffreys in England was such a one; another one, in France, was a man to whom they gave the nickname *head-chopper*.[9] Such men were not born to be magistrates; nature created them to be executioners.

11. On putting warrants into effect

Do we have to go to the ends of the earth, do we have to have recourse to the laws of China to see how careful we must be with

---

[9] The reference is to Jean-Baptiste Machault, *lieutenant-général* of police, not to be confused with his son Machault d'Arnouville, the Comptroller-General.

men's blood? The courts of that empire have existed for more than four thousand years, and for four thousand years also no villager on the fringe of the empire has been executed without the proceedings of his trial being sent to the Emperor, who has them examined three times by one of his courts; after this he signs the death warrant, or a modification to the punishment, or a complete pardon.[10]

Let us not find examples so far away; Europe is full of them. In England, no criminal is put to death whose sentence has not been signed by the King. It is the same in Germany, and almost throughout the whole of the North. Such used to be the practice once in France; it should be so in all civilised nations. Far from the throne, cabal, prejudice and ignorance can dictate the sentence. Those petty intrigues, which the court does not know about, can make no impression on the court: it is surrounded on all sides by the major issues. The Supreme Council is more accustomed to dealing with cases, and is less prejudiced. The habit of seeing everything in a broad perspective has made it wiser and more aware of things. It can see far better than a provincial lower court whether the institution of the State needs to make a severe example of someone or not. Finally, when the lower court has made a judgement according to the letter of the law, which can be rigorous, the Council mitigates the terms of the warrant in accordance with the spirit of every law, which is to sacrifice men only when it is clearly necessary.

12. On being put to the question

All men, being vulnerable to violent attacks or treachery, hate the crimes of which they might be a victim. All are united in wishing for the punishment of the main offenders and their accomplices. Yet all of them, through a sense of pity that God has placed in our hearts, protest against the tortures that the accused, from whom people want

---

[10] 'The author of the *Spirit of the laws*, who has planted so many fine truths in his work, seems to have made a cruel error when, in order to prop up his theory that a vague feeling of honour lies at the basis of monarchies, and that virtue is the basis of republics, he said of the Chinese: "I do not know what this honour is among peoples who cannot be made to do anything unless they are beaten with a stick." Certainly, from the fact that the populace is kept at bay with a heavy club, and from the fact that insolent thugs and rogues are beaten with a heavy club, it does not follow that China is not governed by courts which watch over each other, and that this is not an excellent form of government' (Voltaire's note).

to tear a confession, is made to suffer. The law has not yet found them guilty, and in the uncertain circumstances of their crime a torture is inflicted on them that is far more frightful than the death they will be given, once it is certain that they deserve it. Good God! I do not know yet whether you are guilty, and I need to torment you to enlighten myself; and if you are innocent, I shall not compensate you for the thousand deaths that I have made you suffer in place of the single one I had in store for you! Everyone shudders at this idea. I shall not mention here that Saint Augustine protested against judicial torture in his *City of God*. I shall not mention the fact that in Rome only slaves were made to suffer it, but that Quintilian, remembering that slaves are men, rejected this barbarity.

If there should be just one nation in the world which has abolished the use of torture, if there are no more crimes in that nation than in any other, if moreover it has become more enlightened, more prosperous since that abolition, that is sufficient example for the rest of the entire world. Let England alone educate other nations; but she is not alone; torture has been banned successfully in other kingdoms. So everything is settled. Will those nations which pride themselves on being civilised not pride themselves also on being humane? Will they persist with an inhumane practice on the mere pretext that it is the custom? At least keep this cruelty for acknowledged villains who have murdered the father of a family or the father of a country.[11] Seek out their accomplices, but is it not a useless barbarity for a young person who has committed a few offences that have no after-effects to suffer the same torture as a parricide? I am ashamed to have brought this subject up after what the author of *On crimes and punishments* has said about it. I must confine myself to wishing people would read again and again the work of this lover of humanity.

13. On some blood courts

Would anyone believe that there was once a high court that was more horrible than the Inquisition, and that this court was set up by Charlemagne? It was the judicial process in Westphalia, otherwise known as the Vehmic Court. The severity, or rather the cruelty, of

---

[11] The reference is possibly to Robert-François Damiens' attempt on Louis XV's life in 1757.

this court went as far as punishing by death every Saxon who broke his fast during Lent. The same law was established in Flanders and in Franche-Comté at the beginning of the seventeenth century.

The archives of a little rural outpost called Saint-Claude, in the most awful rocky part of the county of Burgundy, contain the sentence and the minutes for the execution of a poor gentleman named Claude Guillon, whose head was cut off on 28 July 1629. He had been reduced to poverty and, on a fast day, feeling the pressure of a gnawing hunger, he ate a piece of meat from a horse that had been killed in a neighbouring field. That was his crime. He was condemned as if for sacrilege. If he had been rich, and if he had ordered himself two hundred *écus*' worth of supper, while leaving the poor to die of hunger, he would have been regarded as a man fulfilling all his duties.

Here is the [judge's] pronouncement of sentence: 'After having seen all the trial papers and heard the views of doctors of law, we declare the said Claude Guillon to be duly guilty in fact and in law of having removed meat from a horse killed in one of this town's fields, of having cooked the said meat on Saturday, 31 March, and of having eaten it', etc.

What wonderful doctors they were, those doctors of law who gave their opinion! Did these episodes happen among the Topinambous and the Hottentots? The Vehmic Court was far more horrible. It secretly delegated commissaries to travel *incognito* through all the towns in Germany, getting information from the accused without reporting them to the authorities, judging them without giving them a hearing; and often, when they were short of executioners, the youngest judge carried out the duties of the office by hanging the convicted man himself.[12] To avoid the assassinations of this Star Chamber, you needed to obtain letters of exemption, imperial safeguards. Often even they were useless. This court of murderers was only completely dissolved by Maximilian I; it should have been dissolved in the blood of the judges; the Tribunal of the Ten in Venice was, by comparison, an institution of mercy.

What should we think of these horrors and of so many others? Is it enough just to groan at human nature? There have been cases in which it needed avenging.

[12] 'See the excellent *Chronological summary of the history of Germany, and of public law*, under the year 803' (Voltaire's note). The author is C-F. Pfeffel.

14. On the difference between political laws and natural laws

I call *natural laws* those laws that nature points to in all ages to all men for the maintenance of that sense of justice which nature, whatever one might say, has engraved in our hearts. Everywhere theft, violence, murder, ingratitude towards benevolent parents, perjury committed in order to harm rather than help an innocent person, plotting against one's country, are all obvious crimes that are curbed with varying degrees of severity, but always justly.

I call *political laws* those laws that are made for reasons of short-term need, either to consolidate power or in anticipation of misfortune.

It is feared that an enemy might obtain information about a town: the gates are closed, and people are forbidden to escape over the ramparts on pain of death.

People fear a new sect which, parading in public its allegiance to the sovereign powers, plots in secret to evade that allegiance; which preaches that all men are equal in order to impose its new rites on them all equally; which, lastly, on the pretext that it is better to obey God than man, and that the established sect is overloaded with superstitions and ridiculous ceremonies, wishes to destroy what the State has consecrated. The death penalty is stipulated for those who, by arguing publicly in favour of that sect, might encourage the people to rebel.

Two ambitious men argue over the throne; the stronger wins it: he decrees the death penalty for the supporters of the weaker man. The judges become the instruments of vengeance for the new sovereign, and prop up his authority. Under Hugh Capet, whoever had anything to do with Charles of Lorraine risked being sentenced to death, unless he was powerful.

When Richard III, the murderer of his two nephews, was recognised as the King of England, the Grand Jury had Sir William Collingbourne hung, drawn and quartered; he was guilty of having written to a friend of the Count of Richmond, who was raising an army at the time, and who has reigned since under the name of Henry VII; two crude and ridiculous lines in his hand were found: they were enough to have the knight killed by means of a horrible torture. The history books are full of similar examples of justice.

The law of reprisal is another one of those laws accepted by nations. Your enemy has had one of your brave captains hanged, a man who has held off an entire army for a while in a little ruined castle. One of his captains falls into your hands; he is a virtuous man whom you respect and like; you hang him by way of reprisal. It is the law, you say: that is to say, if your enemy has stained himself with a great crime, you must commit another one.

All these laws of blood-soaked politics have their moment in history, and one sees clearly that they are not true laws since they are short-lived. They are akin to that need to eat other people which you sometimes have in a situation of extreme famine: you eat them no more once you have bread.

15. On the crime of high treason, on Titus Oates, and on the death of Auguste de Thou.

People call *high treason* an attack on the country or on the sovereign who represents it. It is regarded as a parricide: thus it must not be extended to crimes which come nowhere near parricide, for if you treat robbery from one of the houses belonging to the State, misappropriation of public funds, or even seditious words, as high treason, then you diminish the horror that high treason or *lèse-majesté* ought to inspire.

There must be nothing arbitrary in our understanding of what great crimes are. If you rank theft from a father by a son, a son's expletive against his father, with acts of parricide, you break the ties of filial love. A son would no longer look upon his father as being anything other than a terrible master. Everything that is far-fetched in the law tends to destroy the law.

In ordinary crimes the law of England favours the accused; but in those involving high treason it is unfavourable towards him. The ex-Jesuit Titus Oates, having been judicially interrogated in the House of Commons, and having given assurances on oath that he had nothing more to say, then however accused the secretary of the Duke of York, later James II, and several others, of high treason, and his denunciation was accepted. First he swore before the King's council that he had not seen this secretary, then he swore that he had seen him. In spite of these illegalities and contradictions, the secretary was executed.

This same Oates and another witness gave evidence that fifty Jesuits had plotted to assassinate King Charles II, and that they had seen commissions from Father Oliva, the General of the Jesuits, for officers who were to command an army of rebels. These two witnesses were enough to have the heart torn from several of the accused, and their cheeks beaten with it. But, in all good faith, is that enough from two witnesses to get those they wish to ruin killed? At the very least, these two informers ought not to have been well-known rascals, at least. It is even more necessary that they should not bear witness to unlikely things.

It is quite obvious that if the two most upright magistrates in the Kingdom were to accuse a man of plotting with the Mufti to circumcise the whole of the Privy Council, the *parlement*, the Audit Office, and the Archbishop of the Sorbonne, it would be no good those two magistrats swearing that they had seen letters from the Mufti; people would be more inclined to think that they had gone mad than to have confidence in their testimony. It is just as outlandish to suppose that the General of the Jesuits was raising an army in England as it would be to think that the Mufti was sending people to circumcise the French court. Yet people had the misfortune to believe Titus Oates, so there is no kind of atrocious madness that has not entered men's heads.

The laws of England do not regard as being guilty of a plot those who knew about it and did not reveal it; they assumed that an informer is as infamous as a plotter is guilty. In France, those who know about a plot, and do not report it, are punished by death. Louis XI, against whom people plotted frequently, passed this law. A Louis XII, a Henry IV, would never have conceived of it.

This law not only forces a respectable man to inform on a crime that he could prevent by wise advice and firmness, but it exposes him still further to punishment for calumny, for it is very easy for the plotters to arrange things in such a way that he cannot convict them.

This was precisely the case with the respectable François-Auguste de Thou, Counsellor of State, son of the only good historian that France can boast of, equal to Guichardin in his enlightened views, and possibly superior to him in his impartiality.

The plot was hatched more against Cardinal Richelieu than against Louis XIII. There was no question of delivering France up to her enemies; for the King's brother, the main instigator of this plot, seeing only a dying elder brother and two children still in the cradle between him and the throne, could not have aimed to surrender a kingdom to which he still regarded himself as the heir presumptive.

De Thou was guilty neither before God nor before men. One of the agents of *Monsieur* the King's only brother, of the Duke of Bouillon, sovereign prince of Sedan, and of the Master of the Horse, d'Effiat Cinq-Mars, had communicated by [word of] mouth the plan of the plot to the Counsellor of State. The latter went to find Master of the Horse Cinq-Mars, and did what he could to discourage him from the enterprise; he pointed out the difficulties. If he had at that point denounced the plotters, he had no proof against them. He would have been crushed by the denial of the heir presumptive to the throne, by that of a sovereign prince, by that of the King's favourite, and finally by the loathing of the public. He was exposing himself to punishment as a cowardly slanderer.

Chancellor Séguier himself acknowledged that when he confronted de Thou with the Master of the Horse. It was during this confrontation that de Thou said to Cinq-Mars these very words, recorded in the minutes: 'Remember, sir, that not a day passed when I didn't talk about this treaty to dissuade you from it.' Cinq-Mars accepted that this was true. De Thou therefore would deserve a reward rather than death in any humane, impartial court. At least he deserved to be spared by Cardinal Richelieu; but humanity was not the Cardinal's strength. It is really a case here of something more than *summum jus, summa injuria*. The death warrant for this good man bears the words: 'For having known and participated in the said plots.' It does not say: 'for not having revealed them'. It seems that the crime was to have known about the crime, and that people deserve to die for having eyes and ears.

All that one can say about such a warrant perhaps is that it was not issued by justice, but by commissaries. The murderous letter of the law was followed precisely. It is not only up to legal experts, but to all men, to declare whether or not the spirit of the law had been twisted. It is a sad contradiction that a small group of men should have someone killed as a criminal whom a whole nation judges to be innocent and worthy of respect.

16. On disclosure by confession

Jaurigny[13] and Balthazar Gérard, the murderers of William I, Prince of Orange, Jacques Clément the Dominican, Châtel, Ravaillac, and all the other parricides of those times, went to confession before committing their crimes. Fanaticism in those deplorable centuries had reached such excesses that confession was just one more way of committing themselves to the completion of their villainous act; it became a holy act by virtue of the fact that confession is a sacrament.

Strada himself says that Jaurigny 'non ante facinus aggredi sustinuit, quam expiatam noxis animam apud domincanum sacerdotem coelesti pane firmaverit: *Jaurigny did not dare to commit this act without having fortified the heavenly bread of his soul, purged through confession at the feet of a Dominican*'.

In the cross-examination of Ravaillac it was apparent that this unfortunate man, when he left the *Feuillants* and wanted to join the Jesuits, had gone to the Jesuit d'Aubigny; that after talking to him about several visions that he had had, showed the Jesuit a knife, on the blade of which were engraved a heart and a cross, and he said these very words to the Jesuit: 'This heart indicates that the King must be persuaded in his heart to wage war on the Huguenots.'

Perhaps if d'Aubigny had had enough zeal and wisdom to inform the King of these words, the best of kings would not have been assassinated.

On 20 August in the year 1610, three months after the death of Henry IV, whose wounds bled from the heart of every Frenchman, Servin, the Advocate-General, of still illustrious memory, required the Jesuits to sign the following four articles:

1. That the synod was above the Pope;
2. That the Pope could not take away from the King any of his rights through excommunication;
3. That ecclesiastics are entirely subject to the King, like everyone else;
4. That a priest who learns about a plot against the King and the state in the confessional must reveal it to the magistrates.

On the 22nd, the *parlement* issued a warrant whereby Jesuits were forbidden to teach the young before they had signed these four art-

[13] Or Jaureguy.

icles; but the court of Rome was then so powerful, and that of France so weak, that this warrant was useless.

One fact that deserves to be noted is that this same court of Rome, that did not wish confessions to be revealed when the lives of sovereigns were at stake, obliged confessors to denounce to inquisitors those whom their penitents accused in their confessions of having seduced them, and abused them. Paul IV, Pius IV, Clement VIII, Gregory XV[14] ordered these revelations. It was a very awkward trap for confessors and penitents. It made a sacrament into a registry of denunciations, and even of acts of sacrilege; for, by ancient canon law, and especially by the Lateran Council held under Innocent III, every priest who revealed a confession, whatever its nature, must be interdicted and imprisoned for life.

But there is worse to come: here we have four popes in the sixteenth and seventeenth centuries ordering the revelation of a sin of impurity, and not permitting the revelation of a parricide. During the sacrament before a Carmelite friar, a woman confesses, or thinks, that a Franciscan has seduced her: the Carmelite must denounce the Franciscan. A fanatical assassin, thinking that he is serving God by killing his prince, consults a confessor on this issue of conscience: the confessor is guilty of sacrilege if he saves his sovereign's life.

This horrible and ridiculous contradiction is the unfortunate consequence of the continual conflict that has existed for so many centuries between ecclesiastical and civil laws. The citizen finds himself squeezed on a hundred occasions between sacrilege and the crime of high treason, and the rules of good and evil are shrouded in a chaos from which they have not yet been extricated.

The confession of one's offences has been authorised since time immemorial in almost every nation. People accused themselves in the mysteries of Orpheus, of Isis, of Ceres, of Samothrace. The Jews confessed their sins on the day of solemn expiation, and they still have this custom. A penitent chooses his confessor, who in his turn becomes his penitent, and one after the other each one receives from his companion thirty-nine lashes while repeating three times the confessional formula, which consists only of thirteen words and which, as a result, does not say anything in particular.

---

[14] 'The constitution of Gregory XV is dated 30 August 1622, see the *Ecclesiastical memoirs* by the Jesuit d'Avrigny, unless you prefer to consult the bullarium' (Voltaire's note).

None of these confessions ever went into detail, none served as a pretext for secret consultations that penitent fanatics have sometimes had in order to have the right to sin with impunity, a pernicious practice which corrupts a salutary institution. Confession, which was the greatest curb on crime, has often become an encouragement to crime itself in times of sedition and upheaval; and it is probably for all these reasons that so many Christian societies have abolished a holy practice that seemed to them to be as dangerous as it was useful.

17. On counterfeit money

The crime of making counterfeit money is regarded as a second category of high treason, and rightly so: it is a betrayal of the State to rob all the individuals in the State. People ask whether a businessman who imports gold bars from America, and converts them into true currency, is guilty of high treason, and whether he deserves death. In nearly all countries he would not suffer the ultimate penalty; after all, he has not robbed anybody. On the contrary, he is doing the State a favour by achieving an increase in the circulation of currency. But if he has arrogated to himself the right of the sovereign, he is robbing it of the small profit that the King makes on currency. He has made good coins, but he is exposing his imitators to the temptation of making bad ones. Death is a lot for this. I knew one legal expert who wanted to sentence this man, who was skilled and useful, to work in the King's mint with his feet shackled.

18. On household theft

In countries where petty household theft is punished by death, is this disproportionate punishment not very dangerous to society? Is it not an invitation to petty theft even? For if it is the case that a master brings his servant to justice for a minor act of theft, and that it costs this unfortunate man his life, the master horrifies the whole neighbourhood. People then think that nature and the law are in conflict, and the law is worthless as a result.

So what happens? Those masters who have been robbed, not wishing to cover themselves in shame, do no more than dismiss their servants, who go off to steal elsewhere, and who get used to robbery. As the death penalty applies equally to petty theft and major robbery, obviously they will try to steal as much as possible. They could even become murderers if they think that it is a way of not being caught.

But if the punishment fits the crime, if the petty thief is sentenced to community work, then his master will report him without any scruples. There would be no more shame attached to denunciations. Robbery would become less common. It all proves that great truth that a severe law sometimes generates crimes.

19. On suicide

The famous Duverger de Hauranne, *abbé* of Saint-Cyran, who is regarded as the founder of Port-Royal, wrote in about the year 1608 a treatise on suicide,[15] which became one of the rarest books in Europe. The *Decalogue* orders us not to kill. It appears that the murder of oneself is no less part of this precept than the murder of one's neighbour. Now if there are circumstances in which it is permitted to kill one's neighbour, there are also circumstances in which it is permitted to kill oneself. You must not make an attempt on your life until you have listened to reason.

Our lives are at the disposal of the State, which stands for God. Man's reason can also stand for God's reason: it is a ray of the eternal light.

Saint-Cyran develops this argument in a major way, and it can be taken as pure sophism. But he is more difficult to answer when he gets to the explanations and the details. One can kill oneself, he says, for the sake of the prince, for that of the country, for that of one's parents.

One cannot see in fact why people like Codrus and Curtius should be punished. There is no sovereign who would dare to punish the family of a man who gave up his life for him. What am I saying? Not a single one would dare to deny him a reward. Saint Thomas said the same thing before Saint-Cyran did. But we need neither Thomas, nor Bonaventure, nor Hauranne to know that a man who murders for his country deserves our praises.

The *abbé* of Saint-Cyran concluded that what was good enough for someone else was good enough for oneself. What is advanced in

---

[15] 'It was printed in a duo-decimo edition by Toussaint Dubray in 1609, with the King's privilege. It must be in His Majesty's library' (Voltaire's note).

Plutarch, Seneca, Montaigne, and by a hundred other philosophers, in favour of suicide is well known. It is a worn-out commonplace. I do not claim here to make an apology for an action condemned by the law; but neither the Old Testament nor the New has ever forbidden a man from taking his leave of life when he can no longer stand it. No Roman law condemned the murder of oneself. On the contrary, this is the law of Emperor Marcus Antonius, which was never revoked: 'If your father or your brother, being accused of no crime, kills himself either to escape from pain, or boredom with life, or despair, or insanity, let his will remain valid, and his heirs inherit by the law of *intestacy*.'

In spite of this humane law of our masters, we still drag people through the dirt; we drive a stake through the body of a man who has chosen to die; we make his memory shameful; we dishonour his family as much as we can; we punish the son for having lost his father, and the widow for being deprived of her husband. We even confiscate the dead man's property, which in effect amounts to stealing the inheritance of the living, to whom it belongs. This custom, like several others, is derived from our canon law which deprives of burial those who die from an act of suicide. It is concluded from this that one cannot inherit from a man who supposedly has no inheritance in Heaven. The canon law, with the title *De poenitentia* assures us that Judas committed a greater crime by strangling himself than by selling our Lord Jesus Christ.

20. On a form of mutilation

You can find in the *Digest* one of Adrian's laws which stipulates the death penalty for doctors who create eunuchs, either by tearing off testicles or by crushing them. The property of those who mutilated themselves in this way was also confiscated. Origen could have been punished for submitting himself to this operation, when he interpreted strictly a passage from Saint Matthew: 'There are those who have castrated themselves for the Kingdom of Heaven.'

Things changed under succeeding emperors, who adopted the asiatic luxury, especially in the Byzantine Empire of Constantinople, of seeing eunuchs become patriarchs and commanders of armies.

In today's Rome the custom is to castrate children to make them worthy of being the Pope's musicians, so that *castrato* and *musica del papa* have become synonymous. Not so long ago, you could see in Naples, written in large letters over the doors of certain barbers' shops: '*Qui si castrano maravigliosamente i putti.*'

21. On the seizure of property for all of the crimes discussed

A maxim accepted by the Bar is: 'Whoever seizes the body, seizes the property', a maxim that is still relevant in those countries where custom takes the place of law. Thus, as we have just said, the children of those who have brought their sad days to an end by their own hand are made to die of hunger there, as if they were the children of murderers. Thus a whole family is punished in every case for the offence of one single man.

Thus when a father is condemned to the galleys for life by an arbitrary sentence,[16] either for having sheltered a preacher in his house, or for having listened to his sermon in some cave or in some desert, his wife and children are reduced to beg for their bread.

This system of laws, which consists of stealing food from orphans, and of giving to one man the property of another, was unknown throughout the whole period of the Roman Republic. Sylla introduced it with his proscriptions. It has to be admitted that an act of theft introduced by Sylla was not an example to be followed. Moreover, this law, apparently dictated only by inhumanity and greed, was not implemented either by Caesar, or by the good Emperor Trajan, or by the Antonines, whose name is still spoken of with respect and affection by all nations. In the end, under Justinian, seizure of property took place only for the crime of *lèse-majesté*.

In the age of feudal anarchy, princes and landed lords, not being very rich, seem to have sought to increase their wealth by means of the sentences passed on their subjects, and that people wished to provide them with an income from crime. With the laws being arbitrary, and the Roman system unknown, strange or cruel customs prevailed. But today, now that the power of sovereigns is founded on vast, secure riches, their treasury does not need to be swelled with the feeble [bits and] pieces of a wretched family. Normally these are

---

[16] 'See the edict of 14 May 1724, issued at the instigation of Cardinal Fleury, and reviewed by him' (Voltaire's note).

given away to the first person to ask for them. But is it right for one citizen to get fat on the last drops of blood from another citizen?

Seizure of property is not accepted in countries where Roman law is established, with the exception of the judicial area of the Toulouse *parlement*. It is not accepted in some places we look on customarily as countries, such as Le Bourbonnais, Berry, Maine, Poitou, Brittany, or at least it excludes houses and buildings. It was once established in Calais, and the English abolished it when they became the masters of the town. It is rather strange that the inhabitants of the capital live under laws that are more severe than those of small towns: this shows how true it is that law-systems have often been established by chance, irregularly and inconsistently, just like cottages are built in a village.

Who would think that in the year 1673, in France's century of greatness, Omer Talon, the Advocate-General, spoke like this in a full session of the *parlement*, about a Miss Canillac: 'In chapter 13 of Deuteronomy God said: "If you should be in a town or place where idolatry reigns, put everyone to the sword with no regard for age, sex or rank. Bring all the spoils of the town together in the public squares, and set the town on fire, together with the spoils, until all that is left in this place of abomination is a heap of ashes. In a word, make a sacrifice of it to the Lord, and let nothing remain in your hands of the property of this accursed thing." Thus in the crime of *lèse-majesté* the King was master of property, and it was taken away from children. After the trial at Naboth, *quia maledixerat regi*, King Ahab took possession of his inheritance. David, having been warned that Miphiboseth had taken part in the rebellion, gave all his wealth to Siba who brought him the news: *Tua sunt omnia quae fuerunt Miphiboseth.*'[17]

It was a question of ascertaining who inherited Miss Canillac's property, property once seized from her father, given away by the King to a keeper of the royal mint, then given by the keeper of the royal mint to the testatrix. And it was in connection with this case of a girl from the Auvergne that an advocate-general made reference to Ahab, King of a bit of Palestine, who seized Naboth's vineyards after having murdered the owner with the dagger of justice, an abominable act which has become proverbial with a view to filling men with a horror of usurpation. Naboth's vineyard certainly had nothing to do with Miss Canillac's legacy. The murder of Miphiboseth, King Saul's

[17] Kings, II.XVI.4.

grandson, son of Jonathas, friend and protector of David, and the seizure of his property, are no less irrelevant to this lady's will.

It is with this kind of pedantry, this frenzy of quotations that are beside the point, this ignorance of human nature, these ill-conceived and ill-applied prejudices, that systems of law have been treated by men with some reputation in their field. Readers are left to judge for themselves what is superfluous in what is said to them.

22. On the criminal process and some different versions of it

If one day humane laws make some practices that are too severe in France milder, but without making crime easier, it is likely that the procedure [set out] in articles of legislation, where the authors seem to have abandoned themselves to excessive zeal, will also be reformed. Criminal legislation seems on a number of points to have been drafted only with the ruination of the accused in view. This is the only uniform law in the whole Kingdom. Should it not be just as favourable to the innocent as it is terrible to the guilty? In England, a simple matter of wrongful imprisonment is corrected by the minister who ordered it; but in France an innocent man who has been flung into dungeons, subjected to torture, can hope for no compensation, for no damages that can be claimed against anyone. He remains forever branded by society as a criminal. An innocent man branded as a criminal! And for what? Because he has had his joints dislocated! He should arouse only pity and respect. The discovery of crimes requires severe measures; it is a war that human justice wages on wickedness, but even in war there is such a thing as generosity of spirit and compassion. A brave man is tender-hearted; should a lawyer be barbaric?

Let us just compare here a few points in Roman criminal procedures with our own.

With the Romans, witnesses were heard in public, in the presence of the accused, who could respond to them, ask them questions himself, or confront them with a lawyer. This was a noble, open procedure, imbued with Roman magnanimity.

With us, everything is done in secret. A single judge, with his clerk, hears each witness in turn. This practice, established by Francis I, was formally sanctioned by the commissaries who drafted the legal regulations for Louis XIV in 1670. One single mistake was the cause of this.

On reading the code *de testibus*, they thought that these words, *testes intrare judicii secretum* meant that witnesses were questioned in secret. But *secretum* means here the judge's office. *Intrare secretum* for 'to speak secretly' would not be Latin. It was a solecism that created this part of our legal system.

Those giving evidence are normally the dregs of the people, and the judge behind closed doors can make them say anything he wants. These witnesses are heard for a second time, still in secret, and this is called *verification*. And if, after this verification, they retract their testimony, or if they make major changes to it, they are punished as false witnesses. So that when a simple man, unable to express himself, but with a true heart, remembering that he said too much or too little, that he misunderstood the judge, or that the judge misunderstood him, retracts what he said on a principle of justice, he is punished like a rogue, and he is often forced to bear false witness simply out of fear of being treated as a false witness.

If he disappears, he is open to conviction, whether the crime has been proved or not. In truth, some legal experts have assured us that the absconder should not be convicted if the crime has not been clearly proved; but other experts, less enlightened, and possibly more widely followed, have taken the opposite view. They have presumed to say that the flight of the accused man was proof of the crime; that the contempt he showed for justice, by refusing to appear, deserved the same punishment as he would get if he had been convicted of the crime. Thus, depending on which sect of legal experts the judge might follow, an innocent man will be either pardoned or condemned.

That the fantasies and errors, sometimes cruel, of vagabonds who have passed their feelings off as laws, should often be accepted as the law, is a great source of abuse in the French legal system.

In the reign of Louis XIV, two ordonnances were issued that were uniform throughout the Kingdom. In the first, aimed at civil proceedings, it was forbidden for judges to deliver judgement by default in civil matters, when the action is unproved; in the second, which regulates criminal proceedings, it does not say that when there is a lack of evidence the accused will be released. Very strange! The law says that a man from whom you are claiming money will not have judgement passed on him in his absence, except in cases where the debt is acknowledged; but if it is a question of life and death, there is an argument at the Bar to find out whether the absconder should be condemned, when the crime has not been proved; and the law does not resolve this difficulty.

When the accused has taken flight, you start by seizing and making an inventory of all his possessions. You do not even wait until the proceedings are over. You still have no proof, you still do not know whether he is innocent or guilty, and you start by imposing immense costs on him!

It is a penalty, you say, with which you are punishing his disobedience of the arrest warrant. But does not the extreme severity of your criminal practice force him to be disobedient?

If a man is accused of a crime, you first of all shut him up in a frightful dungeon; you do not allow him to communicate with anyone; you weigh him down with irons, as if you had already found him guilty. The witnesses who testify against him are heard in secret; he sees them face to face only for a moment; before hearing their testimony, he must bring forward his objections; he must give a full account of them; in the same instant he must name all the people who can support these objections. After the testimony has been read out, he is no longer party to the objections. If he demonstrates to the witnesses either that they have exaggerated the facts, or that they have omitted other facts, or that they have made a mistake in the details, fear of torture makes the witnesses persist with their perjury. If the circumstances that the accused man has set out in his interrogation are different from those reported by the witnesses, that is enough for ignorant or prejudiced judges to condemn an innocent man.

Where is the man who is not horrified by this procedure? Where is the just man who can be sure of not becoming a victim of it? O judges! If you want an accused man who is innocent not to take flight, give him the means to defend himself.

The law seems to oblige the magistrate to behave towards the accused more like an enemy than a judge. This judge has the power to order[18] the prisoner to be confronted with the witness, or to keep him away. How can such a necessary thing like confrontation be arbitrary?

---

[18] '*And, if necessary, confront*, says the 1670 edict, section 15, article 1' (Voltaire's note).

On this point custom seems to contradict the law, which is equivocal; there is always confrontation, but the judge does not always confront the accused with all the witnesses. He often omits those who do not seem to him to have important charges to make, yet such a witness who has said nothing against the accused during the inquiry might testify in his favour. The witness might have forgotten circumstances that are favourable to the accused; the judge himself might not at first have appreciated the relevance of these circumstances, and might not have recorded them. It is thus very important for all the witnesses to be confronted with the prisoner, and that there should be nothing arbitrary about that in [the process of] confrontation.

If it is a question of a crime, the prisoner cannot have a lawyer; so he opts for flight; this is what all the maxims of the Bar advise him to do; but in taking flight, he can be condemned, whether the crime has been proved or not. So a man from whom you are claiming money only has judgement passed on him in his absence in cases where the debt is acknowledged; but if his life is at stake, judgement can be passed on him in his absence when the crime has not been established. What! The law places more value on money than on life? Consult pious Antoninus and the good Trajan; they forbid the condemnation of people who are not present.

What! your law allows a person who has misappropriated public funds, a fraudulent bankrupt, to have the services of a lawyer, and a man of honour is often deprived of this help! If a single occasion can be found when an innocent man would be justified in having the services of a lawyer, is it not obvious that any law depriving him of this is unjust?

Lamoignon, the First President of the court, said against this law that 'the lawyer or counsel who has been customarily given to the accused is not a privilege granted by ordinances or by laws: it is a liberty acquired by natural right, that most ancient of all human laws. Nature teaches every man that he must have recourse to the enlightenment of others when he has not got enough of his own to know how to proceed, and obtain help when he does not feel strong enough to defend himself. Our ordinances have taken away from the accused so many advantages that it is absolutely right to retain what is left for them, and above all the lawyer, who is the most important part. If you wish to compare our procedures with those of the Romans and of other nations, you will find none more severe than those observed in France, particularly since the 1539 ordinance.'

These procedures have become even more severe since the 1670 ordonnance. They would have been much milder, if the majority of commissaries had thought like Mr Lamoignon.

The Toulouse *parlement* has a very strange practice with regard to the evidence of witnesses. Elsewhere half-proofs are accepted, which basically are just doubts: for it is known that there are no half-truths; but in Toulouse quarters and eighths of proofs are accepted. There, for example, a piece of hearsay can be regarded as a quarter-proof; another, vaguer piece of hearsay as an eighth, so that eight rumours that are just the echo of ill-founded tittle-tattle can become a whole proof. This was more or less the principle by which Jean Calas was sentenced to be broken on the wheel. Roman laws required proof *luce meridiana clariores*.

23. An idea for reform

The magistracy is so worthy of respect that the only country in the world where it is venal[19] is vowing to free itself of this practice. People want a lawyer to succeed through his ability to dispense the justice he has defended with his vigilance by what he says and writes. Then, perhaps, you would witness the birth of a regular, uniform system of laws from [the doing of] good work.

Will judgements on the same issue be delivered that are different in the provinces to those delivered in the capital? Must the same man be right in Brittany, and wrong in Languedoc? What am I saying? There are as many legal systems as there are towns; and in the same *parlement* the maxim of one court is not that of the court next door.[20]

What a monstrous disparity there is between the laws of the same kingdom! In Paris, a man who has lived in the city for a year and a day is reckoned to be an independent citizen. In Franche-Comté, a free man who has lived a year and a day in a house on land belonging to the Church becomes a slave; his relatives would not inherit what he has acquired elsewhere, and his own children are reduced to penury if they have spent a year away from the house where their father died. They call this a fair province, but what fairness!

[19] i.e. France.
[20] 'On that point, see President Bouhier' (Voltaire's note).

When you want to mark the boundary between civil authority and ecclesiastical custom, what interminable arguments there are! Where is this boundary? Who will reconcile the eternal contradictions of the Tax Office and the law? Lastly, why are reasons never given for warrants in certain countries? Is there some shame in having to justify one's judgement? Why do those who make judgements in the name of the sovereign not present their death warrants to the sovereign before issuing them?

Whichever way you look, you find contradiction, harshness, uncertainty, arbitrariness. We are seeking to perfect everything in this century; so let us seek to perfect the laws on which our lives and fortunes depend!

Dialogue between a philosopher and a comptroller-general of finance

The Philosopher

Do you know that a finance minister can do a lot of good, and as a result be greater than twenty marshals of France [put together]?

The Minister

I was well aware that a philosopher would like to soften the harsh [image] that people reproach a man in my position for having; but I did not expect him to want to give me cause for vanity.

The Philosopher

Vanity is not so much of a vice as you think. If Louis XIV had not had a bit of it, his reign would not have been so illustrious. The great Colbert had some; be vain enough to surpass him. You were born in much more favourable times than he [was]. One must rise to one's century.

The Minister

I agree that those people who farm fertile land have a great advantage over those who have done the digging.

The Philosopher

Believe me, there is nothing useful that cannot be done easily. Colbert found on the one hand a financial administration in all the disorder into which civil wars and thirty years of plunder had plunged it. On the other hand, he found a nation that was frivolous, ignorant, enslaved to prejudices with the ancient rust of thirteen hundred years [on them]. There wasn't a single man in the council who understood what change meant; there wasn't a single one who understood what the gold ratio was, not one with a notion of what trade was. Nowadays, the brightest people communicate even more closely with each other. The general population still remains in a state of deep ignorance to which the need to make a living condemns it, and in which it has been thought for a long time to be in the interests of the State to keep it; but the middle class is enlightened. This class is very large; it tutors the great who sometimes think, and the small who don't think. It has established itself in the financial [world] since the time of the famous Colbert, and the same thing has happened in music since the time of Lully. Lully could hardly find anyone capable of performing his symphonies, although they were very simple. Today the number of artists who can perform the most erudite music has grown as much as the art itself. It's the same with philosophy and with public service. Colbert has done more than the Duke of Sully; we must do more than Colbert.

At these words, the minister, noticing that the philosopher had a few papers with him, wanted to see them; it was a collection of a number of ideas that could provide plenty of food for thought. The minister took one of the papers and read:

'The wealth of a state consists in the number of its inhabitants and in their labour.

'Trade only serves to make a state more powerful than its neighbours because after a certain number of years has passed it has a war with its neighbours, just as, after a certain number of years, there's always some public catastrophe. Now in that catastrophe of war the richest nation necessarily triumphs over the others, everything else being equal, because it can buy more allies and more foreign troops. Without the catastrophe of war, increasing the reserves of gold and silver would be pointless; for provided that there is sufficient gold and silver for currency circulation purposes, provided the balance of trade was just equal, then it's clear that we lack for nothing.

'If there are two thousand million *livres* in a kingdom, all commodity and labour costs will be double what they would be if there were only one thousand million. I'm just as rich with an income of fifty thousand *livres* when I buy meat at four *sous* per pound as I am with an income of a hundred thousand when I buy it at eight *sous* per pound, and everything else in the same ratio. Thus the true wealth of a kingdom does not lie in gold and silver; it lies in an abundance of commodities of every kind; it lies in manufacturing and work. Not long ago people saw a Spanish regiment on the River Plate whose officers had golden swords, but they lacked shirts and bread.

'I suppose that ever since the time of Hugh Capet the amount of money in the kingdom has not increased, but industry has developed a hundred fold in all branches. I say that we are in real terms a hundred times richer than we were in the time of Hugh Capet; for to be rich is to enjoy; now I enjoy a house that is better ventilated, better built, better designed than that of Hugh Capet himself. The vineyards have been better cultivated, and I drink better wine; manufactured goods have been improved, and I am dressed in finer clothing. The art of appealing to [people's] tastes with a more delicate seasoning enables me to eat as well as at one of Hugh Capet's royal feasts. If, when he was ill, he had himself transported from one house to another, it was in a cart; as for me, I have myself transported in a comfortable, pleasant coach where I can let in the light without being inconvenienced by the wind. It wasn't necessary to have more money in the kingdom to attach a painted body to leather suspension, only ingenuity was needed: and this is the case with everything else. The stone with which Hugh Capet's house was built is being put to the same use as [the stone] in houses being built in Paris today. No more money is needed to build an ugly prison than to construct a pleasant house. It costs no more to plant a well-arranged garden than to cut yews into absurd shapes, and turn them into crude representations of animals. Years ago oaks used to rot in the forests; today they are fashioned into parquet flooring. Sand used to lie uselessly on the ground; now glass windows are made out of it.

'Now the man who enjoys all of these advantages is certainly rich. Ingenuity alone has procured them. Thus it's not money that enriches a kingdom; it's intelligence; I mean the intelligence that directs labour.

'Trade has the same effect as manual work. It contributes to life's comforts. If I need something made in India, some natural product found only in Ceylon or on Ternate Island, these needs impoverish me. I become rich when they are satisfied through trade. I wasn't short of gold and silver; I was short of coffee and cinnamon. But those who travel six thousand miles, putting their lives at risk, so that I can drink coffee in the morning are just a superfluous bit of the nation's workforce. Wealth thus consists of great numbers of hard-working men.

'The aim, the duty of a wise government, thus relates clearly to the workforce and to employment.

'In our part of the world more males than females are born; so we mustn't cause females to die. Now it's obvious that it's [social] death for females to bury themselves alive in cloisters where they are lost to today's generation, and where they nullify the possibility of creating future generations. The money lost in providing dowries for convents could therefore be very well used to encourage marriage. I compare the fallow land you still find in France to the girls who are left to wither away in a convent; both must be cultivated. There are many ways of forcing farmers to make neglected land productive, but there's one sure way of harming the State, and that is to allow these two abuses, burying girls alive and leaving fields covered in brambles, to survive. Sterility, of whatever sort, is either a vice of nature or an attack on nature.

'The King, who is the nation's treasurer, gives pensions to ladies at his court, and that money goes to tradesmen, hair-dressers and embroiderers. But why are there no pensions attached to the encouragement of agriculture? That money would revert to the State as well, but with a greater return on it.

'We know that it's a vice of government for there to be beggars. There are two kinds: those who wander in rags from one end of the kingdom to the other, ripping a few pence for the local tavern off passers-by with their pitiable cries; and those who, in uniform dress, oblige the people to make contributions in the name of God, and come back to have supper with them in great houses where they live a life of comfort. The first of these is less pernicious than the other because, as it goes on its way it makes children for the State, and if it produces thieves it also produces masons and soldiers; but both kinds are an evil which everyone complains about, but which nobody tears out by the roots. It's very strange that in a kingdom with uncultivated land and with colonies inhabitants are tolerated who neither make children nor work. The best system of government is the one which has the least number of idle people. How is it that there are nations, with less gold and silver than we have, whose memory has been immortalised through public works that we dare not imitate? Obviously their public administration was better than ours since it kept more people in work.

'Taxes are necessary. The best method of raising them is the method which best facilitates work and trade. An arbitrary tax is vicious. Only alms can be arbitrary, but in a well-administered state there shouldn't have to be any recourse to alms. The great Shah Abbas, when he created in Persia so many useful organisations, did not found any poor-houses. People asked him why. 'I don't want', he said, 'anyone to be in need of a poor-house in Persia.'

'What is a tax? It's a certain amount of corn, cattle, produce that owners of land owe to those who don't own any at all. Money is just the symbol of that produce. So really tax is only on the rich; you can't ask a poor man for some of the bread he earns, or for some of the milk his wife's breasts give to her children. It's not on the poor, on the unskilled labourer, that a tax must be imposed. When you make him work you must give him the hope that one day he will be in the happy position of paying taxes.

'In wartime I suppose that fifty million more *livres* are spent each year; of this fifty million, twenty disappear abroad; thirty are used to have people massacred. In peacetime I suppose twenty-five of those fifty million are spent; nothing then disappears abroad; as many citizens are put to work for the public good as were slaughtered. All kinds of public works are increased; the countryside is cultivated; the towns are improved. Thus people are really rich through paying the State. During the calamity of war taxes mustn't be used to provide us with the comforts of life; they must be used to defend life. The happiest nation must be the one that pays most; undoubtedly that's the richest and most hard-working state.

'Currency notes are to money what money is to produce: a symbol, a token of exchange. Money is useful only because it's easier to pay for a sheep with a golden *louis* than to give four pairs of stockings for one sheep. Similarly, it's easier for a provincial tax-collector to send to the royal treasury four hundred thousand *francs* in a letter than to have them transported at great expense: thus a bank, a credit note, is useful. In the government of a state, in trade and in the circulation of money credit notes are what winches are to ships in full sail; they relieve men of the loads that they wouldn't be able to move with their bare hands. A Scotsman, a man who was both useful and dangerous, established a system of credit notes in France. He was a doctor who gave his patients an emetic that was too strong. They went into convulsions from it; but just because some good medicine has upset you, does that mean that you have to give it up for ever? From the debris of his system there remains the East India Company which makes foreigners envious, and which might make the nation great. So this system, kept within appropriate limits, might have done more good than bad.[1]

'Changing the value of the currency amounts to making counterfeit money; issuing to the public more credit notes than the total amount of money and goods in circulation amounts even more so to making counterfeit money.

'Forbidding the export of gold and silver materials is a hangover from barbarism and poverty: it's simultaneously a wish not to pay one's debts and to lose trade. It's in effect a wish not to pay since, if the nation is in debt, it must settle its account with foreign countries; it means loss of trade because gold and silver are not only the price of commodities, but are themselves commodities. Spain has retained, like other nations, this ancient law, which is just an ancient misery. The only thing that governments can do is always to break that law.

'Charging taxes within one's own territory on one's own country's goods province by province; making Champagne the enemy of Burgundy, Guyenne the enemy of Brittany, is another shameful and ridiculous abuse; it's as if I were to station a few of my servants in an ante-room to intercept and eat part of my supper when it's brought to me. People have worked towards correcting this abuse, and to the shame of the human spirit, haven't succeeded.'

There were many other ideas in the philosopher's papers; the minister savoured them; he had a copy made of them, and this is the first portfolio of a philosopher to have been seen in the portfolio of a minister.

---

[1] 'At that time the East India Company survived brilliantly, and there were great hopes for it' (Voltaire's note).

Index

Cambridge texts in the history of political thought

Titles published in the series thus far